The Alchemy of Kindliness: A Testament

© 2020 Carol Horne

The moral rights of the author have been asserted.

Parts of this book are based on real events and the recollections of the author about them. Names and descriptions of people and details of conversations and events have been changed and some characters created as a literary device to protect the privacy of others

ISBN 978-1-9163396-0-6

*My thanks to the following
for their part in making this book what it is*

Nigel, my husband and unfailing companion and emotional support –
I can never thank you enough

~

My family in the UK, Eire, South Africa and New Zealand –
the long road softens in time

~

Mary, Helen, Ann, Rose, Lils, Liz, Gini, and all other friends who cared
enough to plough through my first stumbling renditions

~

The Centre for Corporate Accountability (now defunct) –
headed by the admirable campaigner David Bergman

~

Adam May, Psychotherapist, who gave me the 'blame pie'

~

Mairede – for the photo of the actual cottage in the 1950s

~

The Welsh Book Council – for their most useful commentary

~

Jessika and Dafydd who believed in *Alchemy of Kindliness* enough
to want to publish it – may you prosper

~

And finally, with heartfelt kindliness to all those I spoke to
(and those I didn't) who have suffered personal tragedy –
May you be well and happy and free from fear.

Carol Horne, 2020

This book is dedicated to
S M

Prologue

'I never did give anybody hell. I just told the truth and
they thought it was hell.'

- Harry S Truman

'A lie gets halfway around the world before the
truth has a chance to get its pants on.'

- Winston Churchill

'..to invest our system with the virtues of ascertaining the truth or of achieving
fairness between the parties does not stand up to close examination. It achieves
neither.... [This] would, I suspect, come as a considerable surprise to most
members of the public who see the legitimacy of our system in its capacity to
ascertain the truth.'

- Justice Geoffrey Davies, Judge Supreme
Court of Queensland

'We come from the earth, we return to the earth, and in between we
garden.'

- Anon

The Dawn Day of Your Going

Some days
Tremble on the edge of being
Will they, won't they, crystallise and harden
Into shapes I recognise and know,
With whom I can link arms
Down the streets of daylight hours?

Some days
Slink from the hedge bottoms of my waking
Belly-creeping on their prey
Then the sudden lunge and crack of jaws
Dawn and doom together
And my feathers float a trail into the wasteland.

Some days
Are an argument before it's shouted,
But at what? To whom?

Some days are history
A time 'before'
When the kestrel's scream
The wren's trill, the raven's honk
And the robin's invitation
Were fluting heralds of
'I'm glad I'm here'.

Some days
Are gunshots.
A single round.
No echo.
And the pillow is my sudden enemy
Bolt upright I sweat in silence
And wait to fall.

Every day
Is a hill I have to climb.
A different day, a different hill.
A different route on the way to the same summit.
Bring with me I must this heart as heavy as a rucksack
Whose contents can't be eaten
The wrappers binned.

Every day
Brings fellow travellers
Shareholders in this global company
With whom I weep and keen
To whom I reach my arms and hug
On whose shoulders I dare lay my head
Our grim business notwithstanding.

And is it only at this end of things
That we surrender bigotry?
On this one day, if not before,
Opinions and prejudice, those threadbare clouts,
Are cast aside
Jealousy and envy no longer have a place.
There are no bitter fights?

From this day on I am
On my knees in the mud of Kosovo
Prostrate in the rubble of Afghanistan
Pounding the red earth of Africa with my fists
Watering the English snowdrops
With my tears.

The dead have power over you. I don't mean one's own dead – mothers, fathers, siblings, friends – their power of course is to be expected. No, it is the 'other' dead I mean, those you have never met or heard of, who lived out their existence before your path in life intersected theirs in death.

I was just in my fifties, recently remarried and with everything to look forward to, I felt young at heart and young in body; my mind was also young and, in some respects, I suppose, and depending on your viewpoint, could have been described as immature. I know some people mutter 'karma', 'nemesis', accuse my generation of having spawned the moral crisis in society, of being so irresponsible that we took nothing seriously, and deliberately walked on the grass when the signs said keep off. I'm no longer sure what all that meant.

What I am sure of is that I'm no longer the woman I was. If I were to be arrested the police would still be able to identify me from my fingerprints; nevertheless, I could overtake acquaintances in the street, and the wash of my passing would not so much as cause a frown of misplaced memory or draw more than the disinterested glance of a stranger, our recognition of others being as it is, so strongly shaped by the spirit – or its lack.

The stark finality of the events that overwhelmed me forced me into the realisation that I could not go pecking around for ever without a care for the fox who, had I known it, was all the time bellying towards me through the undergrowth, with its slow patient stalking. In the end, it came without warning; was shocking in its sudden pounce and snap. And I didn't immediately understand that my violent passage out of the old world would squeeze me so out of shape that I could never be the same again.

Nor was I to know that one burial would mark my entry into the new world – and another one would be needed to help me walk in it with sure tread.

**

Home

'Home is the place where, when you have to go there, they have to take you in.'

- Robert Frost

October 1946

Although it was not yet the end of October, unseasonable easterlies were blowing a Baltic chill across the fields and the morning light reflected off a faint rime of frost on the tussocks in the home field. Annie sighed. As if life isn't hard enough without this wind. She slipped on the uneven cobbles of the yard and a thin spray of slime and manure splashed her overalls. The ewes aren't thriving and we've the whole winter to get through yet. I flippin' well hate this place, she said to herself as she tucked a rebellious lock of springy auburn hair under her scarf and pushed forward in the sharp teeth of the squall. There's nothing for me here. And that great lump just makes things worse, too. She turned to look up the hill when she heard the collie bark and the running hooves of the small flock as Evan herded them off the hill into the yard. Evan was her older cousin by some five years, from her da's eldest sister, who'd run off to the city, everyone said, before the war, leaving him to be brought up by his nain and taid. Her nain and taid too. Nobody knew who his father was, although gossip had it he was one of the navvies who came over on the boat from Dublin to Holyhead, looking for work on the roads and railways in England and just passing through. She could feel it in her to pity him if he didn't behave so badly towards her.

She saw him swing the stick he always carried at Pabi, shouting the dog to 'Get by'. He had taken to squashing an old twill cap down to his eyebrows, as if to hide in its shadow his shock of bright ginger hair, legacy of the Viking marauders they both carried in their genes. When he was out and about, his hair advertised his presence long before he got close enough to speak, and Annie wondered if the cap was a ploy so she wouldn't notice him until it was too late to get away. His face was red too, and clashed with his hair, though whether this was from exertion, or drinking, or strong feeling, or because he was out in all weathers, it was hard to tell – perhaps all four.

Annie watched him stumble across the yard now with that curious flapping gait of his. He never seemed to know how to set his feet down firmly on the ground and a wet field pocked with holes from the cows was an obstacle course from hell to him – it was lucky he'd never broken an ankle. She wondered idly if he could see properly, he squinted so. Always scowling at me, anyway. And who does he think he is, accusing me of being up to no good? If he thinks I'm going to stay here and put up with it, he's got another think coming. What have I ever done to him to make him hate me like this?

She clenched her jaw to keep from crying. Life was hard enough without Evan trying to make it more difficult. She knew it was he who had persuaded Taid to put a stop to her idea of teaching the infants at the village school, saying she was needed to help with the farm now Nain was gone... she really missed Nain. All she was allowed to do for pocket money was a bit of cleaning and domestic work one day a week for Mrs Simpson up at the Plas, which Nain had arranged before she died. Lucky she did, she thought, because if she hadn't I'd be a slave on this place for Evan, and for nothing. But a shilling an hour's not much neither, how can I save on that?

Annie sighed as she thought back to when she'd first come to the island. It felt a lifetime ago, but was scarcely over two years.

*

Taid met Annie off the train. A small man, like her da, his son, but with the wide shoulders and stocky thighs of a champion wrestler which he had been as a youth at the annual fairs, he greeted her gruffly, hoisted her small suitcase into the cart and helped her up beside him. He smelt faintly of drains, which Annie learnt later was from the sheep dipping. She drew back from his touch; his hands were red and scaly, damp from the psoriasis that had plagued him since a boy, he was always scratching it till it wept. If he noticed her flinch she couldn't tell.

"Trot on, Ziggy," he flicked the whip at the horse's rump. They jolted along the lanes until, "A sad day, a sad day," Taid nodded to himself. Annie nodded too, what was there to say? "We'd liked to've come up for the funeral, bach, but Nain's been proper poorly, see. But we were all praying for you, for the good Lord to make sure you came to no harm." A pause as he looked away; then, as if torn from him, "Mind now, you're daughter of my son and it's your home here for as long you need it."

Nain, though, had hugged her and set down a plate of floury currant buns on the rude plank table in the big room with the range.

"You just sit yourself down, *cariad*, and have a *panad* and a Welsh cake. You're better here than in that great place with those things falling everywhere." She gave Annie a sharp look, "*Duw, duw*, but you look as though you haven't had a good feed for weeks you're so pale and thin."

A stray bomb had hit the small terraced house in Liverpool and wiped her mam out of existence; da was missing in action, they said, presumed dead somewhere in France. Nain didn't say much, it wasn't her way, both she and Taid the type of folk who kept things close; but Annie could feel the hurt inside Nain, when she held Annie tight, smoothed her hair and wiped her tears with a corner of her pinafore. She knew Nain's own loss recognized the pain inside her. She was a fine-boned woman, so small that Annie felt big and clumsy next to her, as though she was some great foundling kidnapped by the faery folk. When she saw her boots next to Nain's on the step she had to laugh at what clodhoppers they looked. She'd obviously inherited her big bones and especially her feet – plates o' meat, as Mam used to say – from Mam's side of the family.

Annie could see how poorly Nain was, the sharp lines on her face and the thin white hair that came out in clumps leaving her pink scalp shining through the strands. Sometimes, when she thought nobody was looking, Annie saw her sit down heavily at the table and lean her head in her hands. But if anyone came in, up she would get, smiling and chirpy as a sparrow, and bustle about showing the face on her as if she was still a girl with a future in front of her, instead of an old lady with little time left for all she'd once imagined.

Annie thought now it was better they hadn't come to Liverpool for the funeral, she doubted Nain would have coped, especially outside of her own territory. As well, Taid, devout Chapel as he was, barely tolerated his son marrying a Catholic, she'd heard Mam say so.

The funeral was a drear affair, that was for sure, little more than a perfunctory stab at ritual really, and the only other people there were two distant elderly female relatives on Mam's side. They'd little enough to say to a grieving fifteen year old girl they'd never met, nor had any interest in, and just melted back into the grim streets out of which they'd crept as soon as the service was over. If she hadn't been in such a state of shock, she'd have had to laugh. There'd been no body to bury. A member of the congregation, Mrs Bolton, whose husband was out in France, took pity on her and took her in, notified the Evacuation Board, and sent a telegram to Nain. The priest at least asked if she was alright and gave her a cup of tea in the rectory before she left with the lady from the Board to catch the train. Mouthed 'God be with you.'

When she went to say a silent goodbye to the house she'd lived in for most of her adolescent years, the grimy little children still playing in the heaps of rubble, all that was left of the street, had gawped and shrilled 'Orphan Annie, Orphan Annie' till she couldn't stand it any more and picked up a cobble and lobbed it at them, her eyes full of tears and a mouthful of blasphemies she was surprised herself that she knew. She was still wondering why God would bother with her when he hadn't cared about her mam, or her da, or the other poor people everywhere, who were being blown up in the war.

'All that church going didn't do us much good,' she thought. Although it felt disloyal, she'd turned away from religion after her first communion, when, to celebrate, she insisted on clacking down the aisle in her first pair of grown-up shoes with little steel-tipped heels, and everyone turned round and frowned disapprovingly. She grimaced at the memory, Blimey, the noise! Load of hoity-toities, I was only a kid after all! But an only child in a street of families with at least three children, more often six or seven, and not allowed to play with any of them. What was that all about? Why was I so scared all the time?'

Because they were loud and rough and pushed and fought and were rude to everyone, she answered herself without hesitation. It could be the priest, or the doctor, or Mr Smart who went to work somewhere in the city in a suit, with a briefcase and with shoes that shone like they were glass – they didn't care. Kids can be flippin' awful- I s'pose Mam was just trying to bring me up right. And when I think of all the mean little tricks they played on people, gluing pennies to the pavement and hiding behind the fence, laughing when some poor person bent down to pick them up... and they stole sweets from the little shop Granny White had on the corner and didn't care that she was old and a widow and hardly made enough to feed a sparrow, as Mam said. She shrugged. They didn't give a mouldy fig for God, so why should I?

Yes, but they'd had fun where she hadn't... never mind God. When they tied a long rope up between two of the trees in the park and balanced a bicycle wheel on its rim, and hung from a stick through the axle, swooshing down like the wind, shrieking and laughing, she would have liked to join in. She winced, remembering their jeers, 'Miss Snooty', 'Watchit you lot, Snooty's spying on us,' or 'Oy, Snobby!' when they caught sight of her bobble hat or her hateful shiny Clark's shoes behind a tree. She hadn't tried to make friends.

I hate you, I hate you! she'd mutter fiercely to herself as she stomped up the stairs to bed. She refused to kiss her mam, the cause of it all, her body stiff and her face screwed up. She'd over-heard Mam say once in embarrassment to a visitor, 'She doesn't like being kissed. I don't know what's wrong with the child."

'Oh, but Annie's such a good girl! Small mercies, Moire," Mam's friends exclaimed when they popped in for elevenses, and sat round in the small parlour, listening to her complainings.

No, I'm not. And I don't care, not one bit, she'd thought. She'd refused to think about the why of it, then, but she'd had plenty of time since. Mam never let her do things like other children, and smacked her if she so much as looked like she wanted to answer back. When she was younger and Jenny her best friend came round to play after school Mam always said, 'You two'd better be good now, or I'll get my stick out, and then you'll be for it." Annie never dared see if she really would. What a little mouse I was. Still am I s'pose.

She felt bad now that Mam was dead, she'd loved her really. And she had given God another chance, she really had – but it didn't look as though he was going to redeem himself.

Dashing the few tears from her eyes, she rescued the milking bucket from where it had fallen, and shook her head, silently shouting No – no – no! over and over again to raise a high whine of mental noise against the sly and slinking memories. She hardly dared even think about Nain and her slow pale shrinking to the ghost of the plump little woman she'd been, her cotton dresses hanging from the jutting coat-hanger shoulders, and that last terrible night when Taid slammed the door of the bedroom in her face, and with spittle and disheveled hair flying yelled 'Bugger off!" at her and Evan. There'd been no doctor and in the morning the vet from over the hill had come and pronounced Nain dead. Like any old carthorse.

There were only one or two well-used narrow paths left now for thinking to travel along, from safe starts to known ends, martingaled like a stroppy horse cowed by the gipsies. She'd been horrified one summer to see one of them, a spindly dark boy, hardly older than her, on his way to Appleby Fair maybe with his family, fill a bottle with pig's blood and smash it between a horse's ears as it reared under him, so the stink of blood running into its nostrils shrank its spirit into submission. That's what I've got to do – to my thoughts.

Too, when it got this bad she didn't dare more than glance across to the mountains with their fiery heads in the sunset and the soft blankets of snow and blue shadows that picked them out clean and stark. Beauty hurt. It hurt because it made her heart open and thoughts dream, so that an onslaught of pain washed through her and all she could do was sink to the floor. She sensed people draw back from her, but it was hard to open up. She knew what she needed was kindness, soft hands and gentle words, but living with men like Taid and Evan, whose sensitivities had been sandblasted by poverty and hard work, and bolstered by the judgementalism of a non-conformist creed, there was no hope of this at home, and no one else to turn to.

She dabbed at the muck splattered on her trousers and turned her back on the yard so she wouldn't have to see awful Evan. Always watching me. She opened the gate into the field and called Kitty, rattling a stick on the pail. Kitty trotted through, udder swinging, her breath exhaling in great grassy puffs. She followed the cow into the barn, tossing hay into the rack. The sweet smell of her filled Annie's nostrils and the gentle rumbling of the cud regurgitating in the barrel of her body lulled her. Kitty liked being milked, by Annie anyway. Her first calving, and she'd had mastitis and was only saved by being tied to the stall on bare earth, no straw in case she ate it, with only a mash of apples, bran and garlic for feed, and her udder having to be hosed down every two hours until the infection went. Hard work replaced the medicines that cost a lot of money, money the farm just didn't make. Annie sat out with her in the byre night after night until she recovered, under an old grey blanket used to throw over Ziggy when he was in a sweat; she couldn't bear to think of Evan's careless hands tugging at her and his rough voice. She lost one of her quarters to the infection, and Evan jeeringly nick-named her Three-Titty Kitty. Kitty wouldn't let the milk down for him since then. I'm glad – serves him right. Not that he cares, the lazy lump.

Resting her forehead against the cow's flank, Annie washed the udder with hot water and started to draw the milk out. This was one of the peaceful times of the day, when she could escape Evan and his bullying ways. If he came into the barn and upset things so there was no milk for breakfast, even Taid would raise a hand to him and curse him for a fool.

*

Not long after, Taid followed Nain. Loveless without her, it was everyone's opinion, as they clustered round the grave down by the little church, that Bron Felen had 'fair wore him out'. He'd given up. Annie felt guilty at how little his death moved her; but then, Taid never bothered to hide much how he felt about me being here, she excused herself. Even so, his presence had at least put a boundary of sorts between Evan and her, and she was apprehensive that the feelings that had been festering between them for so long would now come into the open, and life would become even harder. She was surprised when Evan carried on behaving much as though Taid was still around, and kept aloof. She gradually put her anxiety to the back of her mind, though once, she looked up and surprised him staring across the room at her, with a strangely intent expression on his face, and a quick spurt of unease sent her swinging with her long stride across to the range to poke it and turn her face to its blaze, then out through into the scullery to fold up the washing, still damp and ready to iron. From then on she always made sure to be busy, never at rest, when he was around, especially of an evening, sat on the wooden settle listening to the wireless; and it was no real hardship, for she delighted in all that had to be done, the sense of ordering things.

It was only when Evan drank at *The Bell* that she allowed herself to relax enough to pick up one of the books Mrs Simpson lent her, and sit with her feet curled up in the old chair with the wear on the arms and the stuffing peeping out where Nain used to rest her elbows. She drew it up close to the fire, her fore-arm across her chest, one finger stroking her upper lip as she always did as a child.

*

I'll tell you now, Evan wasn't the man his grand-father was, and it didn't take long before things started to fall apart. The lime wash fell away from the walls, grasses and other plants seeding on the roofs caused slipping slates and leaks, the pond started to silt up and the barns to fall into disrepair. Annie did her best, but some things she just plain couldn't manage. The mainstay of the farm's income were the sheep, see, though the pasture was really too wet and soft and the ewes suffered badly from foot-rot if Evan didn't keep their hooves trimmed, and moved them too late onto the higher rocky ground behind the house. Annie told me, proper distressed, she couldn't bear watching them limp around the pasture, kneeling to grab a few painful mouthfuls. And then Evan, cursing her for being a scold – as though it was her fault he didn't look after them. I'd have a go at him too, mind, he'd listen better to me. His attitude was one of 'What do women know, always bleating on about this and that?' Times've changed I know, but a lot of the menfolk thought this way in those days. Anyway, when he couldn't ignore it any longer he'd shift himself to bring the poor suffering ewe into that small barn at the end there, past the cobbles. You had to pare away the overgrowth and dress their feet with diluted hydrochloric and carbolic acid. You could hear the others on market day talk about him, 'Have you been lately to the Bron? Enough to make you weep, it is ...'' and, 'Not a stockman that one – never was, never will be. Not like old Huw.' But they never said anything to his face.

And Evan's bad temper wasn't helped when the cows and their calves started to scour, then in no time at all became constipated and blood started to show in their urine. After a couple of the cows aborted he was forced to call in the vet.

*

'Red water,' pronounced the vet, washing his hands in the bucket of water Annie brought from the spring, as they stood in the barn gazing at the latest victim.

'What the hell's that?' Evan demanded. He swung his heavy head from the cow to the vet, like a bull sighting its quarry and about to charge.

'It's caused by ticks infecting the cattle with a parasite – have you noticed a build up of ticks in the pasture at all?' the vet asked.

'Nope.' Evan shook his head, and although his management of the land clearly left a lot to be desired, the vet held his tongue, wanting to be paid.

'Death's not usual, luckily,' he observed, 'but the animals won't flourish unless you take the trouble to treat them.' The treatment was linseed oil together with carbonate of ammonia and warm ale. And a 'hope and a prayer', as the vet added sardonically.

'Iesu Grist, man, the blŵdi cows'll get pissed,' said Evan in disgust as the vet disappeared down the track to his next callout, 'and there'll be nothing left for me to have a sup with.'

Annie kept herself occupied well away from him that day. He liked his drink, and the thought of doing without put him in a bad temper. Dilwyn Maesgwyn called by later in the day on his way up the hill to the village from work and suggested going to the pub. When Evan told the sorry tale Dilwyn had to laugh, but when he saw Evan's face quickly changed it into a cough, then turned and gave her a slow wink as Evan laced his boots.

"*Nefi blŵ* – come on, Evan, man," he said, "don't fret. I'll buy you a pint of 'pally ally'," and for the next week or so Evan supped free, courtesy of the men folk in the village.

*

' He jests at scars that never felt a wound.'

- William Shakespeare

November 1946

Annie woke to a strange muffled silence that, like thick oil, overlaid the faintest susurration of the surf. Wrapping the eiderdown round her thin shoulders she padded across to the small window of her bedroom to scratch off the rime and look out over the bay. Large snowflakes were floating down onto the blanket of ivy which covered the walls of the yard. Her bedroom was the loft over the dairy, or 'kitchen', and a warm draught blew up through the gaps between the rough planks, carrying the sweet smell of wood smoke from the range. Down below she could hear the scrape of hobnails on the cobbled floor and the growling of Evan's voice raised against some offence he was hearing on the wireless. A thump on the floor and a shout got Annie moving quickly to dress, and descend the ladder.

The morning started, as every morning did, with Evan's surly looks and his quick impatience to be served his breakfast. If Taid was here he'd have already been out, and wouldn't have come in for breakfast proper until he'd done a couple of hours work, Annie thought. If it wasn't for the fact that she'd have to be out the door herself as soon as they'd eaten, she would have acted cross-grained too, delaying his breakfast and provoking his ill-temper further just for the satisfaction of it.

November – the month in the trough of the year when the darkling days still had many weeks to go before the light's slow return, when the rotting seed-heads bobbed blackly on the banks, to fall and be trodden to mush in the lanes with the drifts of leaves, and the ravens swung like tattered flags in the easterly winds. Annie put away the thought of her seventeenth birthday just gone with all the other things in her life that hurt; it had passed unremembered by anyone except herself. Her birthday depressed her; she could not imagine new life entering the world at such a dead time. Mam used to make her laugh though, telling the story of how she had burst out of her like a champagne cork, along with the pop and whine of the fizzling fireworks reflected in the slow moving river, and how Da had brought home bottles of black stout with which to wet her head. This was when they still lived on the Wirral, before Da's job meant they had to move to Liverpool. Neighbours had brought round dinners, and the milkman had left an extra bottle on the step every day for a whole week. But Da and Mam were ghosts and the bile rose in her gorge at the stale taste of the old family stories without the warmth and affection of those still living.

She stirred the porridge and broke eggs onto the range. She had something to look forward to now, though. Monday was cleaning day at Mrs Simpson's - and Jan, handsome Jan of the bright blue eyes, would come in and have his bit of dinner with her at the big white-scoured kitchen table. Saturday was market day and, if she was lucky, time for a stolen stroll down to the river – with Jan. But today was Friday and choir night – and Jan. Annie hugged herself in anticipation.

*

Mrs Evans closed the lid of the piano, collected the music scores, and everyone crowded round the urn in the kitchen of the village hall, warming their fingers, eager to exchange gossip. Annie sat entranced with her cup of cocoa and garibaldi biscuit, listening to Jan's tales of life in Poland before the war. Jan was such a gentleman and so tall, and handsome with his blond hair and his teasing eyes which followed her about. Although gallant, of course, he had no time really for the silly girls who giggled and nudged each other when he came into the hall, and who tarted themselves up, like that Mavis Jones, with her pink lipstick and mascara and face powder and cheap scent. You wouldn't catch her doing that, though she liked looking at the fashion advertisements in the magazines. No, he saw the underneath of people, and she could talk to him about things that mattered. When he walked her home, as he did more and more often, she talked about her life in Liverpool, and her mam and da, and how horrible it was at Bron Felen, especially living with 'Awful Evan', as they both now called him.

"And you will stay here in Wales?" Jan asked, as they made their way home that night. "Have you not family elsewhere you will go to stay with now war is over? You are clever Annie; you could do many things I think, not just work as slave to your cousin on farm."

"No, no-one else. Leastways, none I know of any more. I did want to stay on at school, I was always winning prizes for writing essays. I was really good at school, and before I came here, Mrs Gordon, the head, asked me to look after a class, as an assistant teacher. Just the little ones, mind, reading and writing and arithmetic. But I really enjoyed it. I'd love to be a proper teacher if I had the chance."

"Future is closed to our peering eyes, Annie. Maybe you will achieve your dream one day. It is important to have dream, go forward." Jan looked away. Annie wondered wistfully what his dream might be and if she featured in it. He never mentioned his future.

*

The next day at market, when Evan went to the pub for lunch with his cronies, and would be gone for a good hour at least, Annie and Jan left the crowd separately, coming together a little way down the path that led to the river, a clear turquoise ribbon from the copper deposits, meandering through the woods and out into the bay. Out of sight, they sauntered arm in arm, ankle deep in the brown leaves from the beech, rare on the island, which lined the path. Annie felt small next to him; such a long, thin man, well over six feet, and she skipped to keep up with his stride. How on earth did he fit in those small airplanes, she wondered. She loved the way he smiled down at her, past his aquiline nose and the planes of his cheeks. She felt oddly tender at the sight of his prominent Adam's apple.

"How did you come to end up here, Jan?" she asked. "I love all your stories about Poland before the war, but I don't know anything much about you. You're a regular mystery man."

To her dismay, his face darkened. The sun was shining; she didn't want dark thoughts to spoil the day. But before she could take the question back, he said, in a rush: "Kolyma. You have heard of it? You do not want to. It is in Arctic circle. Few people survive first winter. My whole family – father, mother, two sisters. When soldiers come, my father whispers 'Go Jan, go in woods!' and thrusts small packet into my hands and pushes me out of back window. I see him, standing in snow in his carpet slippers, arguing. I hear my sisters sobbing and soldiers shouting and cursing. I see them hit my mother with rifle and she falls. Blood is over her face. I want to go to her but I am frozen where I am. Frightened. I must do as my father tells me. One soldier he pulls my little sister, Maria, into the house. I do not go to help," he stopped, his throat working. "Where they are now? Dead? Who knows? I do not know." Jan stopped. He looked at Annie, one hand up to her mouth, the other to her breasts, her eyes wide with – what? Horror? Pity? He turned away. "Poland I left is gone, I can not go back to it. Jan that is me – young, not knowing – he is gone too."

Annie kicked a mole hill in the middle of the path, scattering the earth in soft pellets, said firmly, "The Jan that's here is good enough for me." She thrust her arm through Jan's stiff one.

Silent now and wrapped in their own thoughts, they slowly trod the path along the bank. Annie considered this story. She didn't like it. That people can behave so, frightened her. She has never seen it; except sometimes, in the slide of an eye, the thin snarl of lips, she thought maybe she might detect it lurking. She remembered Mickey. Mickey, at school. Poor stupid Mickey, who stuttered and flinched, and couldn't hear properly because he'd been hit so often round the head, whose clothes always smelled, and who never wore socks. Mr Stotten the village policeman was always being called out to his house, sometimes in the middle of the night, carrying his truncheon and his handcuffs on his bicycle. People talked of course, and Mickey would be away from school the next day. Then one day he would turn up again, his eyes puffed and red. He hated to take his jumper off to do PT but when the teacher made him you could see his thin knobby arms and there would be big blue-black bruises all over his back. Some going green and yellow. One day he was away and Mam and Da told her he was in hospital and would probably never come back to school. When she asked what had happened, Da just shook his head and said, "Animals. That's what they are. They should be put in a zoo."

She'd imagined maybe lions or grizzly bears had escaped from a circus and been wandering round town, and tried to eat Mickey. Much later she heard his parents had been arrested and sent to prison for beating him so badly he had nearly died. Her da was right, too, and Mickey never did come back to school. But what Jan told her was an entirely different order of inhumanity.

A jay screeched, inspecting them, perched on a bare branch and silhouetted against the clear blue winter sky. They pulled apart.

"What happened after you ran off into the woods?" She knew little about Poland, but what she did know made her think of dark fir forests, bears and wolves, snow up to her thighs. She couldn't imagine how Jan managed to survive.

Jan picked up a pebble, skipped it over the water. 'I run, I run through the forest. When I cannot run more, I stop. I have no shoes and I see my feet; they bleed from sharp stones and roots, but I feel nothing. I see figures through the trees and I think it is Russians chasing. I run again till my heart, it feels it will burst. But it was not Russians, and not *leshyi* or *mavkas*, wood spirits and demons I hear old women tell stories of."

"You don't believe things like that, do you?" Annie asked, surprised; Jan seemed such a down to earth person. But who really knew what beliefs people held close, deep inside? They probably didn't know themselves.

Jan laughed then at the incredulous expression on her face, her fine eyebrows drawn up and her brown eyes wide. 'No. I am not usually so believing in such things. But my world, it is turned inside out and I am shocked at what soldiers do to my people. I think, what is normal any more? I cannot trust what I see."

Annie could understand this. She shivered and huddled close, pulling his arm round her shoulders. She cleared her throat. 'So what were the figures in the woods?" She had to know.

'Other people from village, running, running like me, from Russians. I go to town of Lvov and family I know who take me in. But then, I hear whispers of Polish army in France, and I make plans. This is where I will go. It does not matter it is other side of Europe." They turned along a track that brought them back round into town by the church, avoiding the market square.

'I go to Rumania consulate and buy *'billet de libera trecere'*," Jan continued. "This allows me to go to Rumania. I have only little left of money my father gives me, but I pay guide to take me to border, where I must wade across big river. I keep walking, there is nothing else to do. Rumunov are anxious about big Polish rush through their country and do not want to make Russians more angry. I do not want to be prisoner – this is not how I will spend war. I hide in barns in day, stealing eggs from chicken coops and cabbages from gardens in night. I am so dirty when I run hands over my body they are full of lice, and there is much blood on my shirt and trousers." He shudders at the memory. 'I come to Bucharest, big city. There are people there who help Polish to escape." In the autumn of 1939 he left Constanţa by boat and after some weeks docked safely in Haifa, Palestine. By then it was December.

'I visit Bethlehem on Christmas Eve for Mass, and how happy I am to find choir singing is Polish airmen. I think I am believing they are angels," he told Annie, 'and I know everything will be all right."

From there he made his way to Egypt and eventually to Marseilles. He was just eighteen.

"But France surrenders to Germans; it is not safe for me and I come to England..." He stopped, his jaw working.

"Jan, I'm sorry." Annie saw the sheen of wet on his cheeks and heard his convulsive swallow. "You don't have to tell me if you don't want." She took his hand.

"Oh Annie. You are sweetheart, but I think you do not like Jan I am becoming. Angry at everything. Angry at English."

"I understand anger all right, don't you worry. Besides, what have I got to be grateful to the English for? My mam was Irish and my da Welsh; the English did their people no favours."

"I suppose. But I do not like me! I get off boat at Liverpool in summer of 1941. It is hot and much bustling with ships and working men. I am despondent but man shouts at me 'Bloody Frogs, eh mate? They have no balls. You are better here in old Blighty.' At least this is what officer who is looking after us tells me he says. I shout back 'You are right!'" Annie laughed.

"I think 'What marvellous place'. Everywhere I am going, tram conductors refuse me to pay, restaurants give me free dinners, and publicans stand me all beer I can drink. People on street shout 'Long live Poland!' After Battle of Britain we Polish are fêted and toasted wherever we go, and parties are dull affairs that do not have Polish airman. We become real glamour boys of England, and we shoot down more Huns than RAF does. We are heroes." Jan stopped and breathed deeply, took up his story once more.

"This summer, I watch Victory Parade in London – I see Australians, Ukrainians, Czechs, Canadians, Bahamians, Kenyans, even one Fijian – but not single Polish." He turned to Annie again, and she saw the pain in his face. "Why not? Because British government is embarrassed of us! And then," he rushed on, 'two letters I am given; one from Poland – it demands I 'return home without further delay to help in reconstruction of new country'; other is from Ernest Bevin, British Foreign Secretary – it tells me I am 'forthwith released from duty' – and also to go home. But I am hearing bad things about Poland and those who go back. I am shocked. Why do British say they will not let us stay? They must know... I do not know what best to do. Look..."

From his greatcoat pocket he took two envelopes, blotched and creased from much reading, and gave them to Annie. She read them quickly, then read them a second time, her indignation growing. "Well, I'm not surprised you're angry," she said, "This is awful. How can they treat you like this? What do you think you'll do?"

"I cannot decide, so many stories I am hearing."

'I'm sure everything'll get sorted out and you'll be able to go back home sooner or later...' A wistful note crept into her voice as she attempted to reassure him. She couldn't imagine him remaining here, in a country that didn't want him.

'Oh, Annie. I keep asking – Home? Where is home? My parents and sisters – gone. My village and town – they do not exist. Blood covers fields and there are graves of thousands in woods. City where aunts and uncles and cousins lived is now rubble with rats and gangsters running through – and English and Americans have given to Russia! They say Communism is good, but I do not forget Stalin is leader of communists who did massacre at Katyn, and it is Stalin who decides who lives and who dies, not Churchills and Roosevelts.'

'What's Katyn?' Annie asked curiously.

'You do not read newspapers?' Annie shook her head. 'Probably is good not. I am angry when I read them. Many things they write are not truth,' he shrugged. 'Katyn is big forest in Russia. In forest they find mass grave, many thousands of Polish people buried there. Russians say it is Germans who do massacre, and Germans say it is Russians. Churchill wants Stalin for friend and does not believe he is monster. No-one knows what is truth. But stories from people who live there say it is Russians. So I wait.' He paused. Annie squeezed his arm, the words she was looking for dying on her tongue.

'I try not to think about it. I do not tell anyone. It is not easy for people to believe such a bad thing can happen. Mr Simpson, he is very kind. He finds work for me until I know what I will do. So here I am. How do you say it – 'a jack of all trades and master of none'? I mend roofs, dig gardens and shoot pigeons, and put on my fancy hat and drive Mr Simpson in Bentley. I am lucky. Living in stable.'

Annie smiled. 'Over a stable. Horses live in a stable.'

'I work-horse too. Now you know my story and why I stay here.' He turned and looked at her then, his mood lifting, a shyness in his eyes. 'Maybe that is not only reason –'

**

Coming Home

1999 – The cusp of the millennium

I first set foot on Bron Felen on the night of December 31st 1999. Harry suggested we drive over to the island for a drink at *The Bell* in Marchlyn to celebrate his birthday – 'Sixty, not a hooligan any more!' as he said, and I thought I detected a hint of ruefulness. The beer was gassy and the crowd at the bar full of curiosity and sly innuendo, so I was glad to leave when he said he had something he wanted to show me. He drove down a narrow lane towards the sea and parked on the verge by a gateway, took my hand and set off along a sunken track lined with hazels. The full moon floated a jigsaw in the clear night sky as I looked up through the bare branches, and moon shadows dogged our footsteps. I was hardly dressed for an expedition – it was rough under foot, and my Spanish boots kept slipping; my short jacket let in a draught round my middle and raised goose-flesh in places best left to the imagination. But I didn't think of complaining.

The rustling of small creatures deep in the banks accompanied us as we skirted the edge of a brook splashing down into a ferny gully, and climbed a small rise that brought us out below a cottage. I ducked under a rambling rose, which threw out its barbed shoots in disorder, snagging my hat, only to be confronted by a jungle of briars that flowed over the cobbled path to the front door, effectively barricading the house. Defeated, we leant on the little front gate, and gazed at its shabby facade. Harry put an arm round me and I breathed in his clean, slightly acrid scent – a mixture of moorland and metal shavings – and my body cried out at how tight I'd become, how brittle and agitated, how disconnected. My feet settled more firmly on the earth.

I looked a query at him. "I signed the contract yesterday." He gestured to take in the hillside, "I came and sat up the hill here every morning for a week. I didn't bother to go in the house – not that I could have... look at it. Anyway you can see at a glance what it's about. Location. People came and went and I could hear their 'We'll have to pull the lot down and re-build', and 'It'll cost a fortune to put a tarmac road in'. You know, I find it hard to understand how people can be so insensitive; there are hardly any traditional cottages like this left on the island now. It's all concrete boxes and pebble dash. This place is special – I wanted to save it."

Harry was a dour man from a Nottinghamshire collier family, who'd been scolded as a boy for being maudlin if he confessed to 'feelings', and I'd erroneously assumed he had little appreciation for such things.

"How did you manage that?" I asked. I knew properties like this were in the main snapped up before most people off the island even heard of them.

"I happened to be in the right place at the right time, cash in hand." He tapped his nose and winked. "Do you like it, Sarah?"

'Oh Harry, how could I not? It's beautiful. It's one of the most beautiful places I've seen."

I gazed out through the frame of the huge old ash and the sycamore, across the wet sands to the deep black of the sea. Behind the grassy dunes, the wetlands with their thickets of alder and willow gleamed with standing water. A vixen screamed.

The courtyard and barns were too daunting to even think about attempting at night, so we climbed up the public footpath behind the cottage to get a view down onto them. I puffed and panted behind Harry who skipped up ahead, nimbly avoiding the rabbit holes and bracken. It was time to get myself into shape; I'd let myself go these past few years sitting at a desk all day, and my age was starting to show.

The lean-to on the gable end was crumbling under the ivy's gnarled ropes, and we could just make out the wide stone arch in the barn wall, long bricked in, where the hay wains would have disgorged their loads. We sat in silence breathing it in, then, getting cold, walked back to the car along the sunken path, through the icy ford, and drove over the bridge back to the mountains.

The next day, New Year's day, Harry asked me to marry him. I knew he was going to ask, and I knew I would say yes; it wasn't just his kind blue eyes, 'the colour of dishwater, you mean', he laughed, or his strong body, honed from years of mountaineering – I never was much drawn to a man because of how he looked – it was more the attraction of something 'unlike', which tantalized me. I accepted he'd irritate me to screaming pitch and we'd argue about many things, but we'd also have heated agreements and moments of profound recognition. The most important thing was the sense of freedom between us: I would be able to do as I pleased, come and go at a whim, and so would he. I was certain that through it all would run the tough thread of tenderness I felt that night. Bron Felen was to be our launching pad. I like to think he would have asked even had he known the burden our marriage would have to shoulder. I like to think also that I would have had enough regard for him to say 'no' if I had known.

*

At the beginning of our marriage, Bron Felen was never more than a dream for the future, the impact on our busy lives negligible. On fine weekends, if we had nothing better to do and the sky was down hard on the tops of the hills, we would pack a picnic and all the tools we could muster into the pickup and spend happy hours titivating – titivation, because we did not have the resources to do much more. We tore damp plaster off walls, rot-proofed beams, and dug channels for the water that streamed from the inglenook across the quarry-tiled floor and out the front door.

'How on earth did anyone manage to live with a river running through the house like this?' I wondered.

"A hardier breed than us," Harry replied, a favourite comment.

The only room that was sound and dry was the bedroom over the dairy, its air still and undisturbed but with a faint odour of lavender. Over by the small window and looking out over the barn roofs stood a crude version of a four-poster bed – still with its thick horsehair mattress. To put it bluntly, it was nothing more than a plank box with legs, some five and half feet high and long, three feet wide, with one long side open and out of which the person inside could look at the stars. There wouldn't be much room for someone built like Harry, I chuckled to myself as I watched him busy with his sketches and plans, thinking of his six foot three scrunched up inside.

I wondered who had slept there; what were their dreams and did they ever realise them; were they happy and light-hearted, or sad and grey? It was hard to figure; the house looked to have been empty for some time. Although nothing of the personal remained, as I looked around I fancied I caught indistinct shadows of despair among the rafters.

'I don't know how you come up with such things," Harry shook his head at me. 'Generations of people lived and died here over the centuries – everything you can think of must've happened at some point. Why'd you pick on despair? It must be all those haunted house movies you've watched," he teased.

But I never watched haunted house movies, and wouldn't be jollied out of my impressions. I plumped myself down on the mattress.

'I don't know. It just sort of slipped into my mind. And it's not that it feels haunted exactly, not in a bad way. Just sad. As though something bright and bouncy has deflated, like a balloon after a party."

'Well, hardly surprising. It used to be lived in – and now it isn't. End of story. We'll change that anyway."

As he climbed down the stairs, little more than a wide ladder, I sat there and looked out at the ships lining up on the horizon waiting for the pilot boats to lead them up the Mersey. One small house-leek had driven its rootlets into the slates of the barn attached to the end of the house, and clung tenaciously, thrusting its silhouette up into the early evening sky. A shaft of sunshine spread itself inside a corner of the box bed. Suddenly it felt cosy and enticing.

'I'm going to sleep in here tonight," I shouted.

'What? You must be mad."

'What's the difference between sleeping in this and a tent? At least this is dry. Besides, I've always wanted to curl up in a four poster."

'Huh. Some four poster. Not much more than a cupboard."

'Well I'm going to anyway, and if it rains tonight don't come knocking on my door."

'You'd be so lucky. And if the mice keep you awake I might let you back in the tent – if you're very nice to me..."

I swept it out, and that night I curled inside my cupboard with a sleeping bag and a cup of hot chocolate. Now the light was going the atmosphere changed yet again and the reality didn't seem so inviting, but at last I fell asleep watching the white foam of the surf down below the salt marsh, and listening to the young tawny owls practicing their calls.

Nothing dragged me fearfully from my sleep, no ghostly touch or moans or whispers. The old roof creaked as the slates cooled and the rafters shifted imperceptibly, but I was used to such sounds – they belonged to all the old cottages I'd ever lived in. No – it was the smell. Gone was the faint hint of lavender. What replaced it wasn't a smell I recognized. The only way I could think to describe it later was 'dark brown'. A sly old, desiccated, ingrained smell. It filled my nose so that it wrinkled and pulled me slowly from sleep, my lips curling.

Clicking on the torch, I padded shivering round the room pressing my nose against the wainscoting, the floor, the ceiling, shining the light into cracks and holes in the plaster. No matter how I pried, I could not discover its source; the whole room seemed to emanate it. It wasn't the animal smell of putrefying flesh – no mouse corpse trapped under the floorboards; it wasn't dry rot, or wet rot, or bat shit, or decaying vegetation; it wasn't the smell of drains or ditches. It didn't drive me out – it was too subtle for that. It was a smell quite simply that leeched the energy out of me. It robbed the dawn of its silver, rendered it dispirited and dull. It wasn't cold, or hot, putrid or foetid. Just – well, brown. I was glad to get up and go and shake Harry awake.

*

The weather that first summer was atrocious; it may have been warm but the rain fell in sheets and everything grew so fast we found it hard to keep up. We did things inside, if we bothered to even drive over. Then there was a fine, dry spell, and we turned our efforts towards re-building walls and setting boundaries, attacking the thickets of bramble, alder, and spiky blackthorn that squatted the courtyard and field. As I worked, my thoughts turned back to the night in the cupboard, and the memory of that smell would twitch my nose and a dreariness seep into my thoughts.

I wondered about who lived there before. Some odd bits of mail addressed to a Miss Williams were still being delivered to the house – nothing that seemed important, catalogues for farm machinery, insurance deals and such like – and when I called in later that afternoon at the post office to ask them to stop delivering them, it was from the woman behind the counter that I learnt the old lady's name, and Annie, as I came to think of her, stepped closer. I caught myself waiting for glimpses of her life to make themselves known, keys that would unlock the story I was sure was there.

One morning, a sudden downpour sending me scurrying inside, I sorted through some miscellaneous junk piled haphazardly in the corner of a barn, intending to throw it in the pick-up and take it to the tip. Most of it was rubbish, but among the old books and magazines, tins of rusty screws, balls of rotting string, I found an old fashioned bakelite door-handle, caught within it all the colours of the rainbow. I sat on my heels and contemplated it. Tasteless and gaudy, it filled me with sadness – sadness at this evidence of what I imagined was the human quest for beauty in the bleakest of lives, for something to gladden the eye and push aside the worries and fears, the unremitting toil a place such as this must have demanded. That was the only object from the house I found that you could have called 'personal'.

The rest of July passed in a veil of rain and low cloud. The ships moored in the bay hovered between the sea and the sky, floating in an ethereal gouache. We found other things to do and left Bron Felen to itself. There was no hurry.

August brought sunshine and warm winds that sucked the moisture from the ground, and I turned my attention finally to the garden. The daughter of hardy rural stock, I had grown up with gardens and gardening in my blood; without a garden, an empty space yawned at the back of my mind leaving me feckless and unmoored as though I might just drift off and away. I needed the warmth of soil in my hands to earth me, the rising of the sap, the delicacy of tiny rootlets, the fragile meristems.

In contrast to the poor pickings in the house, the garden was a treasure trove. The wilderness had invaded to such an extent that it was difficult to get the gates open, but, once inside, everywhere I looked gave up one delightful secret after another, and I began to sense the special relationship the previous owner had to the garden. To the outside, not the inside. Just like me, I thought, and felt less of an intruder. It didn't surrender any priceless artifacts: a clump of rich deep pink peonies, here in the corner of a wall; rows of bitter-sweet raspberries of a long vanished variety underneath brambles as high as the cottage roof; and the roses! One morning, there they were peeking out from the middle of the enormous buddleia, nodding in the breeze. I wasn't a lover of roses, they smacked of formal Victorian gardens and fussy pedantry, but so ridiculous did they look I had to smile, and scrambled into the heart of the buddleia to cut half a dozen blooms. I was immediately a convert, their old fashioned powder-puff perfume beguiling me. Annie's roses.

I was tempted to call the garden a graveyard, so full of cast-off things it was: delicately engraved old spoons, now twisted and dull, blotched with verdigris; a myriad bottles, fizzing like champagne with bubbles in the ruby and jade and topaz glass; edging a border, a half rotted beam from one of the barns carved with initials and a date, 1780; and the iron rim of an ancient cartwheel abandoned under the privet hedge.

'Look, a scarificator!' I heaved on the tines of another rusting piece of machinery.

'You mean scarifier,' Harry laughed. 'A scarificator's an instrument used to puncture the skin – meaning human,' he added with sly relish, '– for medicinal purposes usually, but I've also heard it was used in some cultures as a kind of social ritual. Phlebotomy, I think it was called.'

'Ok, ok!' I laughed. Trust Harry to know all about it. And 'phlebotomy' – what a word! A word to curl the tongue around.

'D'you remember the old barbers shops used to have a red and white striped pole outside?' he continued mischief in his voice. The red was for blood, white for the tourniquet, and the pole for the stick used by customers to grip and dilate their veins, and...'

'Yuk! Stop!' I clapped my hands over my ears. I might work in a hospital but I left all the gory stuff to the nurses.

*

Autumn came blustering in, and then, just as I was thinking Bron Felen could wait and why not quit my job at the hospital to go and live with him in the South West, Harry's work in Bristol ran out of funding. This meant we had to find a fairly prompt answer to our straitened circumstances. The obvious solution was to move from the house we were renting, buy a residential caravan and live permanently at Bron Felen, rent and mortgage free. The bucolic life beckoned.

*

The arrival of the caravan was an event the village talked about for days. The road servicing the farm was extremely steep, single track and with tight bends which would not allow the passage of a forty foot caravan. We solved the problem by asking a neighbour to bring it along the beach on a flat base trailer with his John Deere tractor.

I was building a stone wall when I looked up and saw the majestic progress of this strange entourage, like desert raiders far out along the beach, making use of the hard-packed sand at low tide's edge. Majestic, because cumbersome, slow and very large. Strange, because I could see little figures running hither and thither so that it looked as if accompanied by crowds of spectators. I almost expected to hear drums and whistles. It described a slow wide arc and scrunched up the shingle onto the road. Abandoning the stone wall I raced down to the lower gates just in time to welcome the procession which by now seemed to have attracted the whole village – women, children, crying babies, along with a sprinkling of men ready with free advice. The feeling of carnival grew stronger, and I almost regretted not laying in crates of beer and cider for the occasion. Everyone followed, waiting for the worst, as it ponderously climbed the field and backed towards its allotted space. We watched, the free advice flying in all directions, while the tractor's owner, as expressionless as a guard at Buckingham Palace in front of his admiring audience, unhitched the trailer; then we put our shoulders to the task, trundled it off the trailer and manoeuvred it into its last resting place. I couldn't even offer a cup of tea, and after a handshaking, smiling, and ruffling of children's hair, the diesel-fume-belching monster summoned its attendants and off they trouped.

*

A day or so later, when Harry was off job-hunting, and I was putting finishing touches to the interior – bookshelves, curtains, bright rugs to hide the gruesome beige fitted carpets, flowers – I heard the whine of the field gate open and the clang as it shut again. I saw a tall silver haired man leaning on a stick make his way towards the cottage up the sheep trod at the edge of the field. I wasn't yet used to the occasional ramblers that walked the public footpath through the property, and in consequence felt guilty and embarrassed at their consternation when they encountered the by now impassable track that traversed the embankment behind the cottage, and had to turn round, grumbling, and retrace their steps. So I felt concern for this elderly walker; he did not seem dressed for outdoor pursuits and was clearly a bit unsteady, even though something in his bearing put me in mind of a military man. Resigning myself to the inevitable help I would be called upon to give, I walked after him and to my surprise saw him knock on the door of the cottage. When there was no answer I saw his shoulders droop. Some instinct made me slow my pace and stop, unsure whether or not to announce my presence, but when he straightened again he looked directly at me, and bowed in a courtly old-fashioned way.

I smiled, 'I'm sorry, nobody lives in the cottage at the moment. We're restoring it. Were you looking for someone? Maybe I can help."

'It is long time ago,' he said, and I drew closer in an effort to understand his strong accent. European – Dutch maybe? But with an added inflection I could not quite place. I nodded encouragement. 'Would you know family living here after Second World War? Williams, their name.'

'Well, yes, a bit. There was an old lady lived here. Annie – Annie Williams. She's dead now. She used to live with a cousin, but he died a long time ago, in the nineteen-sixties I think. There's only an old man left in the village who knew them – Dilwyn... I don't know his last name.'

The old gentleman's face crumpled and a shadow passed across it. He put a hand to his eyes. 'Ah yes, Dilwyn,' he said.

'I remember well.' He drew a breath, straightened, then asked, 'Perhaps... Do you know if Miss Annie ever married – or had children?'

On the surface the question seemed innocent of anything but idle interest, much as anyone just catching up might take, but in it I detected a preternatural alertness, and a feeling of strong currents swirling.

'As far as I know from what I've picked up here and there, she lived on her own, right up to the time of her death. Would you like to see Dilwyn? He could perhaps tell you more. I can give you directions to his house,' I suggested, wondering if I was doing the right thing, but the old man shook his head.

'There is nothing to say. Too long years now.' He looked around again and said, 'I work near here at big house of Simpson family just after war. I am friend of Miss Annie then.'

I thought he was about to say more, but he evidently changed his mind, shook my hand, and went to take his leave.

'Do you want me to remember you to anyone else?' I thought to ask.

'No thank you. Only person I like to see, she is gone. Too bad, eh?'

He smiled, but his face was sad, then turned and walked back along the track to where I could see a car parked on the verge. As he reached it I saw by the fence a young coloured woman with a small child, who were looking at the horses in the field. Of course, that inflection in the voice – South African! Familiar, yet out of context on this Welsh hillside. She turned as he neared. The old man shook his head, then put his arm round her shoulders. They looked back but I don't think they saw me watching them. The little girl jumped up and down tugging on his other hand and her thin high voice reached me, 'See the horsey, Gampy!'

As I listened to the whine of the car's engine labour up the hill and die away and disappear, I wondered about the old man, and his connection with Bron Felen. I wished I'd asked his name, but, as it was, events overtook me and it was not until some years later that I thought to mention his visit to Dilwyn.

*

Dilwyn

Dilwyn. That lover of stories and connoisseur of the heart, eloquent and wistful, kindly, the hang of his head belying the jocular face. Born and bred not more than a couple of miles from Bron Felen, I did not expect to find such a thoughtful one living out his days here. The woman in the post office, enjoying the chance for a good gossip that I afforded her, and with the hint of a scandal flirting in the corners of her voice, first mentioned him.

'Well, well now. From the mountains, you say? You'll be missing them, won't you? Just the sea to look at. Got your hands full with that old place, I expect... My niece makes those cards, collects all the flowers and dries them herself... Has Dilwyn been down yet? I'm surprised. Haunts the place he does. Ah well, he will, he will,' when I shook my head. 'Did you want first or second class?... Lived on his own ever since his wife passed away, though if you ask me he was too interested in her at Bron Felen to grieve much... That'll be two pounds eighty five, with the card... She wasn't interested in him, of course. I mean, I don't think she was quite 'all there', really, you know?" tapping her head. 'What I do know is my Geraint was too frightened to go down the footpath past the cottage in case she came out and swore at him. She didn't like people, and they didn't like her back. Stands to reason, the way she behaved. She put up with old Dilwyn mooning about the place though... It'll be nice to see it tidy, like; got to be a bit of an eyesore."

So his reputation preceded him. The man himself I met one afternoon when Harry and I were struggling to shift a mountain of stones from the middle of the courtyard. I turned round to see a figure standing in the entrance. The sun, well below its zenith, shot a slanting ray past him, dazzling me so I had to shade my eyes to make out more than a halo of white hair.

'Hmm. You're going to be busy." The voice was deep and pleasant with its lilt. He moved into the shadow of the wall and lowered himself onto a baulk of timber. 'Doing it up, are you?" He pleated his face into a grin, 'Can't deny she let it get in a fair state." He tapped a boulder with his stick. 'This lot used to be the gable wall, till it fell down. Buried the cooker. You should've heard her!" He chuckled. 'Lucky she'd gone outside to get something, or she'd've been buried with it."

"Are you Dilwyn?" I asked.

"Someone's been talking, I see. Aye. Dilwyn Maesgwyn at your service."
He reminded me of my dad's under-gardeners when I was a small kid. He lived in one of the dark run-down cottages that were all that was left of the old village, he told us, out beyond the common land, festooned with gorse and heather and willow.

"Aye. Every now and then they have a go at me to move into one of the new council houses down in town, but I won't be budged from here." He poked a weed out of the cobbles, satisfaction evident – whether from the weed or from digging his heels in was impossible to tell . 'Lived here all my life, I have, and die here too, I expect."

Alone apart from a couple of hens and a rooster whose crow, he joked, could be heard on the mainland, and a grumpy old terrier called Bwster. Bwster couldn't walk far any more but made up for it by pacing the boundary of his tiny front garden and growling menacingly at everyone who went by, only to fall on his back and squirm happily if you bent down to scratch his tum. I suspect Dilwyn missed the company of a woman, and I could tell he was one of those men who chat effortlessly to what they call 'the fairer sex' on their terms, without feeling he had to exert his masculinity. He mentioned how he'd seen active service in Burma, and this seemed to have lit a touch paper in him, not put it out as it had for most of those who came back from the war wanting to go nowhere ever again, like my dad.

'I married after the war, not like some who rushed into it before they got sent off and regretted it ever after. Teacher she was. Made it her mission to educate me, too. I took the job of traveling salesman for an agricultural feed manufacturer in the Midlands. Got me out and about. Restless. Couldn't stay put." Apart from a touch of arthritis which crippled his knees in January when the cold air from the blasted Russkie steppes swept across, he grumbled, he was still pretty fit for a man nearing or in his eighties – which he must have been by my accounting. All this he told us in the space of that first afternoon.

After that, he took to wandering down the hill for a chat and a cuppa, a *panad*. Often when I looked up, there he was, leaning against the garden wall or with both gnarled hands clasped over the ball of his famous blackthorn stick, his soft hair blowing in the breeze off the bay.

It was one afternoon shortly Before Fleur, as I took to calling that time – perhaps late November – that I told Dilwyn about the curious night in the box-bed and how Harry had pooh-poohed my impressions of despair. What did he make of it? I asked him. He shrugged as if to dismiss my question, but I saw his eyes turn inward, and it wasn't many minutes before he hurried off along the track, saying he had things to get on with.

*

Aye, despair now... I wouldn't want to think that, but not far off the mark prob'ly. Funny how it started; who'd have thought? It all changed after that Polish lad arrived in the village. Didn't happen all at once, bit by bit, so no-one noticed. In the autumn of 1946, it must've been. Aye, 'cos what followed was one of the coldest winters I can remember.

At the time, all anyone knew was he'd been taken on as a handyman-chauffeur up at the *Plas*. He was friendly enough, though there were times his eyes seemed to be seeing things other folk couldn't. I'd seen that look before, in boys I'd fought with, who never got used to the blood and killing that became their sole business with the world. He was a tall lad, gangling; finely built, you'd say to be polite. Sort of outgrown himself. Always seemed to hold his head bent, most like from having to fit into the Hurricanes he'd almost lived in. Or perhaps just shy, like.

He was pleasant company, if of few words; he liked to drink a pint or two at *The Bell* or the *Prince Llewellyn* in town, and chat about the weather and farming and such. He never stayed over long and he never drank over much, and used to go back to that small room he had over the stables well before closing time. He was a fine tenor, I remember, and joined the local church choir. There weren't a lot of male voices round by then, and he was much appreciated. I'm sure he believed we all accepted him in the village, and so would anyone else have. If the odd visitor happened to notice him and ask who the stranger was, folk'd laugh and say, 'Oh that's Jan' – or Tad, or whatever his name was, I forget now, 'one of them Polish airmen. Works round here.'

They'll tell you folk this way hadn't yet got infected by the propaganda that was building up in the papers in England; the local papers hadn't caught on, that's for sure. I s'pose you could hear stuff on the wireless, but for most of 'em – it was in one ear and out the other, and as often as not spouted by one of that bugger's – that Fascist feller, what was his name? – well, one of his supporters, so nobody in their right mind believed what they said. But it wasn't long in coming for all that.

But the truth now... knotty old problem, the truth, I reckon. What I know is, the truth can be different to what you think. All I've just told you was the 'story', like, that everyone was fond of repeating as if it was gospel – after what happened later, of course, not before. It wasn't how it actually was. When I said he was a friendly man, well, he was – in the beginning at any rate.

Folk'd nod and grunt when he came into *The Bell* and they might stand and listen to him talking on about this and that. But it was rare they'd start the conversation, and when the common courtesies were finished or he ran out of things to say, they'd turn away pretty quick and take up their conversations with each other, like as if to say he wasn't worth the bother, as though he was somehow invisible.

It embarrassed me, aye indeed. When I could, without anyone noticing, I'd end up casual, like, next to him at the bar. He was an intelligent lad, thoughtful – more than some of the daft lot you'd find in *The Bell*. I used to like talking to him.

Ah well, I s'pose, human nature being what it is, it was hardly surprising his welcome in the choir started to get a little strained when the single women and younger girls noticed the interest he was taking in Annie. And it rubbed off on the men too. He didn't think, neither of them thought I shouldn't think – oh, I'm getting in a right old muddle – they thought we didn't see what was going on, and I don't say we all did – or not all of it – but I knew they were getting... 'friendly', I suppose you might say. I don't mind telling you I'd fancied my chances with Annie before he turned up, so I was pretty sharp onto stuff like that. But you have to be bigger than that, don't you? Anyway, it was all innocent in those days; not like now. Mind, Annie was from away too, even though she was old Huw's grand-daughter, so why anyone should've cared about what she got up to I don't know. But people like a good bit of tittle-tattle, don't they, and I think little things like that rankled more and more as times got worse for us all.

Anyway, a lot of them – not me, never me – might have had a laugh, like I said, but it was at him, not with him, 'cos they knew they'd bamboozled him, being folk of, well, a guarded and duplicitous nature, and who can blame them? They'd learnt well enough from history how to present a face that said one thing while their heart said another. And when they said, "Oh, that's Jan – he works round here..." I could hear the innuendo. It was faint but it was there. And the Pole's command of English wasn't so good that he could hear this whispering of the snake.

I've never told anyone this – I saw Evan watching them, too. And I watched him. He kept his head down and squinted out from under the peak of his cap, but I saw him. His eyes watched from the sheep-pens on market day, from the pub on choir night, from the boundary fence at the *Plas*. He saw comings and goings, like I did, tom-foolery and maybe a bit more. His ears were pricked, alert for nuance and deceit as acid as lemons. He saw the Pole holding Annie's hand, his arm round her waist, her head laid on his shoulder when they thought nobody was watching. I was disappointed too, I will admit, but I could let it go. Not Evan. He scowled at the flush in her cheeks and her gaiety; and she could be good fun, mind – but not when Evan was around. He watched them and I watched him.

**

Not much of a farm

It wasn't much of a farm. It sloped to the north and east and as the sun moved through the year it abandoned the land at the end of October, not to reappear on the fields until nearly March. There was a tendency round the edges to ferns, horsetail and moss, liverwort and algae, all the signs of a sour waterlogged land. Watercress grew in the streams that sprang out along the base of the escarpment. Watering animals was not a problem but drainage was a perennial headache, especially when autumnal gales dropped the leaves and blew dead twigs and branches to collect in the culverts.

But the rich deep soil in the home fields grew abundant hay and supported the small herd of beef cows – mostly bullocks – and Ziggy, the half Irish draught horse they used to pull the trap, whose lungs were broken from too much hard work too soon as a colt, you could hear their thin whistling when he galloped. Enough to survive, too little for ease.

After Taid's death Annie decided to carry on keeping a few chickens, penned up because of the foxes, though always easy prey for the heart-faced stoats; and Kitty of course. When Nain and Taid were alive they'd also kept a couple of pigs, usually Welsh, in the piggery next to the house. The black and white spotted piglets gamboled like hairless puppies but grew rapidly, and their appetites soon became so voracious, their squeals so intimidating, that Annie refused to go in with them. Taid used to tease her with stories about pigs devouring human babies, and the farm labourer who cut his leg hedging one day, so badly he couldn't move, and the big sow came and started gnawing the leg before he could be rescued. She wondered sometimes at the relish in his voice when he told her such things.

"That would be old Peg-leg Price, in town," he said. "Never the same since," and shake his head mournfully. Annie, born and bred in towns, gullible, would shrink as he passed them in the street, his wooden leg tapping.

In the curved wall of the piggery was a line of square 'windows' each set with a stone back board and a slot at the bottom, against which she would hurl the contents of the pig bucket and the hot mash, to watch it slide down into the trough below. If she peered in she could see their long snouts and dished faces gobbling the food. When it was time to slaughter them the pig-sticker from the village came and did the deed on a pig-bench, the blood rolling down from the thick neck into the pan set on the cobbles to catch it for the black puddings that were Nain's speciality. Pig-sticking was another time she preferred to be occupied well away from the yard. Pigs, she'd heard, were intelligent creatures and always knew the day they were to be killed; the only way, then, to get them from the sty to the bench would be to put a bucket over their snouts and steer them backwards, squealing to rend your heart and ears.

In the scullery-cum-larder sat the huge slate slab mainly used for preparing the hams which would be cured and then hung in the kitchen, slices cut off whenever wanted. Nain, if she felt well enough, made brawn in the big boiler hung over the range – after soaking in brine for a day, in would go the whole head to be boiled with the trotters and the tail, herbs and shallots till the meat dropped off the bones. Annie would strain the liquor off, it was too heavy for Nain to lift, and help her chop the meat and put it in an earthenware terrine, some of the stock added, a plate with a large weight put on top to press it. Annie thought it tasted wonderful, but the smell when it was cooking was dreadful.

Now, even though Evan cursed and complained, Annie refused to keep pigs. The empty sties became the dumping ground for stakes and ropes and other paraphernalia of a farm; the slate slab that still seeped moisture from the salt heaped on it over the years became home to the miscellany of preserves and cordials which Annie put by and exchanged for the ham and sausages and cuts of bacon he insisted on.

Gardening she loved, even if it meant her nails were broken and her fingers engrained with dirt no amount of scrubbing or washing dishes could remove, so that the girls up in the village oohed and aahed at them, wondering how she could bear to let them look such a disgrace. She knew without thinking what the plants needed, when they needed it, and the regular movements of digging and hoeing, almost a dance, gave space for her dreams, yet anchored her to the urgencies of life.

Annie's mother, Moire, hailed from one of those counties slap bang in the middle of Ireland, and the O'Sullivan family surely had, along with all the others, suffered during the Great Hunger. 'Be listening to what I tell you now, my darling girl,' she told her daughter, as they trudged in their boots heavy with mud up to the allotment, whose soil was thin and salty from the spray off the Dee, but from which, as if by magic, she cajoled so much. 'Watch me, now, and learn. 'Tis the truth; those who know the secrets of the land are those who survive. I learnt this from my mother, and you will be learning it from me, and may Our Blessed Lady, with your willing hands, always provide for you and yours. I haven't much to give you, but this I can.'

Annie always wondered what made her mam marry her da, but now, she thought, now she'd found someone herself, she understood. Dai Williams had been an eager escapee from the poverty of tenant-farming, and had thought himself lucky to be taken on as a machine-hand at the soap factory in Port Sunlight on the Wirral. She remembered how he'd push back the kitchen table, take hold of her mam and pull her dark head onto his shoulder as they whirled round to the tinny music from the big old wireless in its pride of place on the mantelpiece. She remembered the look in her mam's eyes as she smiled up at him. They had stopped dancing, and Mam had stopped laughing, when they moved to the mean little streets in Liverpool where anything green that showed itself was a miracle. Until then, Moire it was who supplemented his meagre wages, with fresh vegetables and fruit, and Annie learnt the art of growing at her green-fingered hands, imbibed it through her pores, osmotically.

'Why do we pull them off? Don't we want as many as the tree will grow?' she asked, thinking what a waste as she dropped the baby applets into the grass. Mam had hurried them up to the allotment in the June sunshine one evening after she'd come home from school, to 'get some fresh air into us'.

'Because the tree has spirit and sap to be growing only so many apples. Any more, and like a woman who carries more than one babe, they'll be small and weak and easy prey to pests and disease. See now, the apple tree, like us, is frightened of hard winter, and wants to be sure it has enough children that will be growing into new trees when spring comes round next year, so it starts with more than it needs, just in case. We're only helping it now. If you look, it's shucking off the very smallest on its own."

"But I thought you told me apple trees need cold winters to have apples..." Annie frowned. It didn't make sense.

"Well, there's the mystery. The tree needs the cold of the winter that's gone in order to fruit well in the summer... but the tree fruits well in the summer because it is scared of the cold of the winter coming... and isn't that just the way of things? We're often scared of exactly what we need to do us good, are we not, now?" She tweaked Annie's puzzled cheek. "Don't fret. One day you'll be understanding things that you can't yet. Come on, let's be picking these greens for supper."

Annie enjoyed pricking out and potting on, could stand for ever sniffing the warm chlorophyll smells of the greenhouse, and even though she was bored by all the time and energy her mam spent growing the leeks and marrows, perfect potatoes, unblemished apples, the showy chrysanthemums and dahlias, just to win a rosette at the local show, the smell she loved best was the smell inside a marquee on a summer's day, that heady mix of canvas, hot trodden grass, ripe tomatoes, cakes, and the perfume of women and flowers and tobacco.

To the meat, milk, and eggs, Annie added all the fruit and vegetables from the garden they could ever need, and every pot and pound and paper bag full she sold she saw was the unlooked for fruit of her childhood. In the towns, the food shortages were screwing people tight. Those with land were lucky; it acted as a buffer against the bitterness and need for a scapegoat that bitterness bred. Even so, uncomfortable incidents threatened in the hostelries where certain of the men-folk gathered in the evening, rinsing the dust of the fields out of their throats and waiting till the children should be put to bed.

One night in *The Bell*, Evan nudged Dilwyn and gestured towards the lone man perched on a stool at the bar, "Him there, see, the Pole. He's one of those foreign boys they're always chundering on about, who're taking all our jobs from us. I listened to the wireless the other night, and they're even training them to speak English proper like, and sending them on courses. Treating them better than us." He spoke loudly in Welsh, and Jan looked towards them. Evan stared back without expression, but Dilwyn nodded pleasantly, said to Evan,

"That's the Polish lad who's working up at the Simpsons. Name's Jan, so old Nobby the gardener told me."

"Oh yes. I know all about him, working up at the *Plas*. In with the nobs more like. That's who our Annie's mooning on about."

'Come on, man. Just friendly, he is, same with all the girls. Not just Annie. No need to be rude. Civil like, that's best. Been enough war and fighting to last us I reckon.

Although he'd not wanted to join up and Taid had provided the excuse, saying he needed his young strength on the farm now he was getting on a bit, Evan's sense of inferiority was galled and irritated, like grit in a shoe, by such seemingly innocent and trivial remarks. To have to sit and listen to all the stories of the boys who had gone out to France and Germany and come back men, like Dilwyn, was hardly bearable. And it wasn't so long ago they'd sat next to each other in the village school and he'd been the boss of the gang.

'Sounds to me like you lot left a lot undone, then," he countered, wiping the froth off his mouth with the back of his hand.

The steady drip of rancour wore into him, and he began to take open affront, 'Why should we put up with what the *blŵdi Sais* dictate to us, anyway? Done that too long, I reckon. If any foreigner puts a foot wrong round here, I'll have him, you wait and see. Surprised at you lot, I am, letting them in and taking our jobs."

They shook their heads and supped their ale, rattled the dominoes onto the table, and said nothing. But no matter how generous and uncensorious they were towards him, he still imagined they were laughing behind his back: 'Cocky sod, who does he think he is?' or, worse, with a sneer, 'Letting his Taid dictate to him!' He could just hear them clacking away after he'd gone out. When he was in one of his dark moods he often took his gall out on Pabi, the Border collie, who would cringe and slink away. The others noticed and thought the less of him, but said nothing.

*

It was a couple of evenings later when it happened. Evan finished his pint, the last of quite a few courtesy of his pals, and nodded to the group round the dart board, "Time to get on home." As he left, he aimed his customary curse and a kick at the dog who was lying in the shaft of sunlight that streamed across the open doorway. He wasn't prepared for Jan, who had just arrived on his bicycle, grabbing him by the shoulder, pulling him backwards away from the dog. He staggered and nearly fell. When he recovered he rounded on the Pole, fists bunched and face even redder. Jan looked him in the eye and said, 'Why you treat him like this? Your dog, he does nothing bad. He does not deserve to kick him like that."

'Wha–? I never –. Dil, Morris? "Evan blustered, and looked round for moral support, the Dutch courage draining away in the face of such a challenge. His drinking companions turned back to their pints. They would not catch his eye. Why should they come to his rescue? They did not feel particularly friendly towards Jan, but he had made Evan lose face and, inside, they were glad. So they pretended indifference. Jan propped his bicycle against the wall and walked past Evan to the bar leaving him standing there.

The bad feeling between them was cemented from that night, and Evan lost no opportunity to insert into his conversation a sly innuendo or carping complaint about the Poles' settling in Britain. More and more, Jan's charm with the girls in the village, but most especially his particular success with Annie, rankled with him. His jealous spite started to fill increasingly receptive ears; they all sensed Jan was different – not only was he an incomer, but he'd been a pilot; and, dazzled by the newly-found heroism of aviation, Jan, in keeping with the now-legendary Polish charm, had transferred those qualities of Poland's dashing cavalry to his exploits in the air, with a canny eye on the admiring glances of the girls and young women.

As conditions worsened, and the cry against the Poles resettling grew louder, the villagers grew to resent the position they imagined he had at their expense, fed by the exaggerated gossip of his special treatment by Mr Simpson at the *Plas*. And if he wanted to suck up to a nob, one of the '*pobl sedd fawr*', what did they care about the loss of all Jan held dear in his life?

*

While Evan focused his malice on Jan, Annie flirted. Not overtly, it wasn't her way, but she was a rapt listener, she made Jan feel interesting and special, and he saw her painted in sympathetic and intelligent colours.

He started to look out for her bright headscarf in the lanes, and felt disappointed if she didn't come to choir practice, or he was out driving Mr Simpson when she came to work. He would make excuses to do odd jobs round the house and yard on Mondays. He dreamt of stroking her rich chestnut hair, which she let down when she came to choir practice, falling to her shoulders, shiny as a new conker. He would offer to walk her home, leaving her at the top of the little track to Bron Felen so that he would not have to speak to Evan. Annie made him laugh, and he enjoyed her quick-witted humour.

'Did you see that bloke with the lurchers hanging round the *Llewellyn* on Saturday? That's Tudur Richards, the rat catcher. You wouldn't believe it but he's eighty if he's a day."

Jan whistled. "He look fifty no more."

"Yes. They reckon during the war he put rat meat in his dinners for protein – but they're filthy creatures and I don't believe it for a minute." She shuddered.

"Oh, and look. That's old Tom Price. See his legs? How bent they are? That's 'cos he always rode a little grey hill pony round the boundaries of his farm…" she grinned. "Story is, if he saw something wrong the other side of a wall, to save riding miles to the nearest gate he'd get off and lift the pony over, then climb over himself and get back on."

"I don't believe this story. Annie, you tease me."

"No, no, it's God's own truth," Annie protested innocently. "Go and ask him. Go on. He won't bite – well, not a great big Pole anyway…"

Another time she pointed out a shifty looking little chap at market who everyone seemed to be ignoring. "Watch out for that bloke, they call him Dai *Pen Rydan*. Best keep clear of him."

"*Pen rydan*? What is that?"

"It means turnip head. You know. It's a big root vegetable, like what the cattle eat in winter. It means he's thick. Stupid. Anyway, he's just got out of the local nick – prison to you."

"Why? What does he do?"

"There was some bloke on holiday, going round on a bike, and he came down the footpath by Dai's place. Well, you're only s'posed to walk on a footpath, and Dai was waiting for him. He got hold of the bike by the handlebars and shouted 'Get back, you bugger, get back!' Well, the bloke naturally refused, and started tugging at the other end of his bike. But Dai was well fastened on. Dai's wife was peering out the window at them, and they both yelled 'Get the police'. It was a stand-off. And when Brian Bryn Bela, the local copper – you know him, round and fat, always standing at the end of the pier when the fishing boats come in – well, he came puffing up, but Dai still refused to let go. Brian had to hold him and get the bloke to prise his fingers off the handlebars one by one, and, when he had, Dai just swung his fist and knocked Brian out cold. The cyclist went hell for leather down the path and got some of the men in the village to go up and see to things, and they carted him off to the cells to cool down for a couple of days."

*

The first time they 'walked out' Jan invited her to go with him to the November 5th bonfire and fireworks on the beach of the little town. He had not come across this charming British tradition before, fireworks and bonfires being banned during the active war years, and when Annie told him the story, it struck him with an amused irony that Sir Guy Fawkes was still being fêted as a villain after all these centuries, especially by the Celtic Welsh who, he learned, had no reason to love the Mother of Parliaments.

'I don't want you going with that slimy Pole, making a fool of yourself and – " Evan blurted at supper, as she was getting ready to go out.

'Well, I'm going, and that's it," Annie interrupted flatly, and flounced out of the house before he could think of anything else to say.

With the revelers crowding the beach and the grass along the Groe, the fireworks had been set up on the pier. They lit up the deep velvet sky, paled the stars to insignificance. Jan and Annie felt as though they'd lost themselves, twirling in the space of the universe, floating hand in hand through the constellations. The small fishing boats that normally tied up to the pier had moored out in the straits, their riding lamps reflected in the mirror calm water. The children dashed about and laughed till they nearly choked in their delight, as they watched their fathers leaping and falling over in their haste to escape the jumping jacks that they insisted were out to get them; and the even littler ones gazed raptly at the bright phosphorescence of sparklers fizzing and sputtering in their mothers' hands.

'You want bake spud, Annie?" Jan stood by the brazier warming his hands.

'Bake spud? You're really learning the lingo," Annie laughed.

'Go on then. Though they're not the same without butter."

They licked the grease from their fingers and strolled along the sea wall and up the small headland to the seat by the cliff edge and looked down on the tide washing the rocks below and over to the mainland with its spread of lights and fires, listened to the faint cheers drifting across as another rocket burst and flowered in the black sky. The night held an implicit promise and both spoke its language.

'I think we should be careful about Evan, Jan, and keep things a bit quiet in the village," Annie said as they ambled back down to the revelry, and Jan understood what she meant perfectly.

*

A bad feeling insinuated itself into the seams of Bron Felen. It followed Annie to Mrs Simpson's and even when she was singing she couldn't get it to dissipate. It hovered in the air and sometimes Annie thought she caught a glimpse of its shadow out of the corner of her eyes, but when she turned her head quickly it dispersed like smoke, like something from a dream that persisted through the day, although she could not recall what. It reminded her of a dream from when she was a small girl, the same feeling reached out from all those years ago and wormed itself through some crack in time into the present.

She was standing on the edge of an abyss. At least it felt like an abyss, but it was only a small one because Annie could easily see the sides and the bottom. Below her lapped a dark lake of steaming manure, like the loads from the local farm Da had delivered in autumn for his garden. A rope stretched from her feet across the void to the other side, and vanished into the murk beyond. She knew she had to cross the rope, that something terrible was behind her. She could not make out what was in front. She put her foot on the rope and felt it give and sway. Stretching her arms out as she'd seen a trapeze artist do in the circus she started to run across. She fought the urge to look down, but the dizzying fumes were rising, her foot slipped, and she fell screaming.

**

Down the line

'So be careful what you wish for
'Cause you just might get it and if you get it
Then you just might not know what to do wit' it.'

- Anon

It's no good. I need to get the telling of it done with. Perhaps then you'll be able to stand back a bit, the way you do in a gallery when you want to distinguish the background from the foreground, see what pushes out and what recedes, what matters and what doesn't.

Our idyll didn't last long. I look at the flotsam of my earlier dream and I still ask, could we have seen it coming? Could we have added up all the small portents and signs over the years and by doing so taken steps to render it manageable – manageable by Fleur herself at least, if not by us? But we had lived the sixties' dream, and boundaries were for other generations. We were pioneers, there were no rules. In the end, of course, it was our children who reaped the result, and Fleur who found she could not reconcile it to life as she ended up living it. And after all, so they said, it was her choice; it was a choice she made. She was a grown up now. And should we not honour, respect that?

Her choice? At least, that's what everyone tried to tell us, perhaps to protect us from the guilt, and shame, and blame – or perhaps because they really believed it. But although I wished to, desperately, I couldn't see where that choice lay. And that lack of choice ended up punching a gaping hole from my womb, down through my perineum, and poured out, a river, between my legs. There are some things you just do not have a choice about. This flight of my soul (for what else could I call it?) buckled my knees and stole my breath, leaving me just enough to caw like the raven in the wind, and thrash like a road kill with its back broken.

Our friends erected a shield against the worst, but all the shields in the world would have been as insubstantial as gossamer against an onslaught such as this. And it was not protection I sought but the harshness of truth and the cold space of my own understanding; whether or not these brought solace or consolation was meaningless to me. I took a big stubborn stick and beat to shreds all the worn out concepts and ritualised phrases. It was like attacking dandelion fluff floating in the air – they danced and wavered, but still they came, clouds of them, blotting out the sun.

I got through it. I nodded and hugged and squeezed hands, listened politely, agreed and capitulated, said 'Maybe', and 'Possibly you're right', and 'I hadn't thought of it that way'.

Against my volition, I found even so I had been busy building defences, armour that clung tightly around my heart – flexible enough to allow it room to beat, and round my lungs enough for them to breathe, and permeable enough for all of me to weep and not drown. My head felt as though it was filled with sphagnum moss, that stauncher of wounds and soaker-up of blood outpourings, that filler of wreaths and hanging baskets – my head, that sponge programmed to get by. I only had to endure long enough to find a space where I could retreat, to wring it out and see what it had soaked up.

I marvel when I see people standing, sitting, talking, eating, drinking, walking at the funerals of their daughters, sons, brothers, sisters, wives, husbands, even though I did the same. How do they do it? Who is pulling the strings? With what iron substance have they been injected that keeps them upright and functioning? Why is the world still spinning? Didn't it stop dead on its axis and fling us all, marionettes that we are, cart-wheeling into space, spilling our gin and tonics, snatching wildly at our nicotine and our drugs, newspapers floating in a meaningless jumble of out of date headlines, dead televisions, i-pods still attached to our earholes? Nope. Here we still are.

*

Winter 2001-2002

The signs of depression were cunning. They didn't come in a rush all at once and flaunt themselves in our faces; they crept in, in the stillness and silence over months, maybe even years. Growing, growing. Stealthily. Ghosts of the past flitted first through her dreams and then her waking hours – a tide of pain like the sea, impervious to any Canute. Then the grasping at straws as to whys, the if-onlys, and the shame of telling anyone what was happening – the guilt, the obsession. The moments of insight, 'Mummy, my brain isn't working right'. Until finally, 'It won't ever end. There isn't any way out," whispered on the beach, on Christmas morning. 'I can't stop thinking about killing myself".

Fleur, Fleur! We stood there, and what I remember now is the splash of her words mingling with the shriek of the gulls and the melancholy piping of the oyster catchers, the feel of her thin shoulders as I wept with her. We all went to see the new Harry Potter that night, drove twenty five miles to the nearest cinema. I don't know what she was watching; it wasn't the film on the screen, but some endlessly repeating internal loop she was locked into, and from which we were locked out.

Next came the rush to the GP, whose remedy was to scream 'Stop it! Stop it! Stop it!' at her during a 'panic' attack. Which guideline did that ever come from? Wasn't she right to panic? But at least he did refer her for a psychiatric consultation, even if in a month's time. A week or so later, a terrified dash at midnight to the nearest Community Psychiatric Centre – any port in a storm – and still the complete absence of meaningful support from the professionals. Then, 'Only two weeks to go now,' we all said to each other, trying to shore up our dismay. Only? Believe me, two weeks was a very big hole down which to fall.

Even then I would not, could not, allow this to be real. I couldn't allow that any chickens might have come home to roost like this. Nothing we had done, or not done, deserved this. The end I foresaw was always recovery and well-being – what a delusion. Always some resource to fall back on – mere wishful thinking.

In the end I had to accept that nothing was connecting with her, and, to my guilty shame, found myself watching her surreptitiously in chemist shops. I breathed an imperceptible sigh of relief whenever she laughed, which was rarely, even if her face was white and her eyes too large. I acted so normal it was abnormal. And I was acting, afraid that it was my perception of reality that was the distorted one.

I can see it now; in so many little ways she said goodbye – random gifts, visits, telephone calls. And I could not rush in where, they say, even angels feared to tread. I could not be the interfering, overbearing parent, mother-in-law, ensconcing myself unbidden in their home, at their table. Her oldest sister came over from France, and I persuaded Fleur to visit us at the same time; they slept in the same bed together, up in the barn we'd converted into an office-cum-spare bedroom, talking through the night. Nothing was changed in the morning; and that old magnet pain exerted its pull and back home she went. Waving goodbye on the train.

Still denying that this was what it was, I turned my back to the hurtling express coming down the line.

*

I turned towards the garden. Of course. Gardening had always been a refuge, and all the gardens I ever had, sanctuaries; they rewarded and solaced me. Distracted me. And this garden drew me more than any before. The sense of sharing it with Annie grew stronger day by day as I worked. I could see her hand everywhere, and as best I could tried to keep the spirit of what I imagined she gave to the garden. Everyone said I had green fingers, meaning I knew instinctively when to cut, prune, dig, weed, water, and feed – and when to stand back. I understood this perfectly – where plants were concerned.

I called Molly, our little Jack Russell, and went out intending to do some much needed digging. As I worked the tranquil plish of the little waterfall from the pond outflow soothed me. Soon I was sweating in the un-seasonal warmth of the January sun. The dappled-ness of the orchard with its old wooden bench set askew beneath the gnarled old plum beckoned. This was where Annie must have sat. I lay on the bench, looking up at the blue jewels of the sky piercing the lacework of the branches, putting myself in her place; but I could not get comfortable. I turned and shifted, lay on my back, my side; gave up and sat up. A little breeze brought with it a sudden sharp mousy smell, and a foetid odour like stinkhorn hit my nostrils. Surely not at this time of year…Where had I smelt it before?… It must be something dead in the hedge, perhaps a rat or a rabbit that Molly had caught and half buried. The boughs creaked and squeaked, like chalk on a board. I began to feel a chill. 'Don't be daft, Sarah' I chided myself, 'just sweat drying and cooling,' and grabbed my fleece. The smaller twigs started to shake and rattle, and I cowered as a shower of the little hard dry fruits which had desiccated on the tree rained down on me. Although afterwards I made a joke of it, at the time it was almost as though they were being deliberately hurled. The hairs on the back of my neck stood up; Molly whined and I picked her up. The breeze dropped and everything became still once more. My unease settled as I hugged the dog's warm body. But inside a drop of fear had lodged. 'I'm losing it,' I said to Molly. 'It's getting to me. I've had enough. I don't think I can handle it."

*

For all of us, fear started as a drop, then became a puddle, a pond, then a lake. It wouldn't stop raining – and the dam burst. She ran out into the morning, when the trees were tossing their heads and all sensible creatures were safe and warm in their burrows and nests, and hid shivering and foetal under a gorse bush. A search party found her after an hour and carried her to the ambulance, and she was whirled forty miles into no-woman's land, to god-knows-where, to a good-for-nothing place, where the greatest problem was a flailing drunk with a broken arm.

She ran off after an hour of waiting, before anyone found the time to see her. I can hear her, 'I've gotta get out of this place...' Still in t-shirt off the trolley past the nurses station with its nurses staring through the waiting room past reception and receptionist staring through the foyer patients' white faces and the revolving doors into the car park people staring.

Harry and I got straight in the car when Johnny rang, the panic in his voice driving us at break neck speed for over a hundred miles. We arrived to be told a friend had found her looking over the railway bridge and persuaded her to re-admit herself.

'Fleur said she wanted to have a wander round, take a look at places where she remembered being happy," she said. In her previous life, gone now, finished. This thought frightened me even more than the overdose itself, because it smacked of a mind made up, undeterred by failure.

'Why did you allow her to just walk out, when you surely must have known she was a serious risk to herself?" I asked the Sister on Casualty, unable to hide my distress.

'We can't stop people discharging themselves," she explained; and 'No, we did not have the power to section her, even temporarily"; and 'It was her choice to leave"; and, the final clincher, 'It's a question of her human rights"

'Her human rights!? What about her right to life?" I asked, taken aback at what was, to me, a cock-eyed perception of priorities.

46

"Who actually spoke to her while she was here?" My jaw muscles tense; sister doesn't meet my eyes.

"Who even tried to persuade her not to leave?" My heart pounds; her mouth becomes a thin line.

"Who tried to stop her?" She goes to the door and opens it, our interview over; my shoulders square.

"Who gave a damn, where was a doctor, what was her triage, and why did you leave her alone in the first place?" Goodbye Mrs Blake, if you want to make a complaint there is a form in the waiting room you can fill in and return to the address on the bottom; the door shuts behind me.

*

Procedures were followed, tests were run, anti-overdose drugs administered. Vomiting, crying, confused, traumatised. Bewailing being still alive. Ashamed she hadn't even managed to get that right.

Even though they thought we couldn't hear them, or perhaps they didn't care if we did, 'She brought it on herself didn't she?" and, 'She was just trying to get attention, like all the waifs and strays we see – cutting themselves and taking drug overdoses – they don't mean it, they wouldn't do it really". Stern, cold, disapproving, in some cases overtly contemptuous. And, the worst, as I stood there in the waiting room, to a thirteen-year old self-harmer accompanied by her hand-wringing mother, 'We've got higher priorities than you, ducky."

Who was meant to care anyway? What, me? I saw in their off-hand manner, their shrugs and indifferent eyes. Me? Overworked and underpaid? Burnt out, this listing temple of Hippocrates, with its certificate-waving priestesses. Yes, I'm bitter. Who wouldn't be?

*

It is tea-time, five o'clock, although the thought of eating or drinking anything sickens me, my throat is solid. We are waiting for the psychiatrist. I am sitting by Fleur's trolley in a cubicle smelling of antiseptic and vomit. I hold her hand. The curtain opens and a bespectacled face peers round the edge, regards Fleur as if she is a butterfly, chloroformed, pinned to a board. Doesn't speak, just stares.

"Who are you?" I ask, holding Fleur's hand too tightly, I can feel her flinch. I loosen my grip, dismayed by the fragility of her bones; appalled at my own reflexive grip grinding them together.

'Er, hmm, Doctor Bryant. Fleur Mason?" He doesn't look at me. She nods. 'Come with me." The face withdraws. I help wrap the hospital gown round her, and she shuffles to the interview room. I panic. This person who seems to be verging on Asperger's syndrome surely cannot be the person who will assess my daughter's mental condition and decide her fate. You might as well ask the rain what it feels like to get wet.

And I am paralysed by the memory of when I was a student and looking for work during the long summer vacation. I went for an interview as a care assistant at the local psychiatric hospital. A person who introduced himself as the duty psychiatrist conducted me on a tour of the unit. We passed along green painted corridors that smelt of strong disinfectant; he pointed out 'interesting' patients (his words) shuffling about in their pyjamas and slippers; and detailed the diagnoses of those who were rocking in various corners. What clinched it for me were the bizarre conversations with others who seemed most eager to accost us. Bizarre because they seemed to make a kind of sense, yet at the same time there was something strangely off-beat and at odds that I couldn't quite put my finger on. Perhaps it was only culture shock, as when you walk off a plane at some far-flung destination, where you can't read the writing or understand what is said – you don't know if you're being offered a cup of coffee or told to bugger off. I didn't to intend to stay long enough to find out. It wasn't so much the bewildered minds as their acceptance of that world as normal. He saw me off the premises and cheerfully looked forward to my joining the team. I already knew – I knew I had been interviewed by a patient as a joke, pretending to be the doctor. And then came the chilling realisation that I couldn't actually tell the difference. I wrote and apologised, and lied, saying I had decided instead to go and do voluntary work abroad.

*

The clock in the waiting room hauls the minutes round with incremental slowness, the torpor that overtakes us is the buzzing of a blue bottle trapped against the glass of the window by its yearning for escape. There has been a long lull in the flow of patients through Casualty, where we are still waiting. Johnny cannot sit still, chain smoking out in the car park, stalking up and down, up and down. I go out to keep him company.

'I didn't know what to do! I didn't think it would come to this. I can't take it any more. I haven't slept for a month. I'm too tired to work, and we can't pay the bills... She just sits on the bed and beats her chest with her fists, crying she can't feel anything! I'm scared..." The litany of his distress and helplessness pours out. I reassure him as best I can. We hadn't known what to do either, then or now. We are hoping these doctors and nurses, the professionals, trained in caring for the bewildered, know what to do.

*

It is nine o'clock. I just heard the town clock in the square chime the hours.
"I'm discharging her. I think she's well enough to go home," the professional announces. There is a stunned silence as we take this in.

"You can't do that!" I blurt. "She's saying how disappointed she is to still be alive. Doesn't that mean anything to you? She'll try again, we all know she will."

"She can't come home, she can't!" Johnny bursts out. "I can't cope, I can't handle it. I don't want her to hurt herself. Please!"

Our voices clamour.

"I'm sorry. I've discussed her case with my consultant and he will not admit her to this hospital."

"But why on earth not?"

"Because these beds are for English patients, not Welsh." Loftily, as though this is irrefutable, impregnable logic. It demolishes us. Never did we entertain the remotest possibility of such a reason.

"The beds in our Unit are limited and if we admit patients from across the border those beds are blocked for our own patients. And they don't just stay overnight or a few days, you know; the Welsh Trusts we deal with do not exactly rush to find a bed for them, and they can be with us for weeks."

But to cast a desperate person out into the night, just to make a point to colleagues over the border, does this sound like sanity?

*

We persist with Dr Bryant, we have no choice. I think of Fleur lying there, white as a sheet, stinking. Tubes in her arm to re-hydrate her. So drugged she couldn't walk without staggering. Take her home? What is this man thinking?

It is a film, a farce. As we argue with Dr Bryant his desire to be rid of us propels us as if by osmosis through the waiting room, into the foyer, through the automatic doors, out onto the pavement. Although I am far from laughing I can't help noticing that for several minutes we hover inside the range of the automatic doors' sensors, and they open and close, open and close, synchronized to our smallest movements, as though in counterpoint with our feelings. Patients and visitors give us a wide berth. It is in danger of becoming a public spectacle. In the end I put a stop to it.

'Now listen carefully, because I want you to be under no illusions. Fleur will try again, we know that, and so must you if you're honest. I don't know what she has told you, but we're the people who know her best and I want what we are saying put on record. Now. If you discharge her and something... happens, well I'm sure I don't need to hammer the point home."

His eyes behind his glasses become owl-like, and off he hurries again.

Half an hour later, he hurries back. There is a bed at *Llanfair*, forty miles away, but no ambulance to take her. If she wants to wait for one, probably in the morning, she can spend the night on the trolley in Casualty. 'She won't be nursed, though," he adds. 'If you want to you can stay with her on chairs in the cubicle or the waiting room."

Before he goes, he writes a letter in which he describes Fleur as suffering a severe episode of major clinical depression, and, in his opinion, a high risk patient.

Despite, or maybe because of, the risk, we decide to take her to the hospital ourselves that night. What can she do but go along with this? Home is not an option. The trolley is not an option. This is the best we can do.

*

We had to agree with the doctor who admitted her to *Ysbyty Llanfair* in the early hours of what was now the next morning, that visiting was best limited to weekends. I don't know why we agreed, perhaps we were all exhausted and the rationale of Fleur having space and quiet, away from her normal life, away from us who couldn't help her – and maybe even, God forbid, made things worse – let us off the hook. So it is that when Harry and I walk through the front door of the hospital later the same day we come to say goodbye. No, not goodbye, see you soon. Au revoir, auf wiedersehen, hasta la vista – see you next weekend.

I wasn't in any space to notice the night before, that the brick walk up to the front doors is so pretty, lined with erica and helleborus, bright drifts of cyclamen, and winter crocuses, their blossoms just opening. I relax; the place doesn't look so bad. The doors aren't locked, and as there is no bell, we walk in and look around. There is not a soul in sight, just an atmosphere of something either just happened, or about to, somewhere else in the interstices of time and space. A Marie Céleste moment.

Harry sits in an armchair in the lounge area that extends all along the front of the building, the seating arranged around the walls; this makes me tense again, a literal 'backs to the wall' moment. A door opens on the other side of the room and through it, shadowed closely by a nursing assistant, comes a young woman, who stumbles and clutches the chair backs for support in a drunken fashion. She staggers past but is oblivious to me, intent on the front exit, headed for the outside. The assistant doesn't look at me either. As she reaches the door the assistant steps in front and steers her back the way she has come. Apart from the sound of heavy breathing their progress across the carpeted room is silent. I shiver; I don't feel quite so relaxed.

I venture along a corridor, and hear voices laughing inside a small office, the door closed and with a sign reading 'Staff Only'. I knock and the voices fall silent. Into the pause that follows pops the thought 'I could just take her away with me'... but before it can take root, a nurse sticks her head out and demands,

"Who are you? What are you doing here?"

I explain who we are and that we are there to visit my daughter Fleur. I can't think of any other reason for ever casually dropping into such an establishment, certainly not 'en passant', on a 'let's call into the Psychiatric Unit' whim; and if we aren't meant to walk in, why isn't there a bell and a secured door? But I don't say any of this.

"If you'll go back to the lounge and wait, I'll bring Fleur to you," she says, her manner abrupt. Have we deprived her of a slice of chocolate cake? Perhaps she is missing out on some juicy gossip? It is a far cry from the kindly reception of the night before, when the night shift welcomed us with tea and biscuits. The flowered brick path disappears as if it never was.

Fleur comes into the lounge, a white and waxen wilted lily. One of the nursing staff later described her in his statement to the police, as 'pale, thin and skeletal'.

"Hi, Mummy", she says in a monotone. I jump up and hug her. Her slumped shoulders and bent head, fingers twisting and restless, makes me want to cry and I turn away to rub the tears from my eyes before they fall, pretending to sneeze.

"Are they looking after you well?" I ask; nothing I have so far seen this morning reassures me.

"I saw the consultant for a few minutes; not for long," she says.

She says, "You should go home, pointless hanging around here. I feel awful."

"Is that what you want, darling?" I say. She nods.

"OK, sweetheart. Shall we have a cuppa first?"

I spot a drinks machine in the corner. "And it'd be nice to see your room. Then I can think of..." My sentence trails away.

'Sure. I'll go and ask." She goes and knocks on the door to the office where the nurses are all still congregated. A nurse opens the door, I can't see if it was the same one, and says, 'Yes?" impatiently. When Fleur comes back she says 'Fine", but Harry can't come because it is a female ward area.

She leads me along a windowless corridor, passing several patients coming the other way who stare at us. She shrinks closer to the wall as they go by. I am filled with foreboding; she is such a sensitive little thing – to be surrounded by these sad, disturbed people in this sad, uneasy place would surely be unendurable. Will she find somebody she can trust? Will there be a nurse or doctor who will empathise and offer kindly compassion? For this, I think, is the only therapy on offer until the drugs kick in, possibly the only therapy ever worth having. Is it even on offer, though? Doesn't it depend on the right sort of human material? I cannot pursue this reflection further.

She has a single room. I'm pleased about this, although it is to prove disastrous. In the corner on the floor by a wardrobe sits her big blue suitcase, still packed, and on the windowsill is a bunch of flowers in their cellophane, starting to wilt in the heat.

'Darling, did Johnny bring the flowers?" I ask. Their lying there unheeded is not a good sign.

'Yes. He came in this morning. Poor man, poor man. Mummy it's no good I'm no good for him I asked him not to come I don't want him to see me here I told him not to wait for me it's too late too late!" she blurts on a breath, bursting into tears. I nearly start bawling myself, the fear rising in my throat. I pull her down next to me on the bed and hug her to me tightly, never to let go. But you can't sit like that for ever, and up I pop again, the irrepressible, soothing, rational person who is such a fraud. But what else could I be? How could I throw off that imprisoning shackle of fear of doing the wrong thing, saying the wrong words, making it all so much worse? So I say sensibly, and so stupidly, Why not wait and see what the consultant says, the drugs are bound to help, and lots of people have a bit of a crisis like this at some point in their lives, and of course you'll get better, you just need to give it a bit of time, and there's a lot to look forward to, just get better first... but she cuts me off, shaking her head, 'It's no good, Mummy. I won't get better. I know. There's no way out. Johnny's better off without me."

Swallowing hard, I don't argue, say, 'Johnny loves you, darling. Surely it's up to him to make up his mind what he wants?"

'He's a good man, a good man – but I'm no good for him," she says again.

'Why don't we put these lovely flowers in some water? Is there a vase?" I get up and look in the little en-suite toilet, more to give myself time to recover than because I think it will help. 'Let's go and ask one of the nurses to get one for us, shall we? Otherwise the flowers will d...," I can't say the word, "...and that would be a shame."

She shrugs. I can see she isn't interested in anything other than the broken record inside her head.

'Mummy, you know the front tooth I had implanted after my car accident? I think the metal's jumbling my thoughts. Perhaps there's some sort of electricity interfering with my brain, do you think I should have it taken out?" she says as we walk back down the corridor, so far from reality that I hold my breath so it can't escape as a moan. When I release it, I convert the moan to,

'Mmmmmmmm. Perhaps mention it to the consultant when you see him, sweetheart?"

Back to the nurses' office we go, bang on the door again, the same nurse says, 'Oh, it's you again." You bloody rude bitch, I think again, have to curb my anger.

'Do you have a vase for the flowers Fleur's been brought?"

'Olga, go and see if you can find a vase somewhere, will you? I'm busy," she turns back and addresses someone in the little room. I hear the clink of cups and saucers and a sigh of exasperation. Another nurse comes to the door, pushes past and marches off without a word. Not a smile between the two of them. We follow. She produces a tall plastic vase from a cupboard, grunts when I say 'Thanks', and heads back to her tea and gossip. The encounter is so intimidating I don't dare ask where we should fill it, and after wandering up and down a few more corridors, we find a bathroom and use the cold tap on the bath.

We go back to her room. I remove the cellophane and arrange the flowers. 'Where shall we put them?" I ask, but the only place is the locker by the window. Fleur picks at the cuticle of her thumbs and I see they are bleeding. I suggest we go back to the lounge and have a cup of tea with Harry, sit and chat for a while in more comfort. But once back in the lounge she sits hunched forward on the edge of the seat, her arms hugging herself and her legs wound round each other. I want to take her in my arms and smooth her out, straighten the kinks, rock her as I used to when she was little, stroke her hair and whisper endearments – but what if she pushes me away? After all, I have brought her here. What have I done? Why am I so trapped in this prison of my own doubt and insecurity that I cannot reach out to my child?

We talk, or at least Harry and I do, but after an hour of cold cups of tea and desultory conversation that is going nowhere we run out of things to say.

"I think you'd better go, Mummy," she says again. "I'm not feeling well. I'll see you next weekend."

She sees us to the door and watches as we walk down the path. As we get to the car I look back and see her half hidden behind the door, still watching. I put up my hand to wave and blow her a kiss. She holds her hand up and blows one back, then turns and moves into the darkness of the building.

*

There was no record that Harry and I had ever visited, I found out later. My grasp of reality by then had become so feeble I could well have believed that I had not gone there that day. Had I dreamt it all? Oh, and I didn't get to see her the next weekend.

People warn, "Be careful of what you want because you might get it." I wanted Fleur to go to hospital; I wanted those who I thought knew what they were doing to look after her and take this unbearable worry away. Things were out of control, and I wanted someone to take control. It simply never crossed my mind to consider if anyone could, or should be, in control of anyone else. Nor if it could possibly be someone's human right to do what Fleur did to themselves.

**

The singing inside

'O for the wings, for the wings of a dove!
Far away, far away, far away, far away would I rove!
In the wilderness build me a nest,
and remain there forever at rest.
In the wilderness build me, build me a nest;
and remain there forever at rest.'

- Mendelssohn, Hear My Prayer

The perfidy, the malice, the cunning...

"They didn't see it coming. Or they just didn't think it had anything to do with them, buried in a little village way out on the edge of Wales." Dilwyn said when I pressed him further for Annie's story. "Annie was an innocent lass for all that'd happened to her, and still lived in a world where the evil underside of life skulked only in the shadows. How could she have foreseen the full extent of what was on its way? And yet, the larger world should have been warning enough.

"When I went to Chester, I couldn't help but notice the turn of the tide; graffiti beginning to appear on walls, 'England for the English'; even round by us the talk in the public bar was mostly grumbles about the lack of jobs and feeding the mouths of foreigners. I can't believe the Pole didn't notice, so why didn't he do anything? And towards the end, when he came in the Bell he mostly drank on his own (though not by his choice), apart from me – I always liked chatting with him, you know me. But it was obvious where things were going – and perhaps I should have said more.

'I s'pose he might've thought he didn't have all that much choice. He couldn't go home, 'cos home didn't exist no more. All the rumours his mates were hearing, about what was happening to them who did go back – arrests, torture, Siberia. I should think that was enough to put going back there with or without Annie right out of his mind. He said the worst of it was the horror of fleeing like a criminal, and how all he had fought for turned out to be a country occupied by a brutal enemy – he meant the Russkies. I wouldn't'have liked to be in his shoes.

'He told me he was thinking of staying here, or somewhere in Wales, not England. He took right against the English. I didn't tell him what I thought about that. And it turned out he did think of emigrating. But he didn't tell Annie. No idea why not; she'd have jumped at the chance, and maybe they'd have got out before anything happened. All these people not saying anything to each other. No wonder the world gets in the mess it does. And Annie blamed me for what happened. As if I could've done anything to stop it."

I looked up sharply as I caught the tremor in his voice and saw him stab at a tuft of grass with his stick. He turned his gaze out to sea so he didn't have to catch my eye. I knew what it was. I was no stranger to what he was feeling. That was a cross we would both carry.

December 1946

'It isn't right for you to be hanging round some *blŵdi* foreigner. What would Nain and Taid think? They'd turn in their grave." Annie jumped, startled out of her reverie, and nearly dropped the crockery she was stacking on the draining board. Evan was stood in the doorway glaring at her.

'I don't care – they're not here to mind, are they?" she burst out, shocking herself. "And what business is it of yours? You're not my keeper. You can't stand the thought of me being friends with someone else, can you? That's what's not right. Why don't you go and find a girl? Jean the Wern, she's always making eyes at you at market, I bet she'd lo…" She gasped as her cousin gripped her upper arm and swung her round to face him. She kicked the pail of milk that was waiting to be poured into the setting pan, and the milk ran a white stream over the floor.

'You dirty little slut", he spat. 'Not all the girls are like you. I've seen you with that foreign bastard up at the *Plas*. He'd better look out or else."

'You leave him alone, he hasn't done anything to you," Annie wrenched herself away. 'He tells me stories about flying and what it was like in the war.

At least he fought in the war." This last came out without thinking, and before she even shut her mouth she knew it would be fuel to Evan's fury.

Evan stared at her, panting, his eyes flat.

"You just watch it, Miss Clever Clogs" he hissed and flung himself out the door into the yard, yelling for the dog. Annie shivered. There was something wrong with Evan, nothing she could put her finger on, and she didn't think he had it in him to do anything really bad, but she resolved to be careful. Just in case.

She threw out the bacon rind and fat, that she could never bring herself to eat, for the birds, and looked up at the gun-metal sky, considering. If the snow would just hold off she would be able to take the bike, even if she had to walk back tonight. She hated walking to the *Plas* in the mornings, she wanted to get there as fast as she could.

The kitchen clock struck the half hour and made up her mind for her, she was running late now. She struggled into the thick heavy coat, already too small, that Nain had bought from old Mr Watts, who had his tailor's shop in a shed along by the pier, and wheeled the bike out of the barn. She set off, shivering in the wind, the weak beam from the front light just enough to keep her to the track. She bumped out into the lane which was iron hard and badly rutted from the cart tracks, swerved to avoid a puddle that had iced over in the night, and stood on the pedals, leant over the handle-bars to go as fast and hard as she could to get warm. Even so, she knew the wool of her mittens would be stuck to the metal by the time she'd got half way there.

Every week Annie picked up off the hall table a thick envelope addressed to the Mass Observation Project, to give to the postman when he called in the morning, and today was no exception. She had noticed Mrs Simpson always spent an hour or so in the afternoon writing at the 'escritoire', as she called it, in the drawing room, so when she came into the kitchen with her list of chores, Annie plucked up courage to ask her about it.

"It's a diary, Annie, and it's so exciting. It's part of a simply enormous experiment called the Mass Observation project. Ordinary people over the whole country are writing for it, and it's all going to be preserved as an historical document."

"What sort of things do you write about?" Annie asked, wondering how Mrs Simpson could think of herself as an 'ordinary' person; and why anyone would ever be interested in what ordinary people thought and did, anyway. Life was pretty dull – 'although perhaps not entirely...' she thought, as she remembered the walk home last Friday with Jan.

'Oh, everyday things, like what we eat, how much household items cost, the weather, conversations with people, places we go. Last week Edward and I took the train to London to visit some old friends, for instance, so I wrote about the journey and what we saw, the clothes we wore, conversations we had, what there was in the shops – how life is. If I feel in the mood I write what I think about things like this welfare state everyone's so excited about. The New Jerusalem."
Annie looked blank.

'Haven't you heard?" Mrs Simpson asked. As Annie shook her head, she frowned, 'Oh, well, it's very complicated – I'll tell you all about it some other day, though I'm not really sure I'm the best person... basically, it means that poor people will at last be able to have access to proper housing and health services and education, free."

She chewed her fountain pen reflectively as she caught Annie's look of doubt. 'I know, why don't you tell me about your life, Annie? You could say what it's like as a young girl in the country, after being brought up in the city. I imagine you're quite observant, and at least you have some basis for comparison."

'I'm not sure if that's a good idea – "Annie began.

'Oh, don't worry. I wouldn't say it was you; it will be anonymous. I'll report it as a conversation I had with a young friend. We can just talk about what you and your friends get up to, what young people are thinking about life, now the war's over. "

This morning was the silver, which she had to clean and polish every couple of weeks, and when she'd finished it was time for elevenses. They sat warming their hands round cups of tea and savoured some *bara brith*, the lovely fruit bread that the baker still occasionally sold when he was able to get a delivery of dried fruit.

It isn't fair, really, Annie thought, you either had to be very lucky to get there before he sold out, or be one of the gentry, and then he'd specially keep some under the counter for you. Like Mrs Simpson. Sucking up to the nobs, everybody was doing it. You had to look after yourself these days, not like when the war was on, and people looked out for each other. No, life wasn't fair, and it was a mistake to think it could ever be; and she'd be surprised if anyone gave a damn about the poor working folk, even despite this 'New Jerusalem' twaddle.

This morning Annie was fidgeting in her eagerness to mention the mutterings she was beginning to hear in town about the lack of jobs, everyone shifting the blame onto the foreigners, the 'misplaced persons' as she heard someone the other day call them, as though they'd been put down somewhere and now couldn't be found. Mr Simpson had friends in high places, and he discussed politics with his wife. She was English and educated, and did not hesitate to speak her thoughts, and although Annie didn't always agree with her, she wanted to know Mrs Simpson's opinions on this.

'Yes, I've read all the nonsense in the papers. Totally irresponsible – it's bound to foment a lot of anger in everyone. They already seem to have forgotten," Mrs Simpson exclaimed, incensed, her carefully coiffed curls trembling with her emotion, 'London would be a pile of rubble, and we would be part of Nazi Germany if it weren't for the courage and skill of the Poles, for instance. Like Jan, here. We should go on our knees to thank them, not bend them to a monster like Stalin." If she saw the slow burn of Annie's cheeks at Jan's mention she said nothing. And Annie tucked away what was said in satisfaction, nodding her agreement.

'I was shocked to see young Elizabeth Roberts outside *The Llewellyn* the other night," Mrs Simpson changed the subject. 'She can't be more than thirteen or fourteen, and she's already hanging about for the boys! Bold looking little thing too. Courting trouble. It was different in my day. Their mothers just don't seem to worry any more." She shook her head.

Annie told her of the young girls in the villages she'd heard gossip about, who had 'given themselves without marriage' to their paramours during the war, and were now leaving the results for their own mothers to look after while they titivated themselves for the local dances.

'What on earth is the world coming to?" Mrs Simpson shook her head. 'I just don't understand it any more."

She handed Annie a copy of a new magazine called 'Woman' to take home. 'You might like this, Annie. Not quite my style, but interesting." It was full of articles on film stars, letters from readers, recipes, knitting patterns, make and mend tips, and a serial 'romance'. Much better than Vogue which she usually took, and which Annie thought was far too posh. On the cover was the photograph of a beautiful young woman. Mrs Simpson tapped the photograph with an elegant finger.

"That's Celia Johnson. D'you know, I met her at a supper party last year. She wasn't at all pretentious, not how you'd imagine a film star, and she told me they spent ghastly hours being bored on Carnforth Station while they were filming Brief Encounter – have you seen it? Oh you really must! – and when the express trains came rushing through they'd all run out of the waiting room with glasses of brandy to watch. What a hoot."

Annie clapped her hand over her mouth, giggling as Mrs Simpson rolled her eyes at the unintended pun. 'What a silly I am." Their laughter ran companionably.

The highlight of the day for Annie was when Jan kicked his boots off and knocked on the kitchen door for lunch, but this Monday Mr Simpson needed him to drive up to Manchester on some business, and Annie ate dinner in the kitchen on her own, glad, for a little time, of the distraction the magazine offered. But her uncomfortable thoughts would not be so easily put aside, and as she sat with her cup of tea they crowded in and the magazine lay discarded. She felt unsettled by Mrs Simpson's confirmation of the building unrest in the country and bad will towards the Poles, and didn't know what to think. Would it affect her and Jan? It would be just her luck if something else came along to smash her dreams, her happiness, again.

Although she enjoyed Mrs Simpson's stories, the pictures they painted of a world so different, so full of promise and ease, made Annie feel restless and cramped. She imagined walking into the kitchen at Bron Felen and telling Evan where to get off, and... She stopped, fearful at the thought of his reaction. She shook her head, scolding herself for being such a frightened mouse. No, not yet, not just yet.

Although Evan's behaviour towards her grew more and more peculiar, Annie refused to be frightened into acting prematurely. "Time will come for it soon enough" was all she'd allow.

She listened to what people were saying: that the pulling together, the best of the British, the camaraderie, support and sympathy for fellow human beings that the long years of the war had engendered, were eradicated as if they never were.

'People are harder, more intent upon looking after Number One. They are more likely to snatch, grab, and lose their temper? Now why is this? What has gone wrong?' JB Priestley was to write, and, when she looked back after all that happened, she could see how right he was. She made her plans; the details were still hazy, but she was resolved – they'd leave Wales, leave England, get married, and go back to his beloved Poland. She didn't tell Jan her thoughts. She didn't tell anyone.

*

'I just cannot believe it!' Mr Simpson's cry in the breakfast room the following Monday as Annie was stringing up some paper-chains in the hallway ready for Christmas startled her. 'Dolly, look at this, in The Times...' Annie could hear the furious rustling of a newspaper, "The Yalta agreement is 'firmly rooted in common sense and equity'. Have you ever heard such ruddy nonsense? Are they out of their minds? ...I'll tell you what they're really saying. In effect, they mean the Poles are the spoilsports at the party. They might as well have said, 'Why don't you clear off back where you came from? We don't need you and your like any more.'"

She refused to take it seriously, it was only Mr Simpson's opinion, but despite herself a drop of fear lodged in Annie's chest; even though she couldn't put it into words, something in her recognized that where public feeling was compounded by a personal grudge, sooner or later something was bound to erupt.

*

She looked out the window of the railway carriage as the train chuffed through the flat coastal plain towards Chester. She pressed her forehead against the glass, relaxed her gaze, and let her eyes glue themselves to the scenery zipping past, right – left, until their attachment pinged and let go. She swivelled her eyes back, right-left, right-left, again and again until she felt almost dizzy. When the glass was steamed up with her breath and she could no longer see out, she sat back and drew pictures in the condensation. Funny to think, she thought, if the train is travelling at sixty miles an hour, then so must my eyes. And not so long ago, she thought, people believed if you went faster than thirty miles an hour you'd die. I wonder what else there is we don't know about, think can't possibly happen, or exist, and in a few years or so will be completely normal?

It was the Saturday after Christmas, and they were on their way to take part in the traditional Choral Evening for massed choirs in the Cathedral. Everyone was a little bit more relaxed and looking forward to it, hard times put aside for a few hours, chatting and laughing, a bar of chocolate doing the rounds. She glanced across the carriage at Jan who was talking to Mrs Evans, the choir mistress. He wore a frown, one arm up behind his head, his fingers fiddling with a clump of hair, the very picture of perplexity. Annie smiled – a typical gesture of his, that meant he was struggling to understand. Mrs Evans had a strong North Wales accent and sometimes it was even difficult for Annie to catch what she was saying. She shut her eyes before anyone caught her watching him. The train rocked along, and this, with the warmth in the carriage and the regular clack-clackety-clack, pulled Annie's thoughts, drifting, into a dream-like state.

She saw Jan, in uniform, in the middle of a clearing surrounded by dark trees. He was bent over peering at a limp bundle lying on the ground at his feet. When he straightened he looked across at Annie, who was crouched at the edge, and his gaze was stony. So you betray me too, Annie. She vehemently tried to deny the accusation, No, no, it wasn't me! but her throat was full of cotton-wool and her jaws flapped without sound. His voice grated like hard rocks thudding against other. She turned and saw a figure digging a hole, the knocking sound a pickaxe striking the frozen ground. The pickaxe rose and fell. The hole yawned bigger and deeper, bigger and deeper, as big as a lake; in it she saw hundreds of corpses, layer after layer, arms and legs entwined, jaws hanging, hands clutching. Postures of agony. Like the hare she had seen at the side of the road, knocked down but not killed outright, thrashing and squirming, bending double and writhing. Soundless, not a wail, not a cry. The image cleared and she saw shreds and tatters of uniforms, the same uniform as Jan's, hanging on the skeletons. The stench of death hit the back of her throat and she retched.

The figure with the pick axe straightened and she saw it was Evan. Jan picked up the bundle and hurled it as though it were a rugby ball at Evan, shouting 'Catch!', so loud it was like a crack of thunder; and simultaneously a lightning bolt seemed to sear the back of her eyes and a piercing whistle rent the air. Her head snapped against the back of the seat, and she woke up, her heart thumping in shock, so real had it been in the wood. But here she was, still rattling along in the train which was now slowing down and pulling into Sandford station. She looked around, nobody seemed to have noticed. Jan caught her eye and winked, slowly, before turning back to Mrs Evans. Slowly she breathed in. Don't panic. Everything's alright. Not long now till Chester. She saw people slide past, and crates of pigeons and chickens stacked on the platform. Something nasty from the dream tried to insinuate itself into her thoughts, mud splashed from a stagnant pond, and she shivered and pulled her coat closer. She felt cold even though the heater under the seat was blasting out hot air, and they were all sat shoulder to shoulder. The porter waved his flag and blew his whistle and the train gathered steam and jerked its line of carriages into motion again. Ten minutes later they were slowing down for Chester General and she was back in the solid world.

*

This was her first time in Chester proper, apart from changing trains when she had come down with her parents from Liverpool to visit Nain and Taid, and all she had seen then was the station with its girders, and platforms, and the people standing like rows of dolls, clutching umbrellas and newspapers. There had been a nasty green-painted waiting room that smelt of disinfectant and dust, and a lady with a tea-urn on a trolley, waiting to get on one of the big long-distance expresses, belching steam out of its stack.

As they clattered across a bridge over the canal, she turned to see the long barges stacking up one behind the other. Then they were pulling in at the station and Mrs Evans was waving them all over to her on the platform. They marched almost in procession, first through the small mean streets by the station, Mrs Evans like a fussy hen in the vanguard, then over the canal and along Eastgate Street, where a blue-jacketed brass band was playing enthusiastically if not tunefully, to the Cathedral. Annie's neck ached from looking up at all the magnificent black and white buildings; Chester was a city that held its ancient history out with pride to its visitors.

The Cathedral itself was a hive of activity, with the members of all six choirs who were taking part milling around, waiting for instructions. They stood there in a big gaggle, their gazes drawn upwards to Heaven by the artful architecture, wondering at the magnificent ceiling, until they were summoned to the quire, where they stared again at the elaborately carved woodwork with its canopies and misericords.

"Annie, Annie" hissed Jan, beckoning her over to him. "Look!" He pointed to a carving of an elephant on the end of one of the stalls. "This man, he never sees a real elephant. Do you see his feet? This elephant has horses' hooves!" They giggled together for a minute until Mrs Evans shepherded them to their places.

The morning passed in a blur of rehearsal until the choirmaster was satisfied. He rapped his baton on the wooden stand, 'Lunch is in the refectory. We'll take a break for a couple of hours. Make sure you're back in your places by four o'clock." Most of the choir hurried off to get a seat for lunch, but Annie and Jan lingered behind, the opportunity to enjoy each other's company without comment and explore the splendid cathedral too good to miss.

A painting of a Madonna and Child on a caterpillar web of silk hung in a glass-fronted box in an alcove, and this gave them an excuse to stand close, Jan having to bend down to see it clearly, so that their heads almost touched and they inhaled each other's sweet breaths. They strolled along the aisles with their faint smell of incense, the candle-light and the echoes of their footsteps creating a pregnant tension. Annie gripped Jan's arm and pointed up – there was a carving of a devil in chains scowling down at them, the Chester Imp, meant to be a warning of what would happen to him if he dared enter the Cathedral.

They went out of the Cathedral precincts along the Rows. It was as though they entered by accident a world long gone, evoked by Christmas with its lights and decorations in the streets, and the old buildings with their tinsel-strewn stalls and shops displaying their wares along the covered walkways. The town was bustling, with everyone come up from the country for the festivities standing in the streets, throwing hot chestnuts from hand to hand, little children running between people's legs and being scolded, and men rushing hither and thither with carts of chickens, their white feathers dropping on the street as they flapped in panic. Several long shiny cars pulled up in front of the famous old coaching inn, and well dressed men and fur-draped women stepped out, to be swallowed up by soft carpets and hushed waiters bearing trays of drinks, impervious to those who stood on the sidewalk and gawked, some without shoes and coats, their hands held out.

"That is me," Jan said, pointing to the stiff-shouldered chauffeurs, chatting in small groups as they waited. 'Not today, it isn't. You're mine today." Annie wound her arm firmly inside his, forgetful for a minute, then withdrew it as he turned to her, his eyes both a warning and a beckoning, 'Let's get away from the crowd...'

They followed the canal path under the railway arches to the Roodee. Apart from an old woman walking a dog further along the river, they were alone. There were no races today, no men winning and losing fortunes, though Annie could almost hear the thunder of hooves along the turf, and the cries of the jockeys, the panting and whistling of breaths, the shouts of the people cheering them on. Today, the only sounds were the plaints of water-birds, small plashings as they ducked under the surface of the river for a tasty morsel, and water voles' quick rustlings in the banks. Here, at last, they were able to relax their vigilance for a short while. They sank onto the grass, and were soon unheeding of the damp, and the debris strewn along the bank from a recent storm.

When it was time to get back, they walked arm in arm as far as the city walls, then separated and approached the Cathedral from different directions and a minute or so apart.

"Where have you been, Annie?" scolded Mrs Evans. 'Go and tidy yourself, you've got leaves and goodness knows what in your hair. Whatever have you been up to?"

'Sorry, Mrs Evans. I went for a walk and some stupid boys down by the river were throwing them about. I didn't realise," said Annie, not daring to look at Jan who was standing with one of the other girls, who sniggered at Annie's discomfiture. Stung, Annie bit back a retort and hurried to the cloakroom. When it was time for her solo in Mendelssohn's 'Hear My Prayer' her pure soprano soared through the cathedral as if on wings, dipping and diving in rhythm with the chorus and the organ, and Mrs Evans' baton weaving patterns in the air.

On the train journey home she sat in a corner of the carriage, watching the dark shapes of trees and buildings rush towards her then gone, listening to the sound of the wheels clacking over the points, and dreaming to herself while the others gossiped about the day. For her, the highlight had not been the singing, at least not the singing in the church, but the singing inside her body which bore her up and flew her out through the window, across the fields, with the thin high whine of the wind in her ears, to the endless snows and pine forests she could see below, the whooshing spray of ice crystals as a horse drawn sledge raced along a bridle track, and the clink clink of vodka glasses in front of a crackling fire.

**

The longest bungee jump

'Don't look where you fall, but where you slipped.'

- African Proverb

Three days later, at a quarter past six on the Tuesday evening, Adam, Johnny's father, rang. I heard his voice, thin, ghostly, as I thought, from traveling through the ether. The only bits I heard, disjointed: '... Fleur... hung... in the hospital... two o'clock this afternoon.'

A red void opened somewhere in my brain, sucked the steel from my knees. For the eternity of a single second, my ears listened dispassionately to this awful wailing. Where had I heard it before? What did it have to do with me? Then I knew. It was the sound of something beloved gone forever, just zapped out of the universe; the sound of women's desolation in the face of tragedy – after bombings and massacres, floods and earthquakes, murder, suicide. I had no choice; it roared out of my lungs borne on a galactic wind, like the longest bungee jump, like the highest roller coaster.

Harry came running. He picked me up off the carpet, and grabbed me as I lurched away on a wild trajectory, threw his arms round me and held me tight. I couldn't breathe, and struggled to push him away. He wouldn't let go. I beat his chest. But there was nowhere to go, the air wasn't any better anywhere else.

It was dark and dense, glue in my lungs. I couldn't seem to scream loudly enough, I wanted the sound to surround me, fill me up, leave no spaces for any thought, or reason or feeling.

Or, if I couldn't stifle them, I wanted to find the seams of things and tear them apart with my voice, sever the universe's magnetic fields, shake apart its atoms, and my wind-milling limbs to hurl the broken bits into the void – then I would have unmade it, time would reverse, and I would prevent those particles from ever finding each other again, from ever combining into the same becoming.

If I ever believed in a God, he left me there. He flew up into the sycamore tree and hooted pointlessly in the nights, until I flung a boot at him and then he flapped away for ever. I saw him go.

*

I rang the hospital, the ward, the nurse in charge – anyone who might happen to pick up the phone, I didn't care. I kept on ringing. Someone, somewhere, knew what I needed to know. On and on, until Harry took the phone from me, and put it down on the cradle, folded me in his arms. This time I let him.

In the end though, I would not be comforted. Out of the shadows they came, scenes picked out and spotlit, playing on an endless stage. I could not turn away. My thankfulness the first time she tried but failed to kill herself, because it seemed that without this desperate act no-one was going to take her seriously, and admit her to hospital and the special care she needed. And even then, did anyone take it seriously? If they did, why were we hearing these stiff condolences and lame excuses, the downright lies, and the shiftiness and evasion as I made my demands for the truth of it.

My wanting Fleur to be in hospital – for her own safety and my relief – condemned her to be surrounded by people who behaved as if they scarcely gave a damn. A hospital that had forgotten how to care – and the world turned topsy-turvy.

I knew the Jesuit saying, 'Give me a child until he is 7, and I will give you the man." It rang in my ears. I had also been brought up by my parents to believe 'they' – whoever 'they' were – had our best interests at heart; that 'they' acted with integrity and wisdom'; that 'they' were skilled, fully competent professionals, superior and always in the right; that 'they' were born to be the rulers, the legislators, the governors – and birthright meant everything. I was the one who knew nothing, was always in the wrong; I should accept my place in the scheme of things and be thankful I lived in such an enlightened place.

Deep down, I saw, I must always have been the closet believer I denied I was. "Why do you always have to argue?" my mother used to ask in exasperation. "Because," I answered.

Because when I was little and asked you, 'Why, Mummy?' you always told me 'Because'. Was I so blind it took such a death to give me sight? Was this my fall from grace? The shock of disillusionment was as great and as heart stopping as a plunge into a deep dark lake on Christmas Day.

*

Johnny wanted an old-fashioned funeral in a church and burial. I was agreeable to that, to think that Fleur would be going deep into the earth, the earth I had always found such a comfort.

The day before the funeral we went to see her. I looked down on the face of my daughter, and felt nothing. Fleur's white hands were crossed over her pale blue dress and I could not believe she wouldn't open her eyes and joke 'Fooled you!'. Her long delicate fingers, I remembered them playing classical guitar. I remembered all the lessons and teachers, the hopes and eagerness. I wondered why the nails and the tips of her fingers were black. I thought she might open her eyes any minute and smile with that quirky mischievousness of hers. I stared intently – but nothing happened. Those gurglings of the mucosal organs, the red warm tide flowing through the intricate arteries and veins, the gentle suction of lungs, all halted.

Hot drops of water fell out of me, dropped onto those cold hands. I saw them with surprise. I struggled to see them as my teacher had always said – 'Water falling, just water falling'. Somehow I'd always thought that meant it wouldn't hurt. My heart was raining. Fleur didn't wipe them away. I looked round the small bare room, with its texts of sympathy on the walls, as if I might find her hiding somewhere. I listened and looked as if to penetrate the material world and find the spiritual entwined amongst its molecules and atoms. Nothing. I left the room and watched my other children go in in turn. They did not deserve, I thought, to deal with this.

*

On the day of the funeral, I, Harry, my son and other daughters, and her father, together with Johnny, and her closest friends, picked basket loads of the fragile horned snowdrops with their bowed heads that reminded me of her, and which carpeted their garden in drifts. In the churchyard the two hundred people that came to the funeral threw handfuls on top of the coffin, until it was piled with their pure whiteness. I would never see the snowdrops on the banks and in the hedgerows without thinking of them falling into the grave of my daughter. Fleur's old school mates sang 'The Rose' by Bette Midler. I could only hear the words at the end: '... the night has been too lonely and the road has been too long, and you think that love is only for the lucky and the strong...'

When I got back to Bron Felen, I couldn't walk further than a couple of hundred yards, I could just about summon the energy to cross the field, and the mud and cold rain of winter reinforced my desolation, sitting motionless in the caravan looking out and away over a grey sweep of watery horizon.

Then came all the mornings of waking up. I ate well, slept like a baby, never dreamed. It was the waking up.

*

When the police told us, faces grave, that the hospital owed Fleur a 'duty of care', I almost laughed. I caught it in time, but I shocked myself. Where had this sudden cynicism sprung from? But of course this was just the beginning. My laughter died. Duty of Care – such a fine sounding phrase, like all the others we were to hear; but make no bones about it, it had no substance, and the facts were plain – there was no care in *Llanfair*. Reading the police interviews later, I found it hard to understand why nobody spoke to her at the hospital – apart from saying breakfast was ready, that is. It must have taken years of slow decline for things to have reached such a pass.

Someone said it could be seen as too much to do by too few with too little money to do it; someone else speculated – and this was only if I was to be charitable (which I wasn't) – that it was the result of the so-called 'Swiss Cheese' effect, where random 'holes' by an accidental 'coincidence' lined up to allow through something 'bad'. In this case, lots of holes and something very bad. Nor did I believe in coincidence. I preferred the theory Harry proposed: 'Scum Always Rises to the Top', with its sequel 'Rot Always Sinks to the Bottom'', but there didn't seem to be precise legal terms for these. 'What about 'Total Incompetence'?' I asked, but had to abandon that when I learned that however true it might be, 'incompetence is not a crime'. Then, where it was lurking at the bottom of the list of potential offences, we might have to settle for ordinary, common or garden, nothing to write home about, carelessness. Like you might mislay your mobile or your glasses.

69

Care, n: attentive assistance or treatment to those in need; concern or interest; watchful supervision; caution in avoiding harm or danger; close attention.

Care, vb.tr: to be troubled or concerned; be affected emotionally.

Careful, adj: thorough and painstaking in action or execution; conscientious; dedicated.

Take knitting... It might seem that I'm going off on one here; stay with me, let me lead you by the hand. My mother was, as were most of her contemporaries, a skilled and assiduous looker-after of my health. Crumpets, toasting forks, balls of wool and clicking needles were my winter comforters. I used to watch fascinated as she took my outgrown jumper, unraveled it, washed, and re-skeined it with the help of my two arms held out stiffly like posts, and another jumper, bigger, fell off the end of her needles a day or so later. What attention to detail, what painstaking application, what proficiency and flair. What dedication to my well-being.

The time came for me to be called to the needles in junior school, and, carrying a thick pair of pink plastic needles, a ball of blue wool, I presented myself to Miss Dodd. It was clear from the outset that I had not imbibed with my mother's milk the capacity to knit. Not only that, I had not inherited the inclination to knit. And to cap it all, I had not inherited the personality or character to knit. But more on this later.

The ball of wool wound itself round the legs of my chair (and others'), or fell in a tangled heap on the floor, the knots resembling nothing so much as careless bird nests, picking up enough fluff to further the metaphor. Plain became purl became a hole became a fishing net. A net for cod, not for sprats. Relentlessly I kept on winding. I sighed, I cried, I threw it on the floor, I kicked it. It never seemed to grow, and it was always lying in wait for me the next lesson. I was sent to repent in the book corner with my back to the class, where I sucked my thumb and learned to read instead.

Mysteriously, and without visible regret on my part, my knitting completely disappeared one week, and I never did another stitch. I was handed some crayons and told to draw a tree instead.

'What happened to your knitting?" mum asked one day.

'Oh, I don't know, it got lost".

'Got lost?" she asked suspiciously.

'Yep. I can't find it. No-one knows where it is."

Which was the truth until the autumn term, when the janitor, alerted by the smell of singeing, found it stuffed down behind the big hot radiator in the classroom, too far gone to resurrect. I never told Mum though, and everyone scratched their heads over how it got there. I kept stumm. And, for the whole of my adult life, I have felt envious of the delicately wrought, brightly patterned jumpers, scarves and hats my friends knit for themselves, their babies, their grandchildren, and their friends. I do repent the burning of the bird's nest. I do.

**

Silica

Outside, the mountains rear their purple heads sharply beyond the straits. Even looking at them overwhelms me with a sense of failure and physical weakness. I am still unable to summon energy to walk farther than down to the beach without losing my breath.

One fine sunny day Harry chivvied me up one of the smaller outliers, and I couldn't tell if it was the effort or grief that caused the tears to fall as I put one foot in front of another through the springing heather. Even driving the car is a burden, especially alone, and long journeys are impossible. After even a few miles I have to pull to a stop overwhelmed by the sheer horror of my loss. I feel trapped, the only freedom my fingers on the keyboard, mining the web for information; and the only place I can go, the garden.

Bron Felen lies at the foot of an escarpment, and the rain falling on the high bog above seeps its slow way down and issues out as springs along its rocky roots. *Botrytis cinerea*, or grey mould, one of the simplest and most ubiquitous denizens of the humid regions of the planet – and this part of the planet is certainly damp – lies in wait everywhere. At least, I thought, we won't suffer from water shortages as global temperatures rose; but, just as the sun's heat drew out their ripe rubiosity, that particularly warm, damp year spawned a grey fluffy rottenness that rampaged through my strawberries. Another facet of my lack of control.

Hunting through the piles of paper, gardening catalogues and books that tottered on every available surface, I unearthed a booklet my daughter in France had sent, called 'Your Garden and the Principles of Bio-dynamics'. As I flicked through its pages I was revolted to read that you could deter rabbits from eating your lettuces by the simple expedient of catching and killing one (rabbit, that is), burning its skin and spreading the resultant ash round the borders of your garden. Although I now, as an adult with a garden, had some sympathy for Mr McGregor and his war on Peter Rabbit, this was not quite my style. But it was when I browsed the paragraph on 'Horsetail' and learnt it could be used to control *Diplocarpon rosae*, or black spot on roses, that my spirit quickened. Silica, so it said, was a major constituent of the cell walls of this *paleozoic* plant; I could attest to the fact that it never fell ill; diseases didn't stand a chance and were casually routed, much as the proverbial water off a duck's back. Botanically it was 'hygro-scopic' – in other words, soaked up water. Horsetail's character was, in short, fungicidal. In theory at any rate. So why shouldn't horsetail be the solution to my strawberry problem? My perception of horsetail and the boggy land it favoured underwent a metamorphosis, and the underneath revealed itself – what I had thought of as one problem might be the solution to another problem. Yet, in the midst of my satisfaction at this discovery, something turgid shifted. I shivered. I didn't need this; I needed to ground myself in what I could only term 'normality'. Gardening usually did this, but here it was, picking away at me, threatening to unravel that comfortable sense of reality. Maybe a deeper understanding was there in me, but it was buried deep, and like a bulb in winter needed the first rays of a spring sun to wriggle their way down, down among the spicules of sand, and leaf mould and loam, and switch it into life.

Harry, meanwhile, sweated and toiled in the house with pick axe and jack hammer, shovels and chainsaws. He employed old techniques and traditional materials wherever he could – shaping every lintel out of green oak sawn from fallen trees, smashing rocks to smithereens with a lump hammer, mixing and applying lime mortar. It took its toll. I watched the superhuman effort that I knew at times tested his physical endurance to its limits. I did not protest or intervene; like my gardening, it protected him from the full impact of the fall-out after Fleur's death – and my growing emotional distance from him.

When the day came to solve the problem of the inglenook and its streams of water I left the computer and went to lend a hand, hoping this might alleviate my guilt. We set to pulling out a succession of fire places and ranges, four in all, stacked one behind the other like pages back into history, before we got to the back wall, where drooped a wrought iron bracket and pivoting arm for the kettle or cauldron. We stood inside and looked up through the sooty tunnel of the chimney at the round disc of sky above, like a blue moon in the heat of the day. To my disappointment our excavations threw up nothing very interesting, just some rotting old nests and birds' skeletons.

Harry disappeared into the next room to make a cup of tea, and I sat on a boulder smoking a cigarette. I could hear him clattering the cups and filling the electric kettle. Then, faintly, as though fighting its way through the haze of dust and rotten mortar that hung in the air, I heard a buzz, a hum. Emanating from somewhere near the back right hand corner of the fireplace, it rose and fell, rose and fell, tantalisingly familiar in its rhythms and tonal lilt, until it dawned upon me that what I was hearing was nothing less than the chattering of a throng of voices, as though at the far end of a cathedral, just audible without my being able to make out the sense of what they were saying.

'Harry!' I whispered loudly. He was only a couple of steps up from me, maybe ten feet away, and there was no door between us. No answer. The voices continued. They grew no louder, but expanded like a lazy bubble being born, and, like the colours that danced and shimmered on a bubble's surface, one voice called high above the bourdon, to sink and another to take its place, while the droning of the rest was the breath that filled it. As I listened it changed, became agitated, vexed even, blown on a wind of irritation. The hairs on my neck stood up, and I raised myself into a crouch, called 'Harry' again, louder. Still no answer. My mind seemed to flex and turn upon itself. Was I no longer in Harry's reality, but a parallel one? Why else didn't he hear me? All restraint left me and I bellowed, 'Harry!!'

The voices stopped and Harry's feet came pounding down the steps.

'What's the matter? Are you all right? You sounded really stressed.'

'I called you three or four times, didn't you hear me?' I said crossly.

'No. I only heard you once, yelling as though I was at the other end of a field.'

'Hmm. Weird,' he said when I described what I'd heard. 'I've read somewhere that stones can actually record sounds. I think it's called stone tape theory. Pretty half-baked, if you ask me,' he continued dismissively, 'and I certainly wouldn't subscribe to it. To do with the resonance of materials like quartz or silica, if I remember right.' Silica again. Interesting... 'It goes against all the laws of physics. But,' he looked at me sideways, a slow grin hiding in the corners of his mouth, 'you never know, perhaps the fireplace did record the sounds of everything that happened in this room since it was built, and it might be that when we unblocked the fireplace it became a gigantic 'acoustic box'. We just pressed the playback button..."

I was too shaken to join in his attempt at humour. 'I don't know. It was eerie. At the beginning it sounded hushed, peaceful. But towards the end it sounded angry, like something horrible was happening. That's when I got scared and yelled for you."

'Forget it, Sarah, don't let it prey on your mind. You've got enough to deal with without stuff like this. Whatever it was it's gone now. Come on, let's go and start dinner, I'm famished."

I forced a laugh, and we left it at that. But it disturbed me. Much against my will, this place was beginning to shake me. I knew there was more to the story of Bron Felen. I would ask Dilwyn. Was he keeping something back? And why?

*

Before I could do so, autumn reasserted itself with wind and rainy squalls. A garden waits for no-one; I co-opted Harry and Dilwyn to help and we loaded bags and boxes with fruit into the pickup and drove them over to Apple Shirley's press. They were ready a couple of days later. I heaved a sigh of relief. I was still in control – just.

Dilwyn didn't drop by for a week. The postman told me he had taken to his bed with a cold, and his knees had flared up – not helped, I supposed, by wading around in long damp grass. Feeling bad at my thoughtlessness, I packed half a dozen bottles of juice into my rucksack and climbed the bank to his cottage. I knocked on the door. A series of hacking coughs followed his shout to come in. Bwster was curled up in his basket, his chin resting on the edge, and one ear twitched a greeting outside the hairy blue blanket that covered him. His master reclined similarly on the sofa under a crocheted patchwork blanket. A strong smell of menthol rose from its folds as he levered himself into a sitting position.

'Here, for you." I unpacked the juice onto the table.

"Ah, medicine. An apple a day, eh, doll?"

He chortled as he saw my gaze fall on the whisky bottle warming in the hearth.

'Perhaps you need harder stuff."

'Doll, the best medicine is someone who cares. Put the kettle on, would you? I'm not decent."

He winced as he lowered his feet to the floor.

"Touch of rheumatics. Get it every year. Good excuse to sit around and catch up on my reading."

On the floor by the sofa were piles of books. While I waited for the kettle to boil, I crouched down to see what he was reading: a biography of Mountbatten nudged shoulders with George Ewart Evans' 'Pattern under the Plough'; Whymper's 'Scrambles in the Alps' lay open at a page with diagrams of Swiss cog railways; the collected works of Jack London.

"That's a real eclectic mix," I said, and the colour flared in my cheeks at Dilwyn's cheeky, 'Pass the dictionary... I'll just look that up!"

"Ellie's – my wife's. Curious about everything. Loved reading, and I loved that about her. I caught it off her, up to a point, but I was never a real bookworm. Liked the outdoors and people too much to sit quiet for long. Times like this though, I like a good story. Read them all several times over by now, still discovering things I didn't see before."

"Oh, you've got a history of Marchlyn. Who wrote it? That must be interesting." I picked the slim volume up.

"You can borrow it, doll. One of them fellers from the university. I remember him coming round talking with everyone. Not long after the war it was. Perhaps 1949. There's a whole chapter about your place in it. It's one of the oldest houses still standing round here."

"Does he mention who lived there? What about Annie?"

He shot me a sideways glance. "He says a bit about the Williams family, nothing about Annie though. I'm related, you know. Some sort of distant cousin, I forget what." He fell silent as I looked for the chapter on Bron Felen, then, "Are you getting a bit of a head of steam up about Annie, now then, Sarah *bach*?"

I closed the book. This was my chance. "Mm. P'raps. I don't know. There's just something about the place. It's like when you meet someone for the first time – you know straight away if you like them and want to get to know them. I felt that about Bron Felen – it felt like home. And the odd feeling it gave me that Annie was someone I knew, or should know. I can't explain it. It's not because it makes me feel good, in fact it often makes me feel pretty weird." I shrugged, and flicked through the pages, hoping this would prompt Dilwyn to open up some more.

"Mm. When we were doing them apples the other day I was thinking about her. Funny. Always keen on the garden, then 'phutt'," he snapped his fingers, "seemed to lose all interest. I remember years when she never set foot in it once. It used to end up smelling like a brewery with all the fruit fallen and rotting on the ground, and the wasps getting vicious drunk. Clouds of them. It nearly drove Evan to distraction. They didn't have much coming in, and growing their own food meant making ends meet. But she would not go in there. It was like she was scared. I couldn't work it out. She came back to it later, like, when she was getting on a bit. Spent a lot of time just sitting on that old bench in the orchard."

"There's something about the house. I meant to ask you."

I told Dilwyn about the voices in the inglenook. "Perhaps I'm imagining it. Harry thinks I am."

"Aye, prob'ly…" He sighed and his voice faded, and that inward look came again into his eyes. I got up and busied myself with making the tea. He would tell me, I was sure, when he felt able. I knew better than to rush him. I would have to wait.

*

You're not far wrong, Sarah *bach*. In fact, I know you're right, though I'm not saying. Something soured and twisted as must've got in among the stones. Something bigger'n Annie and Evan. I'd have to say, now I look back, it was probably life asserting itself, trying to grow, expand, wanting to jump and sing – not just bend its back and wrestle with a patch of dirt…

But when you start lifting your head and looking about, you don't know what the world'll bring your way. Annie didn't, nor Evan. And the Pole, poor bugger. Like a lamb to the slaughter.

**

Boogie-woogie

'Straighten up and fly right
Straighten up and stay right
Straighten up and fly right
Cool down, papa, don't you blow your top.'

- Nat King Cole

A hammer blow of depression has descended on me. No matter how hard or how long I try, every act of trying locks me further on the 'outside' of things. Somehow, I can only enter the inside, breach the boundaries as it were, 'unbidden'. To control myself in civilised fashion, as I feel I ought, serves to strengthen different prison bars, condemns me to a circumscribed world with only the illusion of movement and change for comfort, the obverse of some universal zoetrope, where the frozen images reel giddily past outside the peepholes I create from within. Hundreds and thousands of years roll past and I am where my ancestors walked. I have only moments ago eaten the apple. *Malus domestica.*

Where are those apples, buttery, delicate flesh pink-flushed, or yellow as primroses, russeted and rough and acid? Piles and baskets of them. With all the scab, blisters, dimples, crinkles, and cracks. I used to eat them straight off the tree or freshly windblown with the juice dribbling down my chin. In October the men-folk, bare-chested, cut the grass round the trees with great double-handed scythes for foddering the sheep and cattle when the snows came down to the foot of the fells. People clambered through the branches with baskets and lowered them down on ropes. Old women and children, me among them, bent double picking up the wind-falls and setting them aside for the press. Ah, the press, where fruit becomes nectar.

A part of me keeps attempting to refashion the world out of the past that held my innocence, my ignorance, but it is a place where I no longer fit. I cannot find myself here. It has become a repository for all the wrong paths I took; vortices that gather the rubbish of wasted years; a honey-pot for the irritations and hurts that just won't let me rest, milling around like bees in the wind and rain, stinging, dying, a frenzy of attack from all directions. An onslaught under which to give up is excusable; where it is a rational choice to die.

If I could only make sense of the confusion that bleeds through my mind in the months after Fleur's death. I know within it lies a hope of future, if not happiness, at least a degree of redemption. But even as it promises me this, I pull away; I cannot deal with it, it hurts my head... 'Life' and 'Death', black and white, truth and lies, these brash twins that swagger and swash-buckle their way in broad brush strokes across the canvas of my existence, they threaten to overwhelm my sanity. Why will they not stay at the periphery, on the edges of the subconscious, why must they pester me with their paradox? I can do without them forever edging into the details of my life, like a many fingered tumour. Not a malignant tumour, necessarily, but sometimes it is hard to figure out straight away which is the good and which the bad.

*

January 1947

New Year came and went and the snow that had been threatening finally fell. The mile to the *Plas* this morning meant in places walking through drifts up to her knees, but the lanes, fields and hedges were so beautiful in the moonlight and under the cover of the snow that Annie's bad mood at having to start out so early soon evaporated. The tracks of hares dotted the virgin surface, and those of a weasel crossed the track up by the gate.

As she turned the corner round the garage she saw someone had at least taken a broom to the kitchen path and step – Jan probably, she thought – but they had already glazed over with a treacherous coating of ice. She negotiated them with extra care – it wouldn't do for her to slip and break any bones, right now especially. She kicked off her galoshes in the porch, and looked around, but he was nowhere to be seen. She opened the door and called loudly, 'It's Annie, Mrs Simpson. I'm here."

Stepping into the warmth, she took off her coat, and laid her wet scarf and gloves on the fender by the range. She first sprinkled salt from the salt pig over the steps and then tied her pinafore on, eyeing the huge mountain of dishes and pans piled up in the scullery. She could hear faint music coming from the drawing room, followed by a draught of cold air from the hall as Mrs Simpson came into the kitchen, her pale blue morning dress floating behind her, a cigarette held high between the fingers of her right hand. She wore no make up and Annie thought she looked much prettier.

"Annie, good morning" she smiled. 'I'm sorry about the amount of dishes, we had some people over last night. Forget the silver, it can wait till afternoon, but could you see to the bedroom and dressing room, clean linen please, and what isn't done today will just have to stay undone, won't it? Edward stoked the Aga on his way out, so there's plenty of hot water. I'll be in the drawing room if you want me."

The warmth of the range beckoned. Annie lowered herself into the Windsor chair. Five minutes, that's all... Upstairs was a chill mausoleum with only the one bedroom and dressing room in use, the rest under covers, and there was no coal for a fire in the bedroom except in the evening before the Simpsons retired. The tomatoes get more heat than us! Sometimes, in the summer and autumn, she liked to go in the glasshouses, lined with gurgling hot water pipes from the coke house outside, and sniff the rich air, redolent with the pungent fruit and foliage.

The kettle was singing softly on the hob and the boiler rumbled, Annie's head dropped. It was hard to keep her eyes open...

She woke with a start as a tractor rumbled into the yard, bringing bales of hay round for the horses, and leapt to her feet. Oh my God. The dishes!

The long case clock in the hallway bonged eleven as she finally wiped the sinks clean and dried her hands, red and wrinkly from their immersion in the steaming hot water. She inspected them ruefully. Be lucky if I don't get chilblains on them. Freezing one minute, hot the next. Nain had had chilblains, and Annie used to watch fascinated as she rubbed slices of potato over them to ease the itching.

When she and Mrs Simpson were sat down with their cups of tea and a Rich Tea biscuit each, she nodded towards all the pots and pans, gleaming now from her efforts, on their hooks and shelves: stock-pots, braising pans, boilers, fish kettles, brawn tins, steamers; oval pots, round pots, made of copper, steel, tinned and cast iron; tongs, choppers, saws; and knives galore. And the glassware and china – soup bowls, side plates, tureens, water jugs, carafes, glasses for sherry, water, wine, port.

'So much. I don't know what half of it's for, even."

'Mm, nor do I! We're lucky we've got Eggie – Mrs Egerton from the village – she still comes over to cook when we've got visitors, but she goes home once it's served. We could do with her living in really, but she can't now her husband's back. Poor man. Skin and bone – "

'We didn't have anything fancy at home, though we did have a lovely set of Waterford drinking glasses from when Mam and Da got married. But we never used them, not that I noticed anyway. Probably scared me or da'd break them. Up until – until – when Mam – when I was evacuated – we had this Woolie's matching set of china; each piece only cost sixpence, though there were a few bits gone by then, and we couldn't afford to replace them as were just chipped or cracked. Mam swore Da used to drop them deliberately so he wouldn't have to help with the washing up; she wouldn't let him touch them after the sugar bowl went." She blew her nose hard, and tucked her hanky up her sleeve.

"Times must have been very difficult," Mrs Simpson interjected, reaching out a hand and clasping Annie's.

'Well, Da's wage was nothing special. We were lucky he came home with it at all, lots didn't. He handed it over to Mam regular every Thursday and she'd count it all out and put it in the compartments of this metal cash box she had. So much for shoes, so much for electricity... she'd never use the electricity money to pay for shoes, always said that was robbing Peter to pay Paul."

*

When Mrs Simpson had gone back to the drawing room, Annie mopped down the flagged floor, wondering how it must be if you were rich. She thought about her Uncle Jack. He wasn't her real uncle, he had employed Mam when she first came over to England, and kept in touch with her ever since. He was rich... well, comparatively. She'd never met him, and now never would because he'd been killed in India. He'd sent her a silver Christening spoon, which was with everything else now, underneath tons of rubble. Perhaps someone would find it one day, and wonder who it had belonged to and what had happened to them. He'd given her a beautiful china doll too, called Sally. She'd loved that doll. Mam had knitted tiny dresses, hats and cardigans out of odds and ends of wool, her needles clicking away over the wireless in the evenings, and Da had whistled and hammered away in his shed and made a doll's cradle out of old bits of packing crate. One day, she'd dropped Sally on the road and cracked her head. She'd cried and cried until Mam said they'd take her to the Doll's Hospital in Liverpool. The doll doctor told them Sally would be better in a few days, and had winked at Mam and put Sally on a shelf with a lot of other sick dolls. When they left he'd given her an aniseed ball which Mam had confiscated the minute they were outside 'because of your teeth.' Instinctively, she slid her tongue across her strong white teeth. She still had them at least, even if everything else had broken, disappeared or died on her.

Her mood dipped again, the flood of nostalgia threatening to overwhelm her. She hauled the bucket of dirty water over to the sink to empty it, ran the tap to rinse the mop and looked out the window. There was Jan. At last. Her melancholy disappeared as suddenly as it came. What was the matter with her? Up one minute, down the next. No rhyme or reason to it. 'Get a hold on yourself, girl,' she chided.

Jan was up a ladder bolting back a section of guttering that was threatening to fall under the weight of snow from one of the outbuildings, and had his back to the kitchen. He was wearing a thin threadbare jacket as though he didn't feel the cold. It probably wasn't that cold compared to Poland. Her stomach somersaulted as she looked at his strong shoulders and the play of his muscles, and remembered his arms around her. She leant on the sink for a few minutes watching him work, then leaned forward and knocked on the glass. He looked round and saw her, and grinned and pantomimed an elaborate kiss, nearly falling off the ladder in the attempt. She giggled and waved. She was about to open the window and shout, 'It's no good you being over there...', but the jobbing gardener from the village came round the corner pushing a wheelbarrow full of clay pots. It would do no good to draw anyone's attention to her feelings for Jan, or his for her. This they had agreed.

*

It was almost lunchtime by the time she finished upstairs. As she came down the stairs Mrs Simpson put her head round the door and said, "Goodness, Annie, what a fast worker you are. Take a break and let's have lunch now and catch up on all my chit-chat." She laughed mischievously, she knew how much Annie loved her tales, and Annie had to smile at the tease. Mrs Simpson's birthday ball had been held at the *Plas* the weekend before. They'd hired caterers from Chester, and afterwards she and Mr Simpson had gone down to London, so Annie hadn't been needed that Monday, and had not yet caught up with the gossip.

Annie listened, fascinated, as Mrs Simpson regaled her with gossip about the wealthy and influential people who had attended, even a real Lord and Lady, and what pranks they got up to when they thought no-one was looking, or just didn't care if everyone was looking. No better than they should be, Annie thought primly, though she giggled as Mrs Simpson told her how one gentleman had strode flamboyantly into the fountain waving his cigar aloft clad only in socks and suspenders. Lucky there was no water in it. Then she blushed as she remembered Chester. She got up ostensibly to stir the coals in the range but really to look out the window to see if Jan was coming in for lunch yet, one ear open for the crunch of gravel, the other on Mrs Simpson.

'You should have heard the band, Annie. We danced until we were worn out, you just couldn't sit still." Mrs Simpson was up and whirling around the kitchen. 'Do you know the boogie-woogie?" When Annie shook her head, 'Come on, I'll show you." She pushed back the table and chairs and made a space on the flags. 'I'll be the man; you can follow me."

And off they swung till Annie began to feel dizzy, Mrs Simpson humming the melodies and singing the words when she could remember them. '.straighten up and fly right...' Annie stumbled against a chair and they both fell in a heap. 'Well, we certainly didn't fly right... we'll both have black bottoms," laughed Mrs Simpson. 'In fact, there used to be a dance called the black bottom when I was..."

But Annie was feeling decidedly queer. Her legs were shaky and she felt sick, and before she could move she vomited all over her pinafore.

"... Gracious me. Are you alright, Annie? Do you want a glass of water? Shall I call a doctor? Jan! Jan! Can you come and help here?" she shouted as Jan walked past the window carrying his ladder.

Between them they lifted Annie onto a chair, and Jan untied her pinafore, put it in the sink and ran cold water over it. Annie waved away the proffered glass of water and protested that really she felt much better now, and it was only because she'd got so dizzy.

'Well, you mustn't stay here, you must go home and rest, just in case," Mrs Simpson said. 'Jan, would you walk Annie home?"

'Oh no, please Mrs Simpson, I'm perfectly well now. I can't – Evan will – " Annie panicked at the thought of Evan's suspicion if she went home earlier than usual and he heard she'd been sick again. She had decided to pretend to be suffering from a bout of influenza to explain away the couple of occasions she thought he'd seen, but as he'd said nothing, nor had she.

Mrs Simpson looked at her searchingly.

"Very well, my dear. If you're sure you're feeling up to things. Sit there for another five minutes and Jan will get you some more tea. I won't offer you a biscuit as it might make matters worse. Oh drat! I'd better answer that." The front door bell pealed and Mrs Simpson left the kitchen.

Jan rushed over and took Annie's cold hands in his, pushed a stray lock of hair under her scarf. "Are you OK now, Annie?" he held her away and looked at her searchingly, his forehead creased with worry. It wasn't like Annie to be so delicate. As they heard footsteps along the passage, he hastily turned back to the sink and carried on scrubbing and rinsing her pinafore.

Annie watched him, the longing staring out of her eyes. Such a gentleman. He didn't turn up his nose with high and mighty notions of what was a man's or a woman's work. He might be a foreigner but his manners put most Englishmen to shame, "And a few bloody Welsh and all" she thought, "with their chapel twice on Sundays."

She knew she ought really very soon confide to him what she suspected, but it had only been a couple of weeks and she could be wrong. She'd only started her periods a year or so ago, quite late, and they hadn't completely settled down yet. But deep inside, she was sure. She hugged the knowledge to her, scared, but at the same time, pleased. Pleased? She was over the moon. Now she knew she'd leave Bron Felen, marry handsome, kind Jan, and they'd be off. Good riddance to Evan; he could stew in his nasty little ways on his own. She had absolutely no doubt that Jan would be delighted with the news and agree with all her plans. All they had to do then, was keep Evan, and everyone else, from guessing until they'd gone, because she just knew he would do something dreadful to try and stop them.

**

A bug to squash

She woke up the next morning, nausea clenching her stomach, and reached for the bowl by her bed. Evan had already gone out with the ewes, and she was down in the dairy when he came back in stamping the mud off his boots on the mat. More work, the thoughtless lout, but she didn't remonstrate with him. It wasn't worth it. She'd be at him morning till night if she let herself, and best keep her chagrin for things that really mattered. The black cloud Evan generated and that engulfed her at Bron Felen was eroding her strength; strength she knew she needed to escape. At least she was standing up for herself more now, giving as good as she got – after all she was a Liverpool lass – but if she hadn't threatened him with telling Mr and Mrs Simpson she was sure he would have hit her; the thought of being called a bully in the village and losing the respect of those he thought mattered, those to whom he doffed his cap and fawned, had stopped him so far.

Breakfast – porridge, eggs and fat bacon, and a big pot of tea – threatened to make her retch again. She clamped her mouth shut and turned her attention to the day's chores. It was better to keep moving and doing. Milking Kitty was still a pleasure, although at this time of the year she was about ready to be dried off. She was big with calf and it would be born right for the spring grass. Ah but, Annie my girl, she told herself firmly, you're not going to be around when that happens, so don't even bother to think about it. The garden, neither.... although she couldn't help but think wistfully of the garden. She'd only carried on where Nain had left off, but it had been a refuge from Evan's pestering, and a permanent memorial to all the hopes and joy that had gone into it over the years, to Nain especially. It had wrapped her round in its subtle beauty, fed her spirit along with her body. She realised, with surprise, there were some things she would be sad to leave behind.

The weather was bright but bone-crackingly cold, and within ten minutes of pegging out the laundry it had frozen solid. 'Oh, damn, damn and drat. As if it isn't enough to have to carry gallons of water to heat up on the range, then heave the wet clothes through the mangle'. It was taking more energy than she had. She'd either have to bring it in and thaw it out, or leave it on the line where it would stay stiff as a board for days and days. And then Evan would certainly be stamping and cussing. Oh well, she'd be out of it soon, and see how he liked that. He thought she minded because he hardly spoke to her. Well, he thought wrong. It saved her from telling him exactly what she thought of him.

On her way down to the beach in the afternoon to check on the cattle, she picked an armful of catkins with their bright yellow lambs-tails to put in the dairy. They would brighten up the cottage, and soon spring would arrive, with the primroses, and violets hiding on the banks, and the bluebells a misty blue coverlet warming the woods. Snowdrops were already showing in the clearings – Candlemas bells. Nain said they were the bringers of hope after the harshness of winter, "My mam told me this story, and she heard it from her mam, but how old it is I can't say."

She and Nain, and Mam, were walking through the tangled woods behind the cottage, and the ground was sprinkled with their milky whiteness. Nain knelt down and lightly stroked the waxy petals.

'Ever since the Fall it snowed without stop, and no flower bloomed," she continued, 'Eve sat weeping. She missed the bright gardens of Eden. An angel heard her, took pity and comforted her. He caught a snowflake in his hand and blew on it, and as it fell to earth it became the first snowdrop. It blossomed and so Hope was born."

Mam shivered and said in Ireland they were omens of death and unlucky, they always grew in graveyards and were called the 'church flowers'. No-one dared to bring them in the house for they were a curse.

Annie loved the snowdrops; with their bent heads, they seemed so bashful, and yet they were the only flower to brave the snow and cold of winter. She liked Nain's story best, but somehow Mam's version stuck, and she had never been able to pick them. In spring and summer she filled the house with flowers. Her favourites were the roses – pink, white, yellow – favourites, because Nain's pride and joy. They were scented papery memories now, their petals hidden in her chest of drawers among her underwear.

A sudden gust of wind flung a sheet of foam at her, the sand ran like a beige river coursing across the beach, the fragmites tossed and swayed so in the dunes that she felt she walked through a world whose edges had blurred and liquefied, disorientating her. The cockle diggers were packing up, their buckets and carts loaded down with the shellfish. As she walked along the low water's edge little jets spouted round her as the razor clams disappeared back down their holes. A flock of oyster catchers ran along the surf line, their bright red legs a blur, piping anxiously. She surprised the big grey heron who lived by the freshwater pond, who rose and flapped his slow heavy way towards the mud flats. She stood and watched him go, glad he was surviving; the winter had been so cold the smaller birds were dying of starvation, and she often found their small bodies frozen in the hedges and ditches.

When she got back to the cottage, out of breath from the climb up the field, she could hear Evan in the top field pounding in fencing stakes. 'Bout time too,' she thought, 'lucky the ewes didn't break out.' Kicking off her boots and flinging herself into the wooden rocking chair by the range, she turned on the wireless, but the reception was bad and the ether full of mournful shrieks and sighs, echoing her agitation. She switched it off and rocked. She didn't recognise herself in the person she had become, beset with doubts and fears.

*

'I've got to think what to do, what's best. It's got to be Poland. It's plain obvious we can't stay round here, and anyway it's the last place I'd want to bring a kid up. Narrow-minded lot – parochial, that's it. Look at the way they ignored little Anwen Jones, her mam wouldn't even let her go out in the garden she was so ashamed. She went away and came back with empty belly and arms, but the lads were all throwing sly weighing-up glances at her, grinning and nudging each other when she went by at market, talking about her out of the corner of their mouths. Predatory, that's what they were. Horrid lot. I should never've gossiped to Mrs Simpson about her, talk about things coming back to haunt you. And even if I've got a man and he stands by me... Yes, best we go to Poland, everything'll settle down there soon. It's probably not half as bad as some of them're making out. I'll talk to him on Friday,' she decided, 'on our way back from choir.'

Again she calculated the dates in her head just to be sure, and knew it was no mistake. The baby would be born at the beginning of October. 'A Libra,' she thought. 'Romantic and charming, easygoing and sociable,' she read in her magazine. 'Just like his father', she hugged the thought closer.

'Will he be pleased? ...Of course he will, don't be daft, Annie girl,' she thought. She had the luck to be big boned, which meant there were four months, perhaps five, to make plans and leave before her condition became obvious to all. Time enough.

That evening, dreaming as she darned, she sat the other side of the range to Evan who was mending Ziggy's headcollar, morose and monosyllabic as usual. There was just the sound of the wind in the eaves and the coals shifting on the fire. Evan raised his head and glowered over at her. Quick to the threat, Annie knew it was one of those evenings to do something, anything, to avert the trouble that look presaged. Bound to be about her and Jan, harping on and on. Picking a quarrel with him first usually worked.

'I've had enough of your stinky old socks. Ugh!" and she tossed them on the floor.

"You selfish little cow," he cursed. 'Need to be a bit more respectful, like. Who do you think keeps this place warm, cutting all the firewood, bringing in all the cash? Think you could manage here without me? You must be daft."

Feigning high dudgeon, she lit a candle and took herself off to bed. She picked up the book of Nain's she'd found in the kitchen, but dropped it again unopened on the covers, returned to her thoughts. She nearly had enough saved to buy that pretty set of curtains from Roberts the Drapers for her bedroom... but what was she thinking of? Curtains weren't the most important things now. She was going to need booties, blue ones, a crib with satin ribbon trim and a silver rattle... She woke with a start, the cold starting to penetrate. The candle had guttered out leaving its waxy smoky smell, and in the moonlight that shafted through the small skylight in the slope of the roof she could see bats flitting round the chimney. There was no ceiling in her room, just the rafters and the slates above them with a thin wash of plaster, the spiders wove their webs in the corners, and she could hear the mice scuttling along the big beams that tied the roof together. But she didn't mind, she liked that the outside was so close to the inside.

It was blustery that night, and from her window the lights of the big ships lined up out in the bay, waiting their turn for the Mersey to suck them up and spew them out at the Liverpool docks. She was unable to sleep and lit the candle again, picked up the book that had fallen to the floor- 'Domestic Preservation of Fruit and Vegetables'. It wasn't going to be long before the Seville oranges arrived all the way from Spain; they usually came in during January, those sour, crumply fruits perfect for marmalade with the sugar she'd hoarded. She enjoyed cooking, the slow change from one substance into another over a fire, the stirring and tasting. Yes, she'd get the ironmonger to mend that old jam pan of Nain's, which she'd found hanging in one of the barns, full of rat droppings and virulently coloured moulds. She'd have to get up early to queue at the green-grocers though, because he was bound to run out. She'd take the surplus to market, to barter for the things they wouldn't be able to grow for themselves, like paraffin, and tea, and sugar.

'Good grief, girl. What are you doing still thinking about things like this?' she berated herself. 'I've got to make other plans now. It'll all be different in Poland.'

She thought forward to Friday and how the night might end. A churn of anxiety and anticipation hit her belly and rose up under her ribs, but she chased it away.

'Don't be such a ninny. You've never been wrong about a person yet, and Jan's one of the best. You'll see. It'll all be alright.'

*

The winter of 1946 - 47 was deathly cold. 'A terrible thing, indeed', the villagers shook their heads and gravely agreed. Old people froze to death in their houses like the small birds in their nests, and as he went about Jan listened to the fluttering fade away and still as streams of cold air swept in from over the Urals with their premonitions of blizzards to come. The peaks of the mountains resembled thickly iced cakes, but the coast had so far escaped the very heavy falls. The men grumbled in the pubs that life couldn't get much more uncomfortable. Jan thought of Siberia, said nothing. Shortages of work meant money was not coming into many households in amounts large enough to keep the fire alight and feed the children's rumbling bellies. Everybody was talking of a fuel crisis; and even could they afford it, the reduced pressure of the gas fires round which they sat shivering made hardly an impact on the Arctic temperatures. It turned them mean and rancorous. Did we fight for this? he heard them say when he went to town. He understood; hadn't he used those very same words? But it didn't make things any easier to bear. He also heard that the other Polish pilots, back at base in Derbyshire, had started going into town without their badges to avoid harassment from local people resentful at the Poles for taking what little there was from 'our lads'. Luckily, such deep animosity had not yet reached here, this outpost of Wales – at least not overtly. Though Evan was helping things along.

Jan thought of himself as a pragmatic man and counted his blessings, but even so he felt beset with doubts and anxieties. The news coming in through the Polish Underground was not good; civil war was still raging between the Russians and the Ukrainians in Kresy, despite the crack troops sent in to break it up. Kresy was his family home before the war, and he felt more despondent than ever. He learnt from one of the Poles in the army barracks nearby that many of the survivors, released by Stalin from the Siberian Gulags and who had joined the Polish Army in Europe under General Anders, were starting to gradually filter into Britain, displaced, dispossessed, and he allowed his hopes to be raised. But although he put word out that he was keen for any information about the Zadrzynski family from Lvov, he heard nothing. There was only a faint chance anyway, he knew. His mother had not been a strong woman and he did not see how his father, unused as he was to hard physical labour, could have survived such brutal conditions. He still had hopes that his sisters could have survived, but as time went on he knew he would have to resign himself to being alone.

He found, with some discomfiture since he had always considered himself a genial, easy-going person, that he was beginning to hate the traitorous English, as he thought of them now. Not individual people, no, but as a nation. Not only had they sat back and watched Germany invade Poland, but they had allowed Stalin to have his bullying way. Now his beloved country had been torn apart, and the beautiful Carpathian Mountains where so much of his spirit still resided, were part of the Ukraine. He beat his fist on his knee in frustration, and got up to pace his small room.

He picked up the daily newspaper Mr Simpson left in the back of the Bentley. It made his blood boil to read what people were saying about Stalin. Did they not see what a monster he was? They will see, and they will be sorry. The English have thrown us onto the rubbish heap. After all we did, the Germans we fought and battles we won! he seethed with bitterness. Now everyone forgets. So much for loyalty and honour.

Although her life had been sheltered, Annie was the only person he could turn to who would listen to his outbursts with sympathy and understanding. While Annie's experiences of the world were limited to a tiny part of these islands, and storm troopers had not raped her or battered down her door, she had small glimpses of how people could behave to each other. How people could easily say one thing and think another, smile at you even as all the time they were tearing you to shreds in their minds. How, he thought bitterly, given the right conditions, these so-called decent people could also turn into monsters with no mercy in their hearts for anyone who was 'different'. It was time to go.

He had read his history books. Where his teachers had been at pains to point out how benevolent and generous the colonial British had been, firm but kind, good allies, he had wondered how it had felt to the people in India, or the Zulus, or the slaves on the sugar plantations. Now he knew. The British, he thought, were a ruthless and insensitive people. He had heard Mr Simpson talking about a government minister who had pronounced, "The cliffs of Dover are where civilisation ends," and he had wondered, 'Which side of the cliffs does he mean?'

*

"These people, these members of your government, they stand in their fancy clothes and talk about my country and my people as though we are just things, without feelings. They would pipe another song if Russians knock on their own front doors," Jan fumed. It was Friday night and he was walking with Annie along the road from the village hall to Bron Felen. The moon was full and bright and cast long sharp shadows in front of them.

'Jan, Jan, look. The shadows!" Refusing to be cast down by his gathering mood, Annie elbowed him sharply in the ribs. She needed him in a more receptive one so she could divulge her news. She danced in the road, slipping and sliding on the ice, her red hair flying wild, curling her fingers into shadow talons, reaching out towards a shadow Jan.

"Aagh. Go away, witch!" he yelled, playing the game, and, wrenching a hazel whip from the hedge as weapon, leapt and pranced, thrust and recoiled, his lithe figure elongated in the moon-shadow.

"Stars, hide your fires! Let not light see my black and deep desires."

Annie paused, asked, "Where's that from, then?"

"Your Shakespeare – Macbeth," Jan panted. Annie laughed,

'I bet I know what your deep desires are." She thrust her arm through his, humming 'Me and my shadow'.

*

Later, by the gate though, Jan could not be diverted from his bitterness.

"What is purpose of this big war at end, Annie? It does not make sense to me. I hear many brave words that it was to come to our aid in Poland, that no big country can overrun little country. But this is what Russia does to Poland now! Our government-in-exile in London, which for whole of war organises resistance to Germany and Russia, it is ignored now and made shame of. How can Mr Churchill turn from us in this way?"

Annie had no words to comfort Jan in his anger, but she knew it had its birth in loneliness and fear, because she had nowhere to go either, no home, no family. It might have been only a hundred miles away, but nobody could deny that the truth for her was that it had all vanished as absolutely and irrevocably as Lvov.

"Good night, Jan, my love. I'm sorry about your family. I hope you find them, I really do. See you tomorrow at market." She stayed and watched as he walked back towards the Lodge. 'I'll tell him then,' she whispered.

The big buck hare was crouched at the foot of the bank, and as she approached he bolted across the meadow, zig-zagging to lose the imagined pursuit. Big scudding clouds raced across the moon and darkened the night. There was no light on when she reached the cottage. Pabi growled – the collie was tied up in his usual place, but there was no sign of Evan. 'Odd,' she thought, 'he always takes Pabi with him if he goes to the pub.' Not bothering to go in the main part of the cottage and see if he was there, she boiled a kettle on the hob in the dairy, filled the big stone hot water bottle and climbed up the rough stairs to her room, admiring again the pretty handle she'd bartered last week from Gipsy Bob. Modern. She liked nice things. She'd fixed it to the door herself; no good asking Evan to do things like that – as if she'd demean herself to ask him anything, anyway. Keck-handed. Useless clod.

The edge of the room's chill had been taken off by the banked up range down in the kitchen. She folded her clothes neatly on the little chair by the door, put on her flannel nightdress and the woollen socks Nain had knitted, and jumped into bed.

She was scared, of course, but she knew what she wanted. Mam had always said things would work out in the end if you went for them with the whole of you...

Except they hadn't for her, had they? Unless buried in the ground was 'working out'. Annie shivered and pulled the blankets closer round her, making a nest from which just the tip of her nose peeped. In the morning the window would be a sheet of ice and she would have to dress under the bed clothes. She slept.

*

She woke with a start when she heard quick footsteps in the yard and raised herself in alarm. Then she heard Evan swear and curse at Pabi and the door bang. The clock in the kitchen chimed nine o'clock and she wondered where he'd been, what he'd been doing, but in the end she had no real interest in these questions. From now on Evan was nothing. A fly she would brush off, a bug she would squash...

**

Invite the vultures in

'If it turns out that there is a God, I don't think he's evil.
But the worst you can say about him is that basically
he's an underachiever.'

- Woody Allen

Summer and Autumn 2002

I wanted answers from the Local Health Board. Its Chief Executive, its Medical Director, its Clinical Governance Department. Its Complaints Department. Its nurses, its porters, its cleaners. I didn't fall apart, except inside where nobody could see the rubble. I came out fighting. They must have been sick of me by the time of the inquest. I hoped they were. Even so I could not winkle out a single honest answer. When the police disclosed the results of their investigation the picture that emerged was appalling. More than the sheer incompetence, what shocked was the absence of any moral position – not just of those under investigation, but of the investigators themselves. But what was it I had expected? Quite simply – a nagging, a picking at the bones, a getting in the way, in people's hair, under their skin, in every morsel they ate or drank, until the truth surrendered itself into our waiting hands.

There is a Chinese proverb, 'He who asks is a fool for five minutes; he who does not ask remains a fool forever.' But that's only the half of it, and I could add the other half: 'He who keeps banging his head against brick walls gets a headache.' The only truth which emerged during that long hot summer was that the hospital had the complexity, the finances and the fear to outlast us all. So was it any wonder that the police solved the problem by taking a few aspirin and went about their business of solving more obvious crimes, leaving me the angry champion of a tragically insane cause, an army of one, clutching my aching skull?

The whole thing was an embarrassment of lies, with a hefty slugging of bare-faced denials, leaving a web of knotted lines and scars on my heart that would never fade. Where no-one was ever able to answer the simplest of questions – 'How can you claim to help people, if you can't even keep them alive?'

We waited, and we waited. The summer turned into autumn, held hints of the winter as the temperature dropped, and the warm earth redolent with the smell of decaying leaves contracted, became hard, unyielding. Fierce winds buffeted the caravan. They blustered inside my head too; I lost my bearings and became irritable and grouchy. When I went outside, which was rarely, my eyes would shiver in the gusts, and I saw everything out of focus, through a watery veil. Still we heard nothing, and this silence from those who should have been shouting on our behalf was a crucible that calcined my frustration and anger – that fire at least burnt bright, and in its light Fleur still lived.

Then, without warning, one of the senior managers involved resigned; another retired; the ward sister moved to Newcastle. Soon, I thought, there would be nothing left of *Llanfair* Acute Mental Illness Unit. Not a bad thing perhaps.

*

'Sarah. Is it an OK time to visit? I don't want to come at a bad time."

'No, no, it's lovely to see you." I sigh, but quietly so she can't hear, and put the kettle on. She takes off her coat and plumps herself down on the garden seat in the late afternoon sunshine of the Indian summer that succeeded the gales. Through the half open door I see her kick off her fashionable shoes and wriggle her toes in relief. 'Why don't you tarmac that dreadful track? I'm not trusting my suspension over those ruts, and it's a killer to walk. Are you deliberately trying to keep everyone away?"

Even though I have to smile, I fear we are in for a long session. Eva. A dear friend, one of the best, but determined to call me out. I can see it in the business-like way she is tidying the books on the table. I know she means well, but I'm weary of admonitory finger-wagging about my 'obsessive' behaviour. I bring out the tray and even though I know it won't put her off for long fuss with the paraphernalia of the tea-time ritual. I pour water just off the boil into the teapot, listen to the hissing of the leaves, and catch the fragrant steam in my nose.

'Look Sarah, I know you won't mind me saying this" (won't I?), 'but you're harbouring some very negative stuff, you know, and Harry tells me you've got a bee in your bonnet now about the old woman who used to live here. As if you haven't enough to handle. You have to face things. Believe me, it'll come back and bite you when you least expect it,' she begins as we take our first sips. No treading carefully here. She is plump and cosseted, and although homely, her wealth has meant that she usually gets what she wants. She feels she can order me around. I try not to let it show, but I am irritated. I will do what I need to do as seems right to me.

'Perhaps you're right, I guess it doesn't do any good to store things up," I concede, a gesture of conciliation. 'I suppose you're someone I might be able to talk to about it." There is a pregnant pause. She cocks her head. Is she expecting me to talk? To convert the promise into the gift? Now? How to even begin?

'I don't know if you'll understand," I begin. How can she possibly understand without putting herself in my place, and who in their right mind would want to do that? I love my friend, and I don't want to upset her. No, that's not true; I love her but I do want to upset her. Some perversity impels me to alienate anyone who offers me sympathy, drive them away so that they leave me alone. But I make an effort and try to be agreeable. 'I don't just mean Fleur's death; it's more subtle than that. Do you remember me telling you once about bunging a boot at God and blowing him out? After that life felt– well, diminished, I suppose. Pointless, totally meaningless! So here I am – the full-blown atheist. It was difficult at first, but it's got easier and easier and now I can't understand how on earth anyone gets taken in by such fairy stories."

*

Eva is no priest worshipper but she is a believer in the idea of an ordered universe, a deliberate mind – and so, to my newly opened eyes, full of a misplaced faith in its messengers. She bridles.

'What are you saying, Sarah? What about divine order?"

'A load of rubbish!" I have to kick, I can't stand it. I watch her, miserable at my meanness, as she jerks back, but defiant for all that.

'I can't believe you mean that," she gasps.

But I do. Because, when they sensed the cold truth of the universe, it was precisely then that the preacher men of old seized the moment to weave those soft lying webs that even now reel us in and put us to sleep.

'Oh, come on Eva, don't be so naive. Look how we clutch the myth, thinking to be saved. Saved from what? I'll tell you what – saved from reality."

'What makes you think you know what reality is?" she retorts. Ouch. She has an unerring instinct for my weaknesses.

'I don't. But it certainly isn't something we know by callousing our knees and cricking our necks, peering up and mumbling our entreaties."

'Why not? Prayer takes many forms, and – " I interrupt rudely.

"Are you sitting there and telling me that by the mere power of prayer we can scale the embankment and command the express to stop?" I am safe in asking this, Eva has not been in a bad place in her life. How could she be sure? And will she dare contradict me?

'Of course not, but – " I have her on the run.

'No, Eva. We're red pulp on the line. We're pitiable. Why?" She shakes her head mutely. I have battered her into quiescence. 'Because we abdicate. 'We are poor little lambs who have lost our way, baa, baa, baa.' Don't let's foist the blame for our shortcomings on the universe. It's we who refuse the responsibility for who we are and what we do. The corollary to this cowardice of course is that we then find it impossible to look our end in the face, accept our own insignificant existence." I pause for breath. I notice her look of recalcitrant defiance. I soldier on. 'Don't you see? We invite the vultures in. So don't let's invent a fairy story of happily ever after. Let's face it – we're all bawling infants who refuse to grow up – "

My victory was Pyrrhic. I may have won the argument but I lost a friend. Did I care? Not much. But the truth was I no longer liked myself. This new 'me' was raw and belligerent. She saw enemies too quickly. She created them. It was my fear of, yet my strange compulsion towards, such 'chats' – the provocative rant they turned on in me once the wall of careful tact was breached - that isolated me. Fleur's death had kicked me from infancy, that much was true, but into – well, I wasn't sure where. Adolescence? Somewhere uncomfortable. Out of paradise, anyway, and I didn't want to be ejected from paradise any more than any other person. But of course it never was paradise, because Paradise was ignorance, not innocence.

So I had my adolescent tantrums. I stamped, shouted, and slammed doors, went stumbling off to sulk in the woods, or threw myself face down in the grass choking with anger and tears. With one mighty difference – unlike all three or thirteen year olds, I, at fifty-three, knew why and what for. I wanted the 'State' to take up my challenge and prove definitively that its laws and precepts were founded on moral rectitude, integrity, that they delivered justice. Then I would shut up and sit down. They revealed themselves, of course, to be little more than clever players of what was, to them, only a game. And they were always going to be the winners. Not me.

When Eva left, cold and distant as I'd never seen her, I couldn't settle, my heart was racing. I grabbed my rucksack and walked the three miles to town. Furious thoughts besieged my brain, splashed the acids in my belly, excavated my bowels. I made no attempt to stop them. They were transients, bums, outsiders – like me. I revelled in their raging. But even as I cheered them on, I knew they were not a solution. Their voices were shrill and inconsistent; one moment a thin whining from the sinuses, the next a predatory shout from the heart that people crossed the street to avoid, a lurking blackness from a horror movie needing only an unwary moment to leap and fasten on its prey.

Neither of these voices was attractive. Anger predominated because I liked its heft; but it was proving to be a rough, unwieldy bludgeon, a Stone Age axe which bruised my hands and injured many bystanders; a powerful magnet to the cultish, the brute, the mob; to those already converted – but to the passion, not the cause. I knew it belonged to the impotent, bleeding in chains.

I feel so lonely. I miss you, Fleur. The road was warm with its whiff of silage and disinfectant in the warm breeze – and there I was, talking out loud to myself again. But what the heck, I thought, there's no-one around to hear me this time, and who bloody cares, anyway? I was embarrassed when some bullocks in a field turned their heads and gazed at me. They did not blink, they did not swish their tails, they just stood there and stared. There's always someone who hears.

*

Harry persuaded me to go with him to Ireland for a short break. We flew from an airport in the north of England with one of those airlines whose employees, almost it seems in order to exact penance for the cheap flights, have become expert in the hundred petty regulations that make one's journey as unpleasant and difficult as possible. They are adept at maintaining the dispassionate expression of a professional, yet underneath is the hint of a spiteful glee. A couple of people in front of us at check-in was a woman with a babe in arms and a toddler, hauling assorted coats, pushchair, handbag and a large suitcase.

My attention snapped into focus at the sound of an acrimonious argument with the check in girl, who had found the suitcase to be minimally overweight.

'No, I'm sorry. You cannot transfer your allowance to your daughter. Children under the age of two are classed as infants and do not have a baggage allowance."

'But I've paid for a seat for her – "

'I'm sorry," (untrue, she was enjoying herself) 'those are the rules of the airline."

"Ah, it's only a coupla pounds. Can't you let it through?"

'No, I'm sorry, those are the rules."

'Well what d'you expect me to do, now?"

'I'm afraid you'll have to either leave something behind or put it in another bag."

'Where'll I get another bag, so? And how would I be carrying it with all this?"

"There is a luggage shop in the mall."

"And if I do that I'll be OK?"

"Of course." Slight pause, as she gathers herself for the kill. 'But, as you haven't booked a second bag in advance, that will be forty pounds extra."

'Forty pounds?! Do I look like I'm made of money? Mary, Mother of God!"

"The conditions of travel you agreed to when you bought your tickets do explain this... Madam."

That was all it took, that final word, to send me over the edge and break one of my golden rules when travelling – Mind Your Own Business. Ignoring Harry's hissed 'Oh for fuck's sake, Sarah', I accused the check-in person of being mean, callous, and other no doubt undeserved epithets. Seated behind that desk, to me she was just a faceless clone, and normal polite considerations could be dispensed with. She blinked rapidly, but managed to ignore me. My outburst rippled through the queue, with mutterings of 'Shame!' and 'Feckin' let her go!' and when the supervisor was summoned over to take charge of the developing situation I was encouraged to believe that I'd shown them we customers had some small powers left us. So when I reached the check-in and my own bag was found to be overweight, I refused to step aside and insisted on opening and repacking it on the conveyor belt with studied slowness, blind to the fact that this would not endear me to those same passengers backing-up behind, who had just applauded my championing of a mother of small children. I chose to interpret the baleful looks directed my way as conspiratorial. Harry, who had stood to one side shaking his head while all this was going on, marched off. 'Let him,' I thought. 'I don't care.'

My appetite for confrontation was whetted yet more when one of that arrogant breed of security guards who then, as now, swarmed in such public places, accosted me before I had even reached customs and instructed me to stand on a dingy square of carpet to have my photograph taken.

"Why? Who says?" I demanded. He waved to direct my gaze towards a notice pinned to a pillar saying 'By Order of HM Government'.

"But – why?" I repeated.

"To make sure that the person going through customs is the same person who gets on the plane... Madam." He sighed, impervious, well-trained. There it was again, that word.

"And how are you going to know that, then?"

"Your photograph will be available to the boarding staff at the gate, Madam. Please remove your hat."

I bit my tongue. This well-muscled hulk did not invite tangling with. Snatching off my beret, I scowled in an effort to disguise myself as much as possible and stalked through customs, where I forced myself to ignore the cheeky 'Nice hat' from the younger of the pair. Outrage sparked an all-too-familiar hot flush which crawled up from my diaphragm, out of my collar, round my ears and painted hectic patches on my cheeks. Tight bands constricted my ribs, my breaths came quick and shallow. I noticed when I tried to engage fellow passengers about the scandalous infringements of our human rights that they smiled, to placate me, not quite meeting my eye, and moved off with ill-concealed haste. I was past caring, my grasp of reality long gone. Harry must have hidden in the toilets, for I couldn't see him anywhere.

From then on I missed no opportunities for argument with all and any officials who crossed my path. I was deaf to the exasperation in the impatient lines of people forced to queue behind me at every confrontation. I stood with arms folded. I would stand there till hell froze over. The field would be to the victor. When Harry re-appeared I shrugged him off, spurning appeasement. The victor boarded and I wondered why I felt so ill.

It took me two days to recover. When I did, I was forced to acknowledge I'd escalated a small annoyance into a nuclear disaster. I was alienating all around me. Not just then, all the time... even though Harry hugged me and said it was OK, I knew it wasn't.

**

An unrightable wrong

'The law is an ass.'

- Charles Dickens, Oliver Twist

'Perseverance, n. A lowly virtue whereby mediocrity achieves an inglorious success.'

- Ambrose Bierce

It took *Llanfair* eleven months and eight days to concoct its report into the 'circumstances of the adverse incident', as Fleur's death was now being labeled. As might be expected, managers had skilfully managed their own red faces, painted them white, shifted the blame. Nurses were being dismissed.

We traveled down south to meet with the police and the Crown Prosecution Service and discuss what next. It was the first time I'd been back to the area since the funeral, and everywhere I turned I saw Fleur, heard her voice. The past hurt; the present hurt; there was no future. I could no longer call this part of the planet 'home'.

The police agreed there was every reason to ratchet up the investigation into the senior managers at *Llanfair* and their actions – or more importantly, their omissions. My hopes that we might get to the truth were raised, but, as the weeks rolled past, and the silence closed in around us again, I grew suspicious about what might be happening behind that firmly raised judicial barrier, especially as, however often I asked, the excuse was always that the information was 'sub-judice' – even when it patently wasn't. Letters I wrote vanished into the maw of the postal services, emails snarled up in the web, and when it became clear there was a determination not to reply, I smashed the façade of polite civility, and accused the hospital, the police, everyone in range, of deliberate obstruction, prevarication and obfuscation. Such wonderful words, but as devoid of impact on those they were aimed at as the little scrumpled paper balls on which I wrote countless drafts of complaint only to end up throwing them in the wastebasket.

*

"When life itself seems lunatic, who knows where madness lies?" I warbled, six months later, as we swerved off the M6 into the mire of streets entangling the city. Months when I barely spoke to Harry, when we hardly touched. Months of irritation if he wanted me to look up from the laptop, drink the mugs of tea he made that went cold. There must have been more to life than that, but I don't remember it.

When we finally found a parking space and got out it was in angry silence because of the row we'd just had. I'm no great shakes as a city driver, the only way I survive is by turning my rear view mirror at an angle so I can see nothing of what is behind me. With Harry's, 'Watch out!' ringing in my ears, I had plunged into the city mayhem, with insouciant disregard for the river of traffic, which parted like the Red Sea before and behind me. When Harry unfolded himself from the foetal position he had adopted right up to the moment I turned off the ignition, he was not in the best of moods; and I was – tense. We were on our way to a meeting with the Serious (who I later, childishly, renamed Trivial) Case Officers from the Crown Prosecution Service, who had, they said, now received the police's final report.

Apart from the criminal expense (his words) of getting there, Harry considered even bothering to go was a waste of our time and effort. Rationally, I agreed with him. Emotionally, Birmingham was the only place on the planet I wanted to be, and, loyal to the end, he insisted on coming along to 'look after' me. I ignored his warning, my still faithful *Sancho Panza*. Like the Don, I might be tilting at windmills and, also like the Don, I refused to be swayed by common sense; unlike the Don and his sidekick, no flamboyant or romantic adventures beckoned us on.

Lowly and mediocre as it may have made me feel, I took a perverse pride in my perseverance despite all the odds. Once I had an ankle gripped in my teeth it was difficult to shake me off, and I hung on and hung on, hoping to gnaw away any and all resistance to my view of the truth through sheer tenacity, even though I could see my prize was only ever going to be a solitary foot.

The office looked out on the Bull Ring through large hermetically sealed windows which shut out the pollution and the roar of traffic, but the artificial atmosphere created by the air-conditioning plus the short-pile nylon carpet built up static to such a pitch that every time I put my hand on the tubular steel armrests of the post-modern conference chair I was sitting in, it discharged with an audible snap, making me and everyone else in the room jump. I explained, in a half-hearted attempt to lighten the mood, that I also had this trouble with supermarket trolleys. No-one was amused. Levity, even when it sprang from nerves, was clearly frowned upon. Much later, I concluded the day was a slice, a whole cake even, of black comedy.

The Case Officer sat at the head of the table, her manicured fingers riffled busily through a large file put in front of her by an assistant, and mused enquiringly, 'Now, we are here to –?'

'– right an unrightable wrong.' I couldn't stop myself.

'Sorry, what was that?' she stared at me.

'Nothing, really. Something I read somewhere,' I waved it off. What was the point?

It was clear from the beginning that a deal had been done, and the file marked 'Not for action'.

'I don't get it,' said Fleur's father, Tony, in bewilderment as we trooped out some four hours of futile argument later, 'Why did they drag us here to sit through that farce?'

'I can't believe they ignored all the evidence and the logic. Well, actually, they twisted it; what we just sat through had nothing to do with getting at the truth. They failed to even grasp the core facts,' I chimed in.

'Wrong. Mistake number one.' Harry said grimly. 'They grasped them alright. To sum up what happened here this afternoon? Easy. Directors' duties be damned; law rigged; case dismissed.'

'If it was that simple, why did we have to wait so long for them to make a decision? They could have told us on day one, for all the difference the extra two years have made.'

'Window dressing. To make you think they care. They don't. That they're 'doing' something. They aren't. Why do you think they didn't prosecute those responsible for the Zeebrugge ferry sinking, or the Hatfield train crash, or the de Menezes shooting?' Harry ticked them off with disgust on his fingers. We stared at him. What had these to do with Fleur?

"Mistake number two. To think those who make the rules, make them for your or my benefit. Nope. They've got their eyes firmly fixed on that rainy day in the future when they find themselves out of office, and so run around lining up cushy corporate seats to fall into. If the law made possible the successful prosecution of large companies and public bodies, it would irretrievably spell the death of all those carefully laid plans. After all, who wants to be held accountable for some faceless person's tragic death, and end up behind bars? Crushed in machinery, fallen from height, poisoned, burnt, irradiated – you name it, there are a million ways to die out there due to another person's carelessness. Wriggle room, that's what they created with the so-called law of Corporate Manslaughter. Not worth the paper it's written on."

We stood silently outside on the pavement, and the sheer futility of it all crushed us. A good rule of thumb, I thought, was that if something doesn't make sense you know there's a key piece of information missing. And in this case it was being rammed home to me that this missing piece of information was that they didn't want to prosecute, not that they couldn't – I didn't get as far as the shouldn't. The whole idea of prosecuting the NHS for corporate manslaughter was enough to keep them awake at nights. If you add to that the fact of suicide – what a horror! – I think they thought we should consider ourselves lucky they'd taken it even this seriously. Now it was over to the Coroner. Even though it made bleak sense, Harry's cynicism was hard to stomach, and I felt my eyes fill with tears. We started off to find our car. Which multi-storey had we left it in? All the ramps looked the same.

'Sarah, I'll ask you again in a year or so's time," he stopped, and the passers-by hurrying home from work or shopping give him dirty looks, forced to walk round him on the pavement, 'because it'll take that long, and you'll be wondering what the fuck happened along the way. I know what happens – I've been a works convener and I know every nasty little trick the bosses get up to."

*

So did I have to accept that I was likely to be deprived of success after all, even inglorious success? 'Just hold, don't grasp; just see, don't look; just rest, don't press' – sound advice, perhaps, but ultimately, the only weapon at my disposal was to complain, vociferously and often. It came perilously close to whining. Judicial review? Forget it. Judicial reviews cost thousands. Justice Sir James Mathew said, as far back as the 1800s, and nothing seemed to have changed,

'In England justice is open to all, like the Ritz Hotel...' I chose to interpret this as begging the punch line, '... as long as you have the money.' Without money, or influence, you will not be ushered across thickly carpeted floors to a table in the restaurant by a deferential waiter, respectfully offering plush menus and uncorking costly wines. Without money, or influence, you will never sleep in a palatially appointed room with brocades and silk sheets, chocolates delivered on a silver trolley – not even for one night. And those who do swish between those golden portals? All you can do is stand on the pavement and stare.

*

My innocence toppled with such a crash after that meeting that the dust storm it raised blinded me to all red lights and warning signs. I kept trying with reasoned and reasonable arguments to change their minds, to get them to 'see the light'. Of course, I failed. Reason was barely able to raise its snout out of the cold primeval muck to take a breath before some big hot bottom sat on him with alacrity.

I lowered my head and pawed the ground, became bull-like. Better than a terrier, I thought. The picture of a terrier with its teeth buried in some person's ankle was beginning to irritate me; it was only an ankle after all, however painful it might бe, and that foot was small reward. But a bull... A bull transfixes you with his furious eye, snorts foam and lather, bellows to raise the hair on your head, and his thundering hooves make the earth, and knees, quake, before he tosses you in the air and tramples you into a stain on the earth. Who would not quail in submission before such a force? But I found my opponents wily and fleet of foot, able to change direction in mid-stride, will-o'-the-wisps hiding within the dust I raised in my headlong charges. I was in danger of a coronary, or at the very least of impaling some innocent bystander. What I wanted was the jugular, to gore and stomp and pound! Yes, red, red, red, the colour of blood. Not the bull in a china shop, no, but that snorting, magnificent Minotaur of the labyrinths... But, I remembered, bulls were usually dragged out of the ring by their tails. And anyway, red mists and charges were more Harry's style than mine, and when it came down to the nitty-gritty I didn't have the killer instinct; I found myself back with the English proverbial, snorting and tossing, my horns well and truly stuck in the gatepost, forced to acknowledge the harder you push, the more immoveable the obstacle.

*

It was two o'clock in the morning, my eyes felt gritty and were becoming difficult to focus, and my legs tight and stiff. I got up and walked out onto the verandah for a breath of cool night air. The milky way stretched a broad path across the blackness and I wished I could walk out along it to the edges of the galaxy, zip through astral light shows, dance to galactic music, not pinned down by some pin-striped bloke masquerading as reasonableness incarnate back here on earth. But I couldn't seem to prise myself away from the computer long enough to even go for a walk with the dog on the beach, let alone go star wandering.

I could hear Harry moving in the bedroom and knew he would be awake looking at his watch and wondering why I was again up so late. My determination steeled itself to resist attack. I was always feeling guilty these days about how I was behaving, but it didn't seem to make any difference. I would come in from work, throw a quick 'Hi' in Harry's direction, make indeterminate noises meant to indicate I was interested in his day, then edge towards the computer and my obsession. I was in effect switching Harry off as I switched the machine on, and he knew it. I knew too that it was only a matter of time.

'You're still up,' Harry emerged from the bedroom in his pants and socks and came outside for a pee. His hair stood on end like a small boy's, and my heart lurched. I so wanted to succumb to softness and soothing endearments, yet something in me refused, was hard, unyielding. Cruel.

'Mm-hmm.' I carried on looking at the stars.

'Sarah, don't you think you ought to give yourself a bit of a break on this?' Harry asked. Here it came. 'It's been so long.'

'I know, I know.' So short.

'It's just that I feel you don't give a damn about me any more. It's as though I don't even exist. I've tried to be supportive, you know that. But you ignore me when you come home, you don't come to bed until the early hours of the morning, and then you go to work. I sometimes wonder whether I actually exist for you. It's not good, you know.'

'Mm.'

'I'm not saying you shouldn't fight for the truth, and I respect and admire your determination. But there's no balance in it. You can't let go even if you wanted to. You haven't any life for yourself.'

That was the point. I didn't have a life. I'd offered my life to the non-existent God of my imagination in return for Fleur's, and he'd spurned it as worthless. He had become that great big bird flapping his way from tree to tree.

I had a life I no longer wished to live. But could I say such things to Harry? I thought not.

'I'm sorry, so sorry. I just can't help it.' I didn't feel sorry. I felt nothing. All feeling seemed to have dried up and I was an empty husk. All that was left was this compulsion to hammer at the door of truth, and every time I hammered someone on the other side would barricade it even more tightly shut, or I would look through the keyhole and see it was a deserted building.

'I have to know what happened, how it happened, and those fucking people – so arrogant, they think they can pull the wool over everyone's eye. Well, I won't let them. Even if they do play golf with the Chief Constable. They think they're above the law –'

I went back inside and flung myself on the sofa. Harry followed looking miserable and cold. He sat down in the corner opposite, as far away from me as he could.

'I agree. I can get very worked up about this too, you know, Sarah. You're not the only one who feels upset and betrayed. The police investigation did start a fire underneath some very sensitive bottoms, even if it's got to be us who fan the flames. But it's hard. On us. On top of everything... one of the most shocking things in this whole debâcle has been to see so called respectable people occupying such eminent public positions scuttle and scurry in their desperation to deny any responsibility and escape the fallout. Like woodlice in the cracks of a rotting branch. It's –'

'It's surreal, it's like something from Kafka,' I burst out, 'All they needed to do was give us a genuine apology and honestly acknowledge what we all know went wrong, and I'd have been able to let go more easily. And look at the money wasted on all this legal finagling. Harry, you know I can't handle deceit. I can sniff it out. It eats me up. I don't want to be this way, believe me, I know how dangerous it is, but I can't help it.'

We sat there in the light from the monitor. Harry sighed, got up and filled the kettle, his panacea for all ills. He opened the door of the woodstove and poked the embers into life. I looked at him as the flames lit up his face. He seemed greyer and thinner, his shoulders more stooped, his face more deeply lined. I refused to let how this was affecting him get to me. If I did, I wouldn't be able to carry on.

'How can little people like us make any difference?' I asked. 'I get so frustrated I could cry.'

'I don't know if we can – make a difference, that is. The problem is the people we're up against have got used to sitting in their big comfy chairs, in big offices, with defensive rings of secretaries and expensive legal advisors. They don't come out. They hide behind their committees, and delegates, draft reports and their claims of ignorance. They're not going to jeopardise their careers on Fleur's account, and so they'll fight tooth and nail. And if they can't totally stop the shit from hitting the fan, their status grants them the privilege of dodging it – early retirement, resignation, the sideways step into anonymity. It's not that it's win/win for them, but damned right it's lose/lose for us."

Harry could rant with the best. The problem was his ranting stoked my boiler and it was steaming and ready to burst. I couldn't seem to find a release valve, and the pressure was starting to distort me. I felt my heart racing. I got up and started to pace, but the caravan was way too small, and I had to keep stepping over Harry's feet. I opened the door onto the verandah again, stepped out into the coolness, so agitated I just had to keep moving. Molly bounded in front of me, her waving stump of a tail a beacon of eagerness – ah, an excursion. Sniffing every hole, every tussock. The world an exciting doggy medley of smells and sounds that just had to be explored. What a difference between her and me. The world out there had no savour for me, no excitement. All I was intent on exploring was reams of paper – worthless stuff that probably should have been shredded long ago. Sifting millions of words for those few that fed my conviction about what had happened at *Llanfair*. I didn't stop to ask if it was worth it. If the penalty was too great. If I would regret it. Nor did it occur to me to consider if truth wore only the one face.

It was easy to insist my goal was the truth, but the more I clutched it the more it ran like water through my fingers. I began to grasp the irony that truth made people downright dishonest.

*

I called Molly and we set off in the starlight down the fields to the beach, along paths that smelled of rotting leaves. A fox's scent blew in the breeze, and Molly's nose twitched. On the way back I called her close; I needed her little white rump to follow as we cut through the small ancient woodland, home of red squirrel, polecat, stoat and fox, and where grew the huge hawthorn, to which one night I had brought Chickie, an old red hen, so old she could no longer walk or fly. I gave her a handful of mixed corn, and nestled her down between the hawthorn's spreading roots on a thick bed of ivy with a view of the sea. In the morning she was gone. Not even a feather. I hoped it was quicker than wringing her neck, I was almost sure it would have been. I consoled myself with the thought that she would not have been able to imagine her end, even though some ancient limbic instinct might have kicked in to warn her that to roost on the ground was not safe. Nature clearing up the debris, the weak, and the fallen, supper for the kits or pups, sustenance for the worms and blowflies, and the myriad small crawling insects who are always tidying up.

I stumbled as the thought hit me. I had delegated, to unknown others, two tasks: one had resulted in the death of an old hen; the other, in the death of my daughter. In Chickie's case I knew with certainty the fox would come; but in my daughter's, I had trusted he would not. But, to be sure, the fox had got her. Now, everywhere I looked, I saw foxes.

When I came back in Harry had turned the computer off and gone back to bed. It was four o'clock in the morning and I was cold and shaking. I needed human warmth, consolation. Would Harry be able to sustain this for much longer, I wondered. I doubted it and I felt as lonely as I ever had in my life.

"Hallo, pie," he murmured as I slipped under the duvet, and put his arms round me. He was still here – for the moment.

**

Quick as a flash

January 1947

"You're quiet tonight, Evan. What's up, man? You've been sitting there with a face like a wet weekend all evening."

"No business of yours, is it," Evan snapped. "Always poking and prying you are, Dilwyn Maesgwyn. Bloody leave me be. I'm off, see you tomorrow." He banged his half and half on the bar and went out. We all looked at each other.

"Evan doesn't like that Polish feller and Annie being so friendly with each other. Proper jealous, and him her cousin and all."

"Oh, I don't think it's anything like that," I said, talk like this made me uncomfortable, pricking my own jealous feelings, unworthy feelings that I stamped on, ashamed. "You know Evan, anything for an easy life. He's fed up, isn't he, with that red water disease. It's meant a lot more work, and he doesn't want the bother. And it's cost him a lot of brass."

"Aw, he can afford it, he's tight as a duck's arse, Dil, you know he is. And he's still drinking on us."

'*Nachdi.* Aye indeed. His Taid would have a fit if he saw how his grand-son runs that place. Old Huw kept everything up to the mark," one of the others said. I wouldn't admit it, but I thought the same.

'Still, I wouldn't want to get on the wrong side of Evan, whatever you say. He can be a nasty piece of work when he has a mind to be. And he's never liked the Pole since that time with old Pabi," said another.

'Na, man. You've got it all wrong. It's the other way round, it's the Pole who can't stand him," said the barman. 'I notice he won't come in if Evan's drinking."

"Aye. Maybe. It might be you're right."

Tired now and wanting a bite before bed, they drank up and went out into the icy night. The temperature was plummeting again after the sudden thaw earlier in the week, and big snow cumuli were building up over the mountains, a few flakes blowing in the wind. The slush was starting to freeze, and it was difficult to stand up.

'You two'll not get home early tonight," I laughed as the Hughes brothers, Emrys and Morris, set off on the three mile walk to their farm.

"Aye, typical bloody weather. Never know if you're coming or going. We'll be up before you lazy lot tomorrow, though, and waiting for you at market," they shouted. I went back in for another pint, not much to go home for.

*

Evan felt the hot jealousy rise like bile in his craw as he left *The Bell.* He carried it everywhere with him now, all the time. It pecked at his mind and distorted his thoughts. He knew he was skewed but was helpless in its grip. Whether fencing or ditching or feeding the animals, images of Annie and the bastard Pole were all he saw – holding hands, strolling into the woods, kissing by the gate, pushing their bicycles together, shoulders touching. He heard Annie's laughter, that drove him to madness when all he got from her was sullenness and cross contemptuous words. He saw the sly looks and malicious grins of his so-called friends, as they observed his discomfiture. He heard the insidious whispering in town and at market – behind the pens, in the hardware shop, along the street, on the beach, no matter where he went, until he had to put his hands to his head to block his ears. So loud were the voices that he often didn't hear people speak to him, and his reputation as a rude, difficult man grew. He found it hard to look people in the eyes, his glance shifted and his brows lowered in case he should see what they were thinking of him, or in case, worse, they saw what was in his heart. Pabi bore the brunt, poor bitch; spoiled for the work, panic froze her belly down in the fields at Evan's shout, so the sheep scattered. When Annie was out he crept into her bedroom and searched through her cupboards and drawers, careful to put all back as it was. What he thought he might find he could never answer to himself.

*

In the early days of January his darkest suspicions were aroused. He stood outside Annie's window and heard the retching in the morning, and saw the furtive rinsing of the bowl. He saw the nausea twist her face in the day, and the race to the *tŷ bach*.

'Must be that bug going round,' she said lightly. He nodded at the deceit, but said nothing. He pretended not to notice. His determination grew that he would have it out with that *blŵdi* Polish bastard; show him not to mess with a local girl. To sod off. He wished the camps on him, the torture, the starvation he'd heard about. He imagined the pits and the agony he'd heard tell of on the wireless, and he wished him there. He dared paint 'Poles go home' on the town's sea wall one blustery night while the rigging sang mournfully in the boatyard, and the men of the town were hunkering down round the coal fires in the pubs for a gossip, while their womenfolk cooked their tea. Like a squirrel he treasured and hoarded the bad-mouthing he heard from others.

He strode down the lane to the farm, his hatred pooling like bile in his gut. Snapping the chain on Pabi he turned round straight away and went back to the gate, stood there as his thoughts swung wildly this way and that. His feet trod without conscious volition the narrow path through the woods to the back of the *Plas*. Soft snow showered over him as he blundered past small birch and rowan, he kicked at them in his rage. He would waylay the Pole coming back from the village hall, and settle his hash for good, then and there, tonight.

A lamp threw its beam out of the window above the stable. Evan crept up the steps and, looking in, made sure the room was empty. Without a thought as to the propriety of his actions, he opened the door and slipped in. The lair of his enemy. He savoured his mastery over it. He picked up a book lying on the table, able to decipher the technical drawings although he couldn't read a word of it – airplane engines. Fancy stuff. He hefted the shotgun on the rack by the door and sighted through it. Stupid bugger, he hadn't even taken the cartridges out, ought to know better. He broke it out of reflex and set it down again. He riffled through the small desk and pored over the bundle of letters he found there. All in a script he couldn't read, looked like one of them runes he'd seen once in a magazine. He pulled out a sheet of paper lying on its own in one of the pigeon holes, and was rewarded. 'Dear Annie,' he read. 'I have decided. I cannot stay in this country. A friend of mine is in South Africa and he tell me this is place where we are welcome. There are big opportunities for pilots and engineers. I know you hate life on farm and I understand why. You have no reason for stay here. I am happy if you come with me. Please, I want you to come. I love you very much and it is hard to think of you to stay here with your awful Evan. Perhaps you learn to be teacher you want in South Africa? "

Evan looked fate in the eyes, and knew he had lost. But before the waves closed over his head he would stop their games, for good.

Just then, by the light of the moon, he saw two dark figures pushing bicycles pass along the road by the gate. 'That's them. That's them. He's seeing her home to Bron Felen. Quick. Quick'.

Quick as a flash his hypothalamus flared, vasopressin flooded his pituitary, his kidneys clutched his water tight and his blood pressure shot up to terrifying levels. Quick as a flash he snatched up the gun, jumped the steps and raced down the drive. The adrenalin flew to his feet and they ran as they had never run before. *"Mochyn!* I'll stop you, you bastard, I'll stop your shannanakins!" he screamed. His voice was hoarse and strained, and sounded strange to his ears. He aimed at the bigger of the two figures who had turned at his shout, and pulled the trigger.

Emrys Hughes staggered backwards and fell, tangled in his handlebars, in slow motion to the ground. His eyes dulled and bowels loosened, his breath stopped. His bicycle bell tinged once and the front wheel slowly span.

"Iesu Grist, man. Em, oh my God, Em. Get up, man, get up!" Morris rushed over to his brother. He crouched down and shook him, tried to lift him. Emrys' head lolled back, his mouth fell open; Morris recoiled in horror at the blackness that dripped onto his hands and knew the light of day would show it red. He looked up, seeking who had done this, but the wild figure of the man who had just murdered his brother had disappeared into the whirling flakes carried along by the wind.

*

Cursing herself for a scared little fool for not having spoken to Jan the night before about what was in her heart and her belly, Annie knew she must find the courage – today. She hoped he would be at the market for he sometimes had to drive Mr Simpson to Chester or Liverpool. 'Well, if not today, Monday will have to do. It's not as though it'll make much difference,' she thought, then winced, knowing she was putting it off. But when she and Evan arrived the market had not even started, and the cows were making a racket and the sheep were panting in tight groups in the pens, the dogs lying in the mud and slush and gazing at them, tongues lolling. Groups of men were gathered all over, heads together, their miens serious, and jabbing sticks at the ground for emphasis; the women had not even set out their stalls but were standing by their carts, their shrill voices and quick fluttering gestures suggesting a fox amongst the hens. The babble frightened Annie, who jumped down off the cart and shyly approached one of the groups of women.

'What's going on?" she asked a woman she knew. 'Why's everybody just standing around talking?"

"Aw *dac*, haven't you heard? That Polish feller up at the Simpsons' has gone and killed Emrys Hughes the Twins. Shot him, last night, outside on the road."

Annie's hands flew to her chest and she staggered under the blow of the woman's words. If ever words could knock you down, these were such.

'You left choir practice along with him last night, didn't you, Annie?" asked one of the younger girls, breathless with excitement at the anticipation of juicy gossip.

'Yes, she did. I saw them," piped up young Esyllt the Bron.

The torrent of their voices broke over her, submerging all coherent thought and leaving her gasping for air as though drowning. A freezing river of blood coursed down and out between her legs to fall on the ground. She looked down for the red puddle, but saw nothing. She put her hand on a stanchion for support. She set down the basket, careful not to break the eggs wrapped in newspaper she'd brought to sell. Another woman joined the group and they turned to her, leaving Annie in her still, small space. Snatches of conversation reached her ears, jumbled and meaningless, but at length she understood that Jan was under arrest in the police station in town for the murder of Emrys Hughes.

'Emrys Hughes? Why Emrys Hughes? It doesn't make any sense." Then felt a sinking as she remembered Jan's anger, and his vitriol about what he thought of as his betrayal by her countrymen. 'But he wouldn't shoot anyone. He's a gentle man. He doesn't fly off the handle like Evan does,' she thought. Just then she glanced over at Evan and surprised a look on his face. 'He's glad! He's glad this has happened. He wanted Jan out of the way and now he's thinking he's got what he wanted!" she thought, with a chill.

'When was this?" she asked the woman she knew.

'Sometime last night, I don't exactly know, doll. Just after they left the pub. The other lads saw them leave. Walking they were, because of the ice on the road."

"Who's saying it was Jan? He walked home with me last night. He couldn't have done it," she burst out.

"Well, you should know, I suppose." The woman eyed her curiously and turned away. Annie grabbed her arm and swung her round.

"Yes, but who's saying it was Jan, then?" she repeated loudly enough for the others to fall silent and look at her.

"Morris saw him," said another woman, defiantly. "He ran down from the stables; shouting and screaming at the top of his voice, he was. Morris recognised his voice, and he was shouting in gibberish, Polish probably. He saw him in the moon too, clear as day. Then he raised a shotgun and pointed it at Emrys and just shot him in the chest, then ran back up the drive. They found the gun up there on the muck heap and my brother told me they've found his fingerprints on it."

"Well, I shouldn't think they've had time for that, and anyway of course his fingerprints would be on it if it was his gun," Annie retorted. "That's just daft. He used that old shotgun to shoot the foxes for Mr Simpson. That doesn't mean he used it to shoot Mr Hughes. Perhaps someone stole it."

"It's you that's daft, girl. Who'd go and steal a shotgun round here? There's no tinkers this time of year. We've all got our own, we don't need to steal one. Anyway, he ran off and Brian found his footprints going up to the house, then out the back into the woods. Who else'd be hanging round there that time of night?"

The woman spoke with the certitude and assurance with which her kinship with the local policeman endowed her and shrugged Annie's hand off her arm angrily.

It still didn't make sense to Annie. "Well, it wasn't Jan, whoever it was."

"Ooh, Miss High and Mighty. Think you know better than the police now?" Annie didn't stop to listen to their spitefulness. Putting her basket of eggs back in the cart, she ran out of the market and down the high street, past the ironmonger's with his buckets and mops, barrows and rakes on the pavement, past the greengrocer's sacks of cabbages, turnips and potatoes, the town hall with its boards advertising a public lecture on the 'History of the Welsh Methodist Movement', to the police station. She'd scotch these rumours. Jan was with her, he was with her. He didn't do it, she knew he didn't. She didn't know who had done it, but it wasn't Jan. It couldn't have been.

"Now then, Miss Annie, steady on a bit." Brian Bryn Bela held up his hand at Annie's onslaught of words. "We don't know exactly for sure the young Polish feller did it, see. Just looks awful suspicious, like. The detectives on the case will be asking folk who've got anything to say about it to come forward during the week, and you'll get your chance then." He escorted her firmly out of the station, saying he would make sure to put her name down on the list of witnesses to be interviewed.

'I want to see him. Please can I see him, please?" she implored.

'Not now, Miss Annie. He can't see nobody until we've had a bit of a chat with him. There's lots of things to be done before anyone can see him. You go on home and settle yourself a bit, you'll be doing yourself a mischief getting in a state like this, indeed aye, and you won't be doing the young feller any favours," and he put his hand sympathetically enough on her shoulder and gave her a little push onto the pavement.

Swallowing her fear and frustration Annie walked slowly down past the life-boat station. She sat on the pebbles with her back to the sea wall. She couldn't go back to the market and endure the gossip and innuendo. She clasped her knees and put her head on them. The shingle hurt her backside. A gull tore at the stinking carcase of a fish down by the water, another one circling. The stays on the sailing boats moored out in the straits twanged and whined in the breeze, and a ragged little boy was dangling a string down from the pier to catch crabs. Nothing had changed, it was all normal. But everything had changed. The white mountains rearing out of the bank of cloud looked menacing, their jagged granite slabs pointed towards her like spears. The little boy stamped on the little green crabs he'd caught and pulled them to bits, flinging the legs and bodies back in the water with a vicious glee. The gull stabbed its companion in the chest, drawing blood, when it came to investigate the gory feast. Nothing calmed her. Everything reinforced her sense of dread and doom. Had there been a God she believed in she would have prayed. As it was, she wept, 'Oh Mam, Mam. What shall I do now?"

*

The next week did nothing to allay her fears as the police, the CID called in to investigate the case, continued to block her attempts to see Jan.

'We hear stories you've been seen walking out with Jan, Annie," they said too familiarly, it felt like an insult. 'Bit fond of him, are you? Nice young feller. Trying to protect him, give him an alibi? *Chwara teg*, fair do's, quite understandable."

And then, when she would not change her story, 'You could be charged with obstructing the course of justice if you're lying, mind," and just shrugged when she shouted her denial and burst into tears of frustration. It was plain from their expressions that they didn't believe her, and didn't care if she knew it.

When they asked her to come in and sign her typed statement, she walked the three miles to town over the icy fields, sinking up to her knees in the blown snow in the lanes, sat down shivering with cold and burning with determination on one of the hard chairs along the wall opposite the desk where the Duty Sergeant was standing, and waited. Her heart was thumping a tattoo so hard she found it painful to be still. Other people were being called in to be interviewed, but instead of chatter, there was a watchful silence in the waiting room. People eyed her grimly, no doubt thinking how dare she deliberately fabricate a story to flout the evidence of their own eyes and ears.

As the days passed she noticed the people in the village grow colder towards her. The girls in the choir excluded her from their gossip, and whispered about 'missing our tenor', all the while looking at her from the corners of their eyes. Dilwyn and the other lads no longer called in at Bron Felen on their way up to the village, and Evan took to spending all his spare time at *The Bell*.

Gradually the rumours reached her ears: Morris had definitely identified the murderer as Jan; Mrs Simpson had called the police at quarter past eight, so the shooting must have happened around eight; Brian Bryn Bela arrived at the scene of the murder at half past eight; Mrs Evans the choir mistress said that Jan had left the village hall with Annie just gone seven, which was when she'd locked the doors – little did she know how they'd dallied and lingered in the lane, reluctant to let each other go, before Jan tore himself away – before she'd summoned up the courage to tell him what she had to. Mr Simpson said the shotgun was always kept in the stable accommodation; Evan had left the pub at about half past six and gone straight home.

This last perplexed Annie. When she got home that night she was sure Evan had not been there, even though Pabi was tied up in his kennel. She remembered waking up when she heard his voice swear at the dog and the door bang as he came in. She'd got in about eight and was almost sure she'd the kitchen clock strike nine. What had Evan been up to after leaving the pub?

"You didn't go home when you left *The Bell* like you said, you liar," she rounded on him that evening when he came in from the fields.

"What are you talking about now?" Evan scowled and slurped his tea.

"When Emrys Hughes was shot. Everyone says you left the pub at half past six, but I know you didn't come home until gone nine, because I heard you come in."

"Don't talk stupid. I went out to look at the cows after I got in. Worried about this red water," Evan answered, too pat for Annie; when had Evan ever bothered with the animals after dark before?

"You're lying. I know you're lying. What were you up to? I know something's going on with you," she cried, banging the table with her fist.

'Don't start getting hysterical like with me. It's that precious Pole of yours that's the murderer, not me, isn't it?"

Annie stared at him. His voice sounded funny – flat and coming from a long way off down a tunnel, and he didn't look at her. She shivered as goose bumps raised along her arms. It hadn't crossed her mind to think of Evan as being the murderer, but... why not? It would fit. She flinched at the idea and then it hit her with the force of a hammer blow, as though the thought took substance.

'It was you killed him, wasn't it?" she whispered in horror. 'Wasn't it?" as he shook his head. 'What on earth did you kill Emrys Hughes for? And what were you doing at the Simpsons'. And with Jan's shotgun?" Suspicion hardened into belief, 'You meant to shoot Jan, didn't you? You must've thought it was him..."

'Shut up you stupid bitch. Shut up! Shut up before I shut you up!" Evan's voice rose as he rose from the chair, and Annie cowered as he took a step towards her. He stopped, a cunning smile crossed his face, and slowly he dripped out his next words to make her flesh crawl, as if she had touched slime in the dark,

'You've gone mad, you have. Off your head, isn't it? Yes, that's what's happened to you. I'm going to get the doctor in tomorrow. You don't know what you're saying. That murdering Pole's driven you crazy. Aye, crazy as a coot. A coot. You don't know what's real any more, all these crazy accusations against me, your own kith and kin. Why would I want to kill the *blŵdi* Pole anyway? He was going to take you off with him to South Africa, and good riddance I say. Leave a man in a bit of peace at last –"

Annie gazed at him and said slowly, 'How do you know he was going to South Africa? He never told me that."

Evan blinked. 'Hah, you think you know everything, don't you? He told us in the pub he was going off. Dilwyn'll back me. Well, you won't be going now, will you?" His blustering fanned the flame of his fear and vindictiveness.

As he spoke, Annie knew that her chance of escaping Bron Felen had just vanished, her dream for the future smashed into smithereens. What did that future hold for her now? She sank into a chair. Her thoughts scattered like sardines before a shark, and she heard his voice distantly, as the mutterings and groanings of a shipwreck settling on the seabed. When she came back to herself, Evan had gone. She sat there until the fire went out and the house grew cold. She sat there while the beams creaked and the mice rolled hazelnuts in the wainscoting.

**

Bad weather

Spring 1947

Annie's thoughts bucked and reared, as jittery as a horse fed too many oats. Pull on the reins how she might, she could as well curb them as fend off the attacking eyes of people, always watching her; some with pity, but most with relish, many with contempt. She retreated into the garden, thinking its sheltering walls and hedges would be a shield, its demands a distraction. It was almost obscene, she thought, as she straightened up from weeding, how the garden pushed so much out of the earth, so voluptuously, while something in her shrank and withered even as her body swelled. The notion took hold and she conceived almost a horror of the garden and its fertile mockery: the satin lushness of the spinach, the red roundness of the beetroot, the winking peas filling their pods till they burst.

She fled from the garden. To still her agitation and to focus her mind, she forced herself to sit immobile for hours on end, like the boulder that crouched in a field; round which the animals grazed, on which the birds perched and

119

hopped, against which the rain dashed and hail bounced, and on which the snow softly settled, concealing its splits and cracks, splashes of bird shit and owl pellets; on which the sun shone by day and melted the snow, which froze to glass at night, so hard you would have needed a chisel to make a mark. Curious passengers on the great Liverpool liners crossing the bay on their way to Nova Scotia shouted to the captain to slow the screws as its chill brilliance flashed in their telescopes, and having heard this was all the current rage, exclaimed excitedly 'Look, look! A chunk of space debris.' High flying fighter pilots ferrying their planes glanced down through the cirrostratus and were dazzled, reporting the strange phenomenon back at base to sceptical commanders, who nevertheless wrote it up and passed it on, just in case.

Evan was forced to walk round her, his unease wearing a path in the soft pine boards. The only time she got up and moved from the kitchen was if someone from the village ventured by, knocking on the door from curiosity, not kindness. Then, snatching up a basket, out she would hurry, across the yard as if on her way to collect the eggs, and there stand, behind a barn, only coming back in when they had gone on their way. When Evan insisted the doctor visit because Annie was behaving like a crazy woman, she forced herself to laugh and chat, made cups of tea and opened a precious tin of biscuits; the doctor went out the door without a glance towards Evan apart from handing him the bill. It was not Annie who looked the fool.

Evan saw through what he called her tricks, so for a while, out of his growing fear, he made an effort to ingratiate himself. He brought cups of tea which grew cold and lined up like lead soldiers ranked for battle; fed the fire with wood only for Annie to sit watching it go out. She sat through his wheedling cajoleries as though they were the merest whispering of the meadow grasses in the summer, and of no more significance.

He tried another tack. He raged with hot denials and banged his fists on the table, any hard surface would do; he punched holes in the soft lime plaster of the scullery wall, he bruised his knuckles on the iron-hard wood of the inglenook lintel; the planks on the door to the potato store sprang apart at his frustrated kicks. Annie sat through his violence as though it was the faintest of thunder storms rumbling on the distant horizon.

When he saw that no matter what he did she would not be moved, desperation gathered in his dread and distilled it to a cunning but credible essence. He had left the pub early with a headache and come home. The dog had been barking furiously at something in the fields and he had been worried about his animals and gone to check on them. He had found a calf down with red water, and one of the just-born early lambs had been mauled by a fox. He'd brought it in but it died. No he hadn't heard any shots. Annie was sticking up for the Pole because they were lovers. Only natural. He was sorry and all that, even if he never trusted the Pole, but it wasn't fair of her to put the blame on him. By dint of constant repetition at every opportunity he almost convinced himself, and won over the credulous nature of others who might have doubted the truth of it.

*

April and May came and went. While the lawyers argued over whether he would be tried in a military or civil court, Jan languished in prison, bail refused; Annie's spirits sank as her hopes of seeing him vanished.

The village gossips got to work. I reckon as there was something going on between her and that Pole. Serves her right. She had it coming, flaunting herself the way she did. And, Evan was right, see. He knew that Pole was up to no good. And now look. Murdered someone. And, gone peculiar, she has. Always thought there was something not right about her.

*

'What else were we to think?" Dilwyn said, when I asked him, knowing how it must have been for Annie, the guilt and the shame, the anger, and the rumours abounding. I was intrigued but not yet disturbed by the links starting to bind Annie's life to mine. We were sitting on the little patio, enjoying a *panad*, and I pressed him to talk.

'She didn't take care of herself, let things go. Looked a proper mess. Apart from the odd time she was forced to come into town, when she dragged a comb through her hair and put on this shapeless old coat – God knows where she got it, it looked like one of Huw's – she spent all her time on the farm in an old pair of dungarees. I still used to go by there odd times to have a chat with Evan, but really to get to see Annie though she kept well out of the way. That was how I heard she'd told the Simpsons she was giving up working for them 'cos she wasn't well, so she said, suffering from a bout of that stomach trouble that was going round... You wouldn't remember, wouldn't have been more'n the spark in your da's eye, but after the torrential rains we had that spring folk were falling like ninepins. *Cryptosporidium parvis*, it was called, and it could lay you low for weeks. I remember what it was called 'cos it had this rhythm, you could sort

121

of chant it. For some reason I can remember words if they have a rhythm. Like 'rosebay willowherb', once I learned 'da da dadada' I never forgot it. But I knew that wasn't what was the matter with her, even if she wanted folk to think it was."

*

Evan scoffed to himself. He reckoned he knew what was up, but he kept it close, sure that if Annie wanted to hide it from others it must sooner or later turn to his advantage. And if the stupid cow thought he was going to put up with a bawling snotty infant she had another think coming. He'd turf her out, see how she liked that. Go back to Liverpool and live on the streets for all he cared.

In the meantime it suited him to pretend. He couldn't stand to think how his pals'd laugh at him if they knew the truth. Him mooning after her all these years, and her choosing some foreign bugger over him. He could just imagine their sneers and the sly glances they'd cast his way at market. He'd be a *blŵdi* outcast. That's what they all thought anyway, if the truth were told, couldn't wait to get one over on him. And he bet the Pole would've scarpered fast enough once he knew what was what. And, the thought chilled him as it took hold, the Simpsons could easily decide not to renew his tenancy on those bits of pasture at the bottom. They liked Annie. They might take her side against him. He wouldn't have enough to raise a proper flock or keep any cattle. Where would he be then? After all, family should stick together, shouldn't they? Not fight against each other. He'd have to try to make his peace with Annie somehow, but wrack his brains as he might, there was no way he could see of doing that – save confess, which he could not.

Even deeper, the sluggish remains of shame shifted now and then in the silt of his conscience, and he felt sick at heart. He forced himself to carry out the chores of the farm, took to staying late at *The Bell*. The commiserations of his mates, even if he didn't believe them, shored him up and added strength to his lies.

*

At the end of May Mrs Simpson came down to visit Annie, concerned with the gossip she had heard about her parlous state, and to see if she could help. She had been genuinely fond of the bright little Liverpool lass, and was shocked to see her deterioration, unkempt and apathetic. She persuaded her to walk down the path to the beach and stroll through the dunes, Annie's mood grudging and resentful.

'My dear, I hope you won't take it amiss, but I can see you're not well and I really would like to help in any way I can," Mrs Simpson started.

'I'm alright. Thanks. But I don't need any help. It's only this stomach bug that's going round. I'll get over it," Annie dismissed the gesture stiffly.

'It's also because of Jan, isn't it," Mrs Simpson insisted, gently enough, 'and this business with Emrys Hughes? Oh Annie, I know you were fond of him. We thought he was a very nice young man too, and very well recommended by Lord Marchant. His father was a friend of Lord Marchant. Did you know that? No, well. So we didn't believe what they said at all in the beginning. But it does look now as though he did shoot Emrys Hughes and – "

'He did not! He can't have. I know he didn't. He was with me all the time before he got to your place and saw the police there and everything. Why won't anyone believe me? They believe that idiot brother of his, Morris, who's blind as a bat and useless as a can of turned milk. I've told them over and over again and it's like they don't want to believe it could be someone else, someone local, one of their own. Oh no, they'd rather think it was someone from away. Protect themselves, huddle together and send some poor innocent person to the gallows."

'Well, that's hardly the tone to take Annie if you want people to listen to you. People don't like hearing what surely sounds like malicious ill-will to them, and –"

'– but you must know how it is. Dilwyn Maesgwyn was telling me once about those men before the war, somewhere down on the Lleyn, who set fire to some buildings –"

'Penrhos airfield, yes. It was a bombing training school."

'Well, he told me the Welsh down there hated the English because of it, and –" Mrs Simpson held up her hand. 'I'll tell you the true story, Annie, because Mr Simpson knew the judge who tried the case in the Old Bailey. What angered the Welsh so much was that the English government had put the bombing school there even though half a million Welsh people protested against it. They felt the English didn't care about the fact that the Lleyn was home to their culture, and they said they didn't want it used to promote what they described as 'a barbaric form of warfare'. I can understand how they felt. Because the verdict couldn't be agreed in Caernarfon, the case was tried in London and three of the leaders were imprisoned. They became heroes to the Welsh. Unfortunately, it was because they made such a song and a dance about it that the Germans learned about the existence of the airfield and bombed it later in the war. The Government brought in a squadron of Czech soldiers to protect it, and now it accommodates Poles like Jan who want to stay in Wales."

'If you asked me, though I know you didn't, it was because they don't like people from away, pure and simple. It doesn't matter if they're English or Polish or Czech it seems to me. Some of the folk round here have family down there on the Lleyn. Why would it be any different?"

'But even if there's something to be said about the problem of hundreds of Poles staying in Britain, Jan wasn't a threat to anyone round here, Annie, he was just a simple handyman. In fact everyone seemed to like him –"

'Jan wasn't just anything. And he wasn't much liked neither, though everyone smiled and acted all nice. He was always a foreigner to them, and they talked about him behind his back. Like they did me, and all. They're going on strike everywhere now because the Poles want to live here – I heard it on the wireless. They're talking about it in the Houses of Parliament in London, even. They don't want them here," Annie burst out. Gone was the deference she usually showed, and she burned red and angry. 'You used to be on their side. What's changed? And what makes you think you know anything about what goes on round here? You sit in your big house and go off to London and posh parties, and you don't know the half, nor care, about what goes on in people's heads anywhere else. How would you like it if someone in the street shouted 'Go home' to you? He told me, he can't go home – they're shooting lots of them that go back, or sending them to prison in Siberia."

Mrs Simpson tried to interrupt Annie's flow, but once started Annie wasn't going to be stopped. It was about time she told someone a few home truths. She was sorry it had to be Mrs Simpson, but she wasn't an ignorant country person so she should have known better, and she should have known that Jan would never do anything like that. Surely not. Oh, the English betrayed everyone.

She rounded on her. 'And why aren't you and Mr Simpson sticking up for him? You could put a good word in for him. They're charging him with murder and they could hang him, and you'd just sit by and say nothing! Well, don't come by here no more, I don't want to talk to the likes of you. You're no better than you should be either in spite of all your posh ways, naked people at parties and having affairs with each other all over the place. So leave me alone. I don't want to talk to you."

Annie turned and marched back along the path, shaking inside her coat. She didn't regret what she'd said one bit; it was about time she said what was on her mind. And if Mrs Simpson was against Jan, then she was no longer her friend.

But she was shaking because she had been shaken. If gentry like the Simpsons believed Jan could have done it, what could she say that would make any difference? Could it be true that he...? No, no, how terrible to even think such a thing. Well, all she could say was what she believed was the truth, if only people had the ears to hear it. Surely they couldn't believe Evan's story, when everyone knew how he hated Jan? But the lads in the village were closing ranks, and it wasn't Evan they were shutting out. Could it be she did have it wrong? Even Dilwyn seemed unsure... No, no, no. Jan couldn't possibly have... Oh, it was all so confusing. She hated them all.

'Mam, mam, what can I do? What will I do with this babby if Jan goes to prison? Or worse? I've got no-one and nowhere to go.' She flung herself down in a patch of marram grass that hid her from the path and cried her desperation.

*

She steeled herself to talk to Dilwyn. She knew he was soft on her and she liked him too, even if he was Evan's friend. He was thoughtful and serious and didn't lark about like the others, and if anyone was up to putting in a good word for Jan it would be Dilwyn. But as soon as she broached the subject, he put up his hand, said sympathetically enough,

'I know, Annie. I know you want me to say it couldn't've been him. But I don't know it wasn't him, see. And nor do you, if you're honest. You might think you know him, and I for one will always say he was a decent bloke, but none of us really knew him. None of us knows what might have gone on inside him. See, there was no reason for anyone to shoot Emrys Hughes, so it must've been a mistake, whoever shot him. All I know is what we all know. I've thought and thought about it, and I've come to my own private conclusions. If you're wanting me to say about the bad feelings between Jan and Evan, well I already have, don't worry. I'll tell it to the judge like it was, but that doesn't mean anyone's going to believe me. There's lots who'll say different, too.'

Annie's brow pleated, and her lips became the thin slash of a knife wound. Helplessly he watched her shut herself away again. It was like someone putting up their summer clothes when winter came in, folding and packing them tightly into boxes, mounting the ladder to the loft, then closing the door on them till the better weather came round. Darkness and cold, silence. He was suffused with dread at what might come of all this. He wondered if better weather would ever come round again for Annie.

**

Here comes the chopper

Spring 2003

The Heart of Wales train clattered its way through the halts and stops on its way south. Harry sat by the window, looking out as first the Cambrian mountains then the valleys unrolled. It was all I could do to resist the awful pull of that familiar but now hostile outside. I kept my eyes firmly on the pages of my book – 'The Role of the Coroner'. The coroner was going to be the single most important person for me during the next three weeks of the inquest, and her verdict would ring through the rest of my life. I did not have high hopes.

Nevertheless, this forced reading on the British judicial system at least opened my eyes to the semantics reposing within the precision, or calculated imprecision, both, of legal definitions. For instance: the Coroner's primary task was to officially and publicly establish how a person died. Such a little word, 'how'. Before now I had thought of it as a simple word. Honest in its declaration, perhaps. But 'How', leading to 'Death by Suicide'; 'How', leading to 'While the

Balance of her Mind was Disturbed'? Okay. Fine. Neat. Is that it? Next, please. That wasn't what I wanted.

'How' in its wider meanings of 'To what extent', and 'In what circumstances', though, was a whole other ballgame. It permitted, in effect, a narrative. It permitted a judgement and analysis of the events – and the other actors. Now I saw that one small syllable as a searchlight illuminating the whole complex inter-reaction between 'society' and homo sapiens. In short, this 'how' had the power to lay bare and dazzle those creatures who ran and hid, sliding from the light, keeping to the shadows.

Simultaneously, as I was about to discover, it was processes of definition and analysis such as these that utterly demolished, destroyed, reduced to rags and tatters, any dignity or privacy in the dying and the dead. And, for that matter, in the living and the grieving.

*

I am sitting in a large room, on a grey plastic chair that has its back against a wall. Next to me, out of the corner of my eye, I can see Tony. He is wearing a suit, which saddens me; he never wears suits. The last time he wore one was at Fleur's funeral. The atmosphere of the room is hushed and everything looks grainy and blurred, as though someone had taken a deep breath and blown all the dust off the furniture to hang in the air. The windows that line both sides of the room are high and the sills are at head level. You could be forgiven for thinking you were in chapel waiting for the Lord to come. All you can see is sky and drainpipes. It is clear there is an accounting to be held in this room; the magisterial step and mien of the officer who showed us to our seats was meant to impress this on us. It left no room for doubt. But by then I was cynical enough to think, 'We'll see...'

We are sitting at the back of this room and at the front, imposing in its bulk, is a dais, with a high wood-paneled facade. I can just see behind it the top of a chair. Below this dais is a woman, her grey hair in a severe bun, who takes no notice of us, and keeps shuffling papers like a deck of cards. Her face is without expression, to her this is nothing special, just another working day. There is a live computer monitor and keyboard on the desk in front of her, with a printer next to it, into which she carefully inserts the neatly aligned stack of paper. I notice what looks to be a recording device and a set of large head-phones.

Another police officer is standing in front of a small door along the right hand side of the room. I wonder who it is who will come through it. It must be the Coroner. I later discover it is the connecting door to the police station. Through which prisoners come. The guardian of the door is a cartoon caricature of an officer, so typical is he of the policemen I have always imagined: tall, broad, his feet apart, and hands clasped behind his ramrod back. He stares ahead, and did not acknowledge our entrance. I start to wonder if we are actually a material reality to anyone there, but I can feel the cotton of my trousers rubbing my thighs, and my boots make a clumping sound on the floor when I get up to go to the toilet.

We wait. So much waiting, I should be good at it by now. I can feel my jaw tense in anticipation of what Goliath is going to crush us during the next three weeks. By the end of that time, I think, I will have memorised this room in every detail, for ever. People I have never met before will come and go, and I will remember their every word and gesture. I will never know them as people, they will be actors on a stage, but I will know them more intimately than my closest friends, even though, as I'm sure will be the case, they will have been coached so that much of what they say will be 'full of sound and fury, signifying nothing.'

*

I have never been to this town before, nestling in the foothills. It hardly qualifies as a town, being what I would call a large village, with shops and a couple of cafes and a few pubs, a school, a chapel or two and a church – and the building in which is this room. The courthouse. Round it, in an untidy sprawl, shuffle rows of council houses, and further out, stride villas with large gardens and two cars in the drive.

Last night Tony and I booked into a hotel in town so we could be here bright and early this morning. During supper, the proprietor kept gliding in and out of the dining room through different doors as though on castors, and every time he passed he would pause by us and ask, "Everything all right? All okey dokey? Just say if it isn't," and then sashay on his way without waiting for an answer. Kafka-esque. He seemed caught up in some endless loop, or perhaps he was practicing his lines for some Amateur Dramatics production. Or it could have been because we were the only guests staying there. It is not exactly a town that I imagine anyone would want to visit as a tourist, even in season, and the disrepair of the hotel and the musty smell of mildew that made me sneeze in the dim corridors added to this impression. I would, if I were normal, have appreciated his concern, but in my current frame of mind the whole thing was frighteningly surreal. I wished he would stop. I was getting fed up with pretending to be nice. All I wanted was to be left in peace without the stale smell of old ashtrays and spilt beer on the carpets, and without feeling I ought to make conversation with the obligatory old local with a teardrop on the end of his nosey nose. I didn't go to the bar for a drink afterwards, but retreated to my room and spent an hour or so arranging and rearranging yet again all the papers I had brought with me.

Tony told me that the evening in the bar had been given over to the discussion of a piece in the local newspaper that week. A man who had recently retired to a nearby village had, it seemed, been singled out as a target, and one of the locals, for his own reasons, had spread rumours that the man was a practicing homosexual, probably a paedophile into the bargain. One night as he was walking home he was set upon and raped by two men wearing dark clothing and balaclavas. He committed suicide the following week. The police had been unable to break the gathered silence as to who might have perpetrated this act, the press smelt carrion, and normal life for the villagers ceased from that moment on. Neighbours spied on each other, and arguments broke out. Fights erupted in the street, and the pubs were more or less empty.

We cancelled our booking this morning and took a self-catering cottage a couple of miles away for the duration.

I can't rid my mind of the story, which runs like a tic through my brain, to the accompaniment of a cacophonous piece of music. Peckinpah's 'Straw Dogs' springs to mind.

I have to calm my nerves, so I get up and tiptoe out the imposing front doors into the concrete yard that fronts the street, and roll a cigarette. As I stand there smoking, several cars draw up and disgorge a procession of people who walk past me into the building. I study them as they file by and wonder which face belongs to which name. The names of all the people who would stand up there before the court, whose accounts I would be hearing, are branded in smoking letters on my brain. It is like a children's storybook in which you have to guess who Mr Tappit is, or Mrs Rumple, from how they look or behave. Real life of course is not that simple – but almost. When I go back in everyone has sat down and there is a subdued murmur of voices.

Seated at desks in the middle of the room, with huge files and books on the floor and covering the desks before them, are the three barristers with their assistants, each team representing someone who has a personal vested interest in the outcome of the next three weeks.

All at once the officer by the small door nods to the severe woman who stands up and declaims loudly, "All be upstanding". With one accord we all shoot up, like a flock of starlings at dusk. A section of the wood panelled wall behind the dais creaks open and in strides a tall woman, her spectacles glinting in the fluorescent lights. She glares at us and sits down. We all sit down. Several minutes pass. Nobody says a word. I fight to suppress a ticklish urge to cough, cowed despite myself by the pomp and panoply. I watch the coroner with fascination. Mrs Parson. She is thin lipped and austere enough to be one. She will be my redeemer or my condemnator. The only sound is the whirr of the severe woman winding a tape in the tape machine. Digital recording hasn't made it this far. She clicks a button and her recorded voice erupts loudly, repeating the 'All be upstanding'. She nods to the coroner, evidently satisfied.

With this, the undertow lets go, my head breaks the surface and I can breathe again. I blink and look around. For an instant I had been dragged back into that deference for authority I have spent the last two years shouldering aside. Now, all I see are paper people. It makes no difference what their jobs are, what they wear, how they look or sound, who outside this room nods and bows and scrapes to whom. When they open their mouths they will be reciting what I already know they have been rehearsing, they will be puppets, puppets of their own making, pulled by the strings of their own fears.

*

I wish I could say I felt something over those three weeks, but I was an empty husk. The only feeling that penetrated my defences was the weariness of inevitability. 'Come on, surprise me,' I begged. 'Tear up the script. Look away from the dots. Hold up your hands. Come out, come out of your boxes.' But I knew they wouldn't, all reciting to themselves, 'Here comes the chopper to chop off our heads!'

*

The coroner is a forbidding woman; she has the habit of dropping her heavy framed glasses down on her nose and peering fiercely over the top at the person on the witness stand. I grow to like it; it presages the discomfort of doubtful integrity under question.

Our barrister, Robert Cubby, is a cheery man who wears a navy suit with wide electric blue stripes and a red bow tie – it is difficult to look at his face when we talk, the suit takes centre stage; Mr Titmarsh, a small man much on his dignity and who later earned himself the sobriquet 'Toady' from us, represents the hospital; and a faintly Irish Mr McCarthy is there on behalf of the nurses.

Every day we walk from the court along the high street to a café where we eat lunch. The high street is typical of a small town in this area of Wales, dominated by the hills surrounding it and with a strong feeling of coal. The pits and the heaps are disused and grown over now with heather and coarse scrubby vegetation, but it still brings to mind dark shafts and tunnels, hardship, and voices raised in song. The high street is long and wide, and everything that happens, happens there, if it could be said that anything at all happens. But I know this is glib rhetoric, from Tony's conversation in the hotel earlier. It happens here, as everywhere, in the woods, in the backstreets, in homes, in people's hearts. The buildings are two-storied and pebble-dashed grey above the shop fronts. The predominant colour is grey or dingy white. It is the sort of street you hurry along with your head down, even when the sun pokes its head over the hilltops. For the whole three weeks we are there it rains every day, either strong pelting rain or a soft drizzle. The wind always blows straight along the street directly from the chapel standing square at the top and frowning severely down it.

The café we choose as our lunch time venue looks like an old fashioned 'Tea Shoppe' from the outside, with chintz curtains, and nets that obscure the lower half of the window so you can't see out or in, just the tops of people's heads as they rush past to the sound of crying children. Despite the attractiveness of the curtains, the inside is nineteen fifties' style – the seats are hard benches and the tables formica-topped, in austere rows, the pictures on the walls of chocolate box kittens, and the flowers plastic. The tea is served in stainless steel individual pots with UHT milk in little containers. Lunch is a choice of cod, chips and peas; burger and chips; egg and chips; sponge pudding and custard and apple pie and custard. Sliced white bread sandwiches are available with a variety of fillings, such as cheese (with tomato or onion), egg (with or without cress) and Coronation chicken. Tinned soup and soft white baps spread with margarine.

We sit there, convinced that everybody knows why we are there. There is an invisible cross on our backs that marks us as 'involved in court proceedings' – at least, invisible to us though not to the townspeople. I have to fight the temptation to ask Harry to look at my back to see if there is anything written on it.

'What do you think of her then?' Johnny appeals to Tony on the second day.

'Pretty scary. When she tore into the police yesterday, whoo! If she's like that with everyone else then I reckon we'll get what we want."

'Do you think so?' I interrupt sceptically. 'I wonder. Perhaps it's all a show, like a drama on television, done up to impress, but still as useless as everything else we've had to do with so far.'

'What do we want then?' Johnny asks.

Good question. The whole thing fills him with fear as he runs the gamut of his, and Fleur's, local town every day. People he hardly knows in pubs nod to him then turn and whisper to each other, and conversations hush as he goes into shops. The stands outside the newsagent's carry the day's headlines, blazoned large: 'Coroner pours scorn on police incompetence' and 'Catastrophic failures contribute to local musician's death'.

'The truth, I suppose. But I'm not optimistic.'

'No. It's like the whole picture's missing and all they're doing is picking about in bits of it. And those bits don't add up. Not to me, any rate. But they don't take any notice of the likes of us.' Johnny is becoming bitter.

'I thought Carpenter was exposed pretty much as a liar though, didn't you?' Tony says with satisfaction.

'Yes. What a creep. He came up and loomed over us when I was talking to Dr Singh – you know, the nice doctor when we took Fleur in to *Llanfair* –and heard me thank him. All he said was 'Oh yes, Dr Singh's going to be an excellent psychiatrist.' Patronising arsehole. He didn't introduce himself, but he must have known I was Fleur's partner, and he never said anything about being sorry.'

'Let's hope this has finished his career, then.'

'I wouldn't want any other poor sod to be in his clutches.' Harry interjects. I am surprised at this. He has stayed remarkably silent throughout the proceedings. He tells me afterwards that he has never felt so shocked.

'If I were you,' Robert says, satisfaction in his voice, when we return from the café. "I would consider making a formal complaint to the Royal College of Psychiatrists regarding Dr Carpenter's professional conduct."

'Can I be bothered?' I think. If ever there was a closed shop that's one. But Robert is fighting for us now, something about the proceedings has jump-started him.

The senior nurse in charge of Kilvert Ward is summoned. I am open mouthed at her arrogant denials. After a particularly self-excusatory exchange between her and Toady, Robert can take no more, and leaps to his feet brandishing a report I gave him earlier – one of those the hospital sent me to keep me quiet, but which they now regret, for in it is damning evidence of their dishonesty. The coroner had not allowed that it was relevant to the inquiry, but now the senior nurse has made a serious mistake and quoted something from it, and its relevance cannot be ignored. The court usher advances and passes it to the Coroner. The Coroner reads rapidly, "Very well, Mr Cubby. I will order a brief recess for discussion. Half an hour, ladies and gentlemen. Mr Cubby, Mr Titmarsh, Mr McCarthy – I will see you in my chambers."

The Coroner billows her way out, followed by the scurrying barristers. We find ourselves out in the dripping dampness having another drizzled cigarette.

When we return the witness is recalled; the Coroner, her glasses perched on the end of her nose, redoubles her glare. I am mesmerized. Toady is definitely rattled. The witness is demolished.

"I'm so sorry. I know it was my fault. I should have been more careful. But I was so busy it just flew out of my mind. I must have misunderstood what I was told. I should have read the notes." The nurse on the stand is crying. She stands there and I can see the tears run down her cheeks and damp patches appear on her blouse.

"Well done, Sarah. Good bit of research there," Robert turns to me. "We've got enough now to support a private action against the hospital at least."

I should be pleased, but I'm not. Another person's life damaged. Is there no end to it? I do feel a brief stab of satisfaction that 'Toady' has been put out of countenance, but this is overlaid with a weary acceptance of its final unimportance. How inglorious success haunts me.

*

The days fly past, and my brain feels at times as though it will short circuit through overload. As witness succeeds witness, my convictions about what had gone wrong at the hospital are confirmed. The list is never-ending: reports not read, medical records not read, care plans changed for no clinical reason, observations ignored, alerts not actioned, rails not removed. Small, mean sins, all of them. The overall competence – well, although I get Robert to argue that the correct description is 'sub-standard', I think the subtlety escapes the Medical Director who, when he is finally called to the stand, insists on calling it 'sub-optimal'. Or, as Harry said, perhaps not. Nevertheless, the shit does hit the fan and well and truly spatters the walls of *Llanfair*. I hope they will be scrubbing for some time to come.

Despite this, and though I sense what we wanted is within our grasp, it feels as though doom is descending on me. A black shadow that has been lurking barely on the periphery of my vision, only to disappear when I snap my gaze towards it, is now clearly visible. When I look up it has become a lift car inexorably descending the shaft where I stand at the very bottom. Or maybe it's just that train coming.

I forget about it when the Coroner asks the final, and crucial, question of the inquest. Here is where the hospital can be generous in defeat and make some sort of reparation. Undo the dirty work of years.

'Dr Magg. I am required to deliver a verdict in accordance with my duties as Coroner. I shall be asking the learned gentlemen of the law for their advice to aid me in my deliberations, but, as Medical Director and the representative of the Hospital Board, I would ask you to reflect on what you have heard, and tell me if you think Fleur's tragic death can be linked to any of the serious failings identified in the course of this inquiry.'

For an instant, everybody holds their breath.

'No, your Honour, I do not.'

The collective exhalation sounds like a wave tranquilly breaking on a sandy shore; but it resounds in my ears like the grating of trillions of grains of the universe against each other.

But when the Coroner sums up, she disagrees. I could rush up and hug her. Her narrative verdict concludes:

'Fleur's death was contributed to by a catastrophic failure in the systems in place at *Llanfair*, together with significant omissions on the part of some individuals concerned with, and responsible for, her care and for the physical surroundings in which she found herself... In my judgment it can properly be said that Fleur's death was contributed to by neglect.'

*

You might think that given such a resounding confirmation of the truth that I was convinced of from the beginning, I would have been released from my entrapment there and then. I thought the black shadow had vanished but I was wrong. Instead it had crept forward under cover of my petty triumph, and insinuated itself inside me, inside the cells and fluids and bones and flesh, and whenever I spoke afterwards you could hear its bark and howl in my voice, sending people hurrying for cover, cowering and cringing. An ectoplasm of the soul. I wanted those pale-bellied creatures that still stalked the darkened management corridors at *Llanfair* exposed to daylight, and this desire corrupted me. It twisted me in unimaginable ways. Although I left the court punching high, my heart was still bleeding – and that train was still coming.

I ask again, and again. I'll probably always ask. What did I expect? I had been, and was still, pursuing a holy grail always in front, just outside my reach. To begin with all I did was turn my head to look for it. Then, slowly, with close attention to every stalking footstep, right foot, left foot, right foot, left foot, I crept towards it. By the end I was running, looking neither left nor right, arms stretched out and yearning. I offered up my flesh and the gods ate.

I always imagined the truth stood still. Then I saw it wave from the top of the hill. I went rushing over and like the rainbow's end, it was gone. Now I saw it dance out there in the bay. I learned to swim and it became the bright scales of the darting fish I could never catch. The truth was that the truth I needed to perceive was the truth I never wanted to see. Other people tried to tell me. I'd drive myself mad, and for what? They were of course right, but not for the reasons they thought, and only partly.

And all the time Truth was shadowing me, lurking round the corner, watching me through a window, its reflection in the glass. It sat next to me on the bus, asked for directions in the street, tapped me on the shoulder, grabbed me by the arm, and finally stared me in the face, blocking all movement in any direction until I stood. Still, silent. Until I said, 'Hi, haven't I seen you around somewhere?"

**

Resonance

' We may agree, perhaps, to understand by Metaphysics an attempt to know reality as against mere appearance, or the study of first principles or ultimate truths, or again the effort to comprehend the universe, not simply piecemeal or by fragments, but somehow as a whole.'

- Bradley, 1846-1924

Summer 2004

We celebrate our move out of the caravan with champagne. Life for a while seems expansive, almost care-free, after our years in the cramped space of the caravan. It is of course an illusion. Inside this skin I am still shut tight, as taut as a drum.

I notice the house exudes a curious spirit. Old and tough certainly, like the glistening membrane of an eyeball, and the despair in the rafters has faded now, but there also peeps forth a soft soul as in the depths of an infant's pupil. I can't quite fathom it; it doesn't cross my mind that it is Harry's soul. The sole trace of any historic aesthetic inside remains the multi-coloured shimmer of that plastic door handle. Who spotted this treasure, in the hardware shop window perhaps, and thought, 'Just right for that door; brighten up the place a bit.' Who took up the screwdriver and screwed it to the rude plank door, stepping back to admire the shimmer as it caught the evening sun through the tiny window, strewing coloured motes over the lime-wash. Who tore it down and tossed it carelessly onto the floor in a heap of rubbish. And why? The thin packing-case partitioning walls we tore down, labelled 'Tomatoes from Spain', and 'Produce of Holland', the false ceiling contrived out of old roughly cut aluminium sheeting, aircraft grade, tacked to two by one battens – were these by the same hand, out of the same imagination and dreaming? The same hand and mind twisted and bent out of shape by some unfathomable misfortune? I couldn't tell.

*

Harry has gone to bed and I sit curled up on the sofa with the book about Marchlyn that Dilwyn had lent me and which I haven't had time to read before. I flip through the pages until I get to the chapter about Bron Felen.

> 'The small cottage below the village of Marchlyn and known as Bron Felen is two hundred and fifty years old. It was built when one Thomas Williams, the 'despotick sovereign of the copper trade', owned and worked Parys Mountain, the copper mine on the island, and furnished the slave trade with its products. It was built on the threshold of agrarian reform and the Methodist Revival; when the Rebecca Riots took place in Carmarthenshire; when the canal-side flour mills in Chester were first erected.'

Ty Bron Felen – named for the profusion of gorse that spills a yellow river around it. The house I have come to inhabit and which wraps itself about me like a shawl, or a shroud. It is hard to tell which.

According to the book, nobody who was anybody in terms of influential, rich, or famous, ever lived here – the reason for its inclusion in the book being that it was a 'fine example of a traditional peasant dwelling' of the time and place. I can believe it. Basic, unadorned, thrown together in parts it seemed, when we first arrived it was more or less still as it had been originally, apart from the single huge brass tap which dispensed cold water from one of the springs in the hillside via a pipe through a rude hole punched in the back wall, and through which a bitter draught whistled; the floor was of unglazed quarry tiles laid on a thin layer of concrete over the bare earth. At times of heavy rain, water sprang out of the fireplace from a confluence of myriad small runnels, and over the decades this had worn a channel across the tiles in its hurry to leave through the front door. Annie cannot have had an easy old age.

There are no foundations – it stands on bedrock – and the walls are built with stones hewed out of the same hillside, where now hawthorn and holly grow in their own secret hollow. The oldest wall still standing is the back wall, the one that faces west, and looking at its curves and sags it is clear that whoever put stone on top of stone was no mason.

Apart from the two feet thick stone walls, the dominant feature is wood. The oak lintels, the roof timbers, the staircase, the window frames and shutters; I never realised how many colours wood came in, from the palest cream, fading through red to the darkest brown, and what patterns and whorls of grain, and the cracks and burrs in them.

The inglenook is large enough to sit inside, and set to the right of the main room, which is unusual but seems to be the custom for the meaner dwellings of the area. The main beam supporting the chimney is oak, charred in places where the fire must have leapt and caught until someone managed to douse it in time. The main timbers in the roof are scarred and crudely hacked. This, then, is the house that is the dream, and the bane, both, of my and Harry's lives.

*

Maybe Harry is right, and it doesn't matter what manner of house, mansion or hovel, elegant or ugly, the same griefs and longings, laughter and resentment, love and happiness, depression and hate flourish inside. Do a building's structures merely reflect a wealth, or dearth, of materials and resources? Is the soul not a component of their construction? I think no, Harry is not right These buildings of pre-industrial times, constructed by hand and with backbreaking effort, hold an indissoluble connection to an internal world; and in the smaller things, too, history tending to preserve the flash and flare of the spirit – the creative, the finer perceptions, the nobler urges, the appreciative. The cherished things we keep for others to find after us: door handles, wrought iron candlesticks, a bit of stained glass, roses and lilac, mosaics patterned with stone and shell and broken crockery.

Bed beckons. I close the book and poke the fire, reflecting that old bitternesses, rude instincts without the leaven of love, are more likely to result in things which are literally torn down, swept up and burnt, or buried in the ash heap, or under trees softly spring carpeted in primroses and snowdrops. So the ugly has a habit of vanishing. While the stones rest in their beds and watch it all.

*

"You might be interested in meeting someone I know. She's into all sorts of odd stuff, like – herbal medicine and standing stones."

I couldn't help but smile at the unintended slur. A lifetime had passed since I'd told Dilwyn about the night in the box-bed – what could have been more insignificant? – and I promptly forgot about it again until a few days later a woman arrived on our doorstep. She was a dumpy little figure, looking to be in her seventies, with a large green furry hat that resembled an inverted flower pot on her bright red hennaed hair.

"Hello, there. I'm Tylluan, it means owl in Welsh," she said cheerily.

"Oh! Hi! Really?" I replied, taken aback.

"Oh, this," she said, indicating the notebook in her hand, although it was the most normal thing I could see about her. "I'm not from the council, don't worry."

I hid a smile.

"Dilwyn told me you needed me. I'm what you might call a geomancer. Feng Shui? Ley lines?" she cocked her head and looked at me.

Not waiting for a response, she breezed on, "Alfred Watkin, he was the first, you know. He mapped the ley-lines on the Welsh borders. Brilliant man. Self taught of course, but quite an authority. Well respected. This place is on a ley line, you know." She must have noticed my blank face, because she changed tack. "Dilwyn told me about you and the cottage, and I thought I might be helpful. I can see you're having trouble with water," eyeing Harry's exertions. Harry was just then struggling in jeans and t-shirt with pick axe and flexible pipes, and submerged in plans of how to drain the land immediately adjacent to the house and alleviate the worst of the mud. He stopped to shake Tylluan's hand, pushing the hair out of his eyes to take her in.

"Always a problem," she said, "either too much, too little, never where you want it. But flowing water can really be very potent – although it is of course as destructive as it is creative. Anyway, I've brought the tools of my trade with me –" she broke off to rummage in the plastic bag she'd put down by her feet, and flourished a large tape measure and compass, "– and people have said they found it quite useful in small ways, you know."

I threw a quick glance at Harry, but he had gone back to his digging, head down; he professed to hate what he called 'all this mystical nonsense'. But although he always made out he was a complete sceptic, we had talked before now about getting a dowser in to find the best spot for a well. I threw up my hands, metaphorically – I was not the person to be changing his opinions. Stubborn man that he was.

"You will have to be very careful here, there is a lot of stagnation round you," Tylluan's voice interrupted my thoughts. A frisson touched the hairs on my neck and snapped my attention back to her. What was she talking about? Then I noticed she was pointing to the horsetails, ferns and reeds, and relaxed. A mistake, I realised later, but at the time I had no real concept of how the internal and external might influence each other. "*Equisetum telmateia*," she pronounced. "One of the larger horsetails. It's presence here indicates water, lots of it; horsetail likes to live with its feet in the wet."

In early spring I had noticed a strange fruiting body emerge all over the garden, only to disappear a few weeks later, to be replaced by a plant that resembled nothing so much as a gigantic green bottle-brush – this was indeed *Equisetum telmateia*, and it thrived in the company of the bucklers and harts tongues, lady and shuttlecock ferns, those other lovers of damp and shady places. I liked it; a prehistoric pteridophytic jungle was thriving on my doorstep – peeking up between the flowers, poking through the shrubberies, and crowding round the garden shed. It didn't take me long, though, to realise that nothing deterred *Equisetum*; it proved impossible to destroy, which somewhat spoilt my appreciation of its atmospheric effect. I spent vain hours pulling and composting it, only to see it thrust up again and again, in even greater colonies than before. Tylluan was right – it all seemed to declare obstruction, snarl-up and impasse.

"You will have to take strong measures to control it," she continued.

"Oh? Yes... What? What measures?"

"Ditches?" Harry put in sarcastically, his blue eyes challenging. Tylluan smiled, dipped her head to acknowledge the humour.

"Ditches certainly. There are other things that will help, too," she answered crisply. "I will need to have a look around before I can give you proper answers. With your permission?

"Oh. Of course."

She handed me the tape measure and compass, folded and put the plastic bag in her pocket, and started to sketch a plan of the cottage. I saw Harry's hackles rise and shook my head at him, mouthing that I'd stay by her the whole time, although what trouble he thought she would get up to I couldn't imagine. But I knew Harry and people with notebooks, peering and prying.

With me a pace or so behind handing her the tape and taking up the end in difficult spots, Tylluan spent the next hour or so wandering around and making copious notes. Several times I tried to ask what she was seeing and doing, but she shook her head, put her finger to her lips, smiled – then carried on. Gradually all the anxiety I felt died away and for a small space of time a forgotten peace crept into its place.

When she had finished and we were seated on the step with mugs of tea, she said, 'I haven't come across such complex lines before. I need to spend some time with this if it's going to be of any help to you. I need to look a few things up. There's something here I can't quite fathom, some sort of blockage...and I don't mean just packed clay or a blocked ditch," she threw at Harry before he could make another quip. 'What I'm talking about here is not necessarily a material blockage." Harry and I stole a glance at each other, Harry clearly thinking what he needed was spade work, which Tylluan wasn't offering, and he had no need of help of the sort she was. My take on it was more ambivalent – had she sensed my fractured spirit, could she help me in some way? I felt a pull, and resisted; I didn't need her help either. She shook hands with us and picked her way down the public footpath that wound round the hill and disappeared into the wood.

Afterwards, we laughed off her 'psychic twaddle' as Harry put it, but, I have to confess, despite the unease she engendered as of something – uncomprehended – I quite liked her. When I next saw Dilwyn, I asked him if he'd introduced her to anyone else on the hillside, but he shuffled his feet and shook his head. Said simply, 'Not to everyone's taste, Tylluan. But I thought you'd appreciate her, doll." And, again, I didn't know whether to cry or laugh, be flattered or insulted.

We discovered her 'remedies', as she called them a week or so later, hand-delivered in the mailbox at the end of the lane. Ditching did, of course, figure in it, seriously. It didn't take geomancy to tell us that. More than the mere facts though, I was impressed by the connections she drew, the poetry of the vision she laid out for us. The resonances.

'...Water' she wrote, 'the life blood of the planet, running through its flesh of earth and bones of rock. Obstruct it and it will cause the land to suffer a stroke, its heart to stop. Just as obstructed blood causes death, so death in turn congeals the blood. Water is a vibrant, a potent, symbol. Its absence desiccates, dries the earth, the flesh, to dust to blow in the wind. Or its stagnation gives rise to sickness and disease, an immune deficiency of the body and the mind, and of the land. Unhealthy thoughts flourish like the bacteria, the slime moulds, the viruses... Remember that the surface of water reflects your world back at you, but underneath it is not as you would know it...'

A sudden image of horsetail flashed through my mind. Sunk in my misery I hadn't given it another thought; but hadn't it shown me a glimpse of the paradox deep inside the stuff of things, warned me not to look just to the surface? Hoping to have a chat with Tylluan about this, I asked Dilwyn when he appeared later that afternoon if he'd seen her recently, but to my surprise his face flushed and he dropped his eyes and rubbed at a patch of mud on his sleeve, "That woman's hard to pin down, *bach*. Never know where she is or what she gets up to; a law unto herself." He shook his head, "Always seems to turn up when she's needed though." My disappointment was sharp, but I let the matter drop, sensing his deep embarrassment. At what, I had no idea. I convinced myself I did not need Tylluan's eccentric understanding to show me how the world worked.

Nevertheless, the links Tylluan made between landscapes and people and their moods and modes of being, had the effect of making me feel part of the world, placed me firmly within it. One phrase in particular stuck in my mind, 'There must be a propitiation.' I trembled at it. Did she mean what I thought she meant? And was it because I didn't propitiate, that life took the turn it did, and led me to where I have eventually come? If that place is good or bad?... I cannot tell.

**

Adversaries

June 1947

The trial was listed for the first week in June. Reporters besieged the area again despite the unseasonable weather conditions prevailing, which kept most people indoors during the day except those whose business was in the fields. The village, the whole island, hummed with speculation. Although several of the locals pointed the pack in the direction of Bron Felen, the hounds were kept at bay by Pabi's menacing jaws. Samuel Parry, laughing so hard someone had to slap him on the back when he inhaled some beer, told a group of amused drinkers in *The Bell*, Dilwyn amongst them.

'I was out looking at the ewes and saw one of them newspapermen as wouldn't give up go round the back and down the bank. It wasn't long before I heard them young bullocks run up the hill from Bron Felen, and right after that out he came again. White and bleeding, he was, and the bullocks round him, stamping and blowing. Had to fight his way through that old thorn hedge at the top of Huw's old potato field he was that scared."

"Aye, only wanted to sniff him, prob'ly. He must've been that daft he thought they were bulls, out to get him and pawing at the ground, like," the landlord put in.

'Na. But someone's been talking," another of the men chipped in. 'I saw Melchior Bryn Môr, the old bugger, spend more than was good for him and his cronies in The Llewellyn the other night, and when did he last have the ready to drink like that?"

"Aye. And what about young Elen over at the bakery? My Olwen said she was showing off one of those new-fangled kitchen gadgets they advertise in the Post, what costs a fortune in the posh shops in Chester."

And children pedaled bicycles round the lanes where there was never money before for such luxuries.

The village drew in tight and squeezed Annie out, and she watched and listened with growing fear, and Dilwyn with trepidation, as the general opinion, stated with more than a hint of relish, hardened; and that Jan would be found guilty and hanged for the murder became a foregone conclusion. Apart from an occasional infanticide nothing much ever happened on the island, and this was a rich seam of man's essentially sinful nature to be mined. The local ministers thundered in the chapels, admonishing their flock to stay away from the evils of drink and envy. Several of the ten commandments enjoyed an added outing, and Evan sowed further rancour and resentment among those who, for less than salutary reasons, shirked the sanctimonious attendances at church.

Annie's strong frame was still able to absorb the swelling of her belly. Her thin legs and arms told a different story, and her cheeks, hollowed by fretting, she reddened with the rouge Mrs Simpson had given her. Thankful for her constitution and the cold, wet weather this summer she was able to put off the prospect of binding her belly to deceive. Instead, she wrapped herself round with one of Huw's voluminous old jackets so that it was scarcely possible to discern her real shape. So she escaped comment from those few whose eyes would always scrutinize others, their shoulders hunched now by the gales and rain, and whose busy eyes were kept scanning the ground for safe footing.

*

The day before the trial Annie stood a long time on the beach, her head-scarf and jacket fluttering in the on-shore wind, staring at the mass of cumuli threatening to the north over the mountains of the Isle of Man. Fingers of wind-harried cloud pointed south, towards her, through the sky of palest blue that overhung the Isle of Anglesey. Overhead a raven fought off a buzzard, cart-wheeling and dipping, filling the air with its raucous cry. The buzzard glided its lazy way to and fro above the cliff eyeing the young ravens preparing to leave the nest. The aerial battle disappeared behind the hill, then reappeared a quarter of a mile away. Backwards and forwards, backwards and forwards, the two adversaries soared for more than an hour before the buzzard, seeking easier prey flapped off over the trees.

*

Annie stood in the street, her back to the Castle, looking up at the imposing bulk of the Crown Court with its Ionic columns and the Statue of Justice on top of the portico. It all had the effect of making her feel small, intimidated. Her court shoes, which she only wore to funerals, pinched, and her breathing came fast. Even though she knew she would not be allowed in until it was her turn to give evidence, nothing would have kept her away on this day, the start of Jan's trial. It was a two hour long journey by bus to get to town, and she set out to walk to the village at first light, buoyed up by the hope that she would get a glimpse of Jan as he was brought into court, and that seeing her there would reassure him she had not abandoned him. The bus coughed its way through the villages picking up people as it went. Annie, sitting on her own at the back, could hear her name murmured in the low voices from behind the headscarves and the collars turned up against the flapping wind. By the time the bus pulled into the *maes* it was so full that people were standing in the aisle, dangling off the roof straps. But the seats round Annie stayed empty.

She got off the bus and clutched her coat closer as a blast of wind blew across the square, feeling the glances of those who were already clustered in their twos and threes round the entrance to the court building, hoping for a seat in the public gallery, as barbs that exposed her soft parts, and tore her, letting the stuffing leak out. She was relieved when they filtered inside, and she was alone in the grey gloom of the drizzle sweeping across the straits. A stray page from an abandoned newspaper smacked wetly round her ankles, and fine droplets clinging like a halo to her hair grew heavy and fell, sliding down her neck. Ignoring the discomfort, she waited, sure that Jan would appear any minute.

The police officer on duty looked over at the forlorn figure standing across the street, recognised who she was. Moving out onto the steps he said, 'If you're waiting to see the accused, they bring them in from the cells under the court, you know. If I were you, I'd go home. Can't do any good standing there in the rain." As he told his wife that night, she looked a poor enough thing, not much about her, and hard to know even if she was all there, for all the thanks he got for his kindness. When he looked out again half an hour later she had gone.

*

The witness stand threatened like a pulpit. How many had stood there in its lifetime, to be heard and judged, not by God, but by other people, Annie wondered. A heterogeneous crowd of murderers, thieves, swindlers, drunks, together with angry, indignant, or broken victims; men and women, both the perpetrators and their victims, like as not bewildered by the turns life had taken to bring them to this place. She stepped up and turned to the face the court. If a court artist had been there, assessing her with his cold sharp eyes, out of his sweeping charcoal strokes would have emerged a defiant and self-possessed, plump figure, stick thin arms and legs, shoulders pulled back, the long chestnut hair caught up by two slides at the temples to flow and gather round a rosy dimpled face; the tremble of her hand impossible to detect unless held in another's, even as the hectic pulse beating in her ears could not be heard by any except herself.

Row after row of faces stared back at her, some pleasantly, some frowning, others curious, scornful, hating – most of all hating, she knew. She steeled herself not to succumb to the terrible temptation that whispered, 'Look, look – over there, where Jan is sitting, ignore the guards by him, let your eyes lock with his, never let him go.' She fixed her eyes on Mr Davies.

She placed her hand on the bible, and, unable to pretend, recited the oath with a lack of enthusiasm that did not endear her to the deeply religious elements in the jury.

"Yes, Jan walked me home," she nodded. "He wanted to talk about Poland, and how frightened he was of going back. He really missed his home. He'd been trying to find out news of his family from some of the refugees who were coming over, but nobody had heard of them. He was very upset and I told him I understood because I lost both my parents in the war, too." She omitted Jan's opinion of the British and their treatment of Poland. "We always stopped at the track to Bron Felen and carried on talking; he never used to go any further in case he ran into Evan." She stopped, frightened of what must come next. Yet it had to be. "Evan hated Jan. I never understood why. He was always saying offensive things about him in my hearing. He didn't like it that he was my

146

friend. So we tried to keep out of his way. Jan walked back to the *Plas* from there."

Led gently by Mr Davies, the barrister retained to act for Jan, she recounted in a voice rendered thin and tremulous by her emotion how Evan had become obsessively jealous about her, "All we were was good friends, it was only other people's nasty minds that thought different," she repeated, her knuckles white as she clutched them tightly in front of her. When the spectators realised what she was imputing, there was a buzz of outrage. Annie kept her eyes fixed firmly on Mr Davies looking neither right nor left save for the briefest glance in Jan's direction, and clenched her fists so her nails bit into the palms, drawing blood. Afterwards she threw her bloody gloves away.

'I don't know anything about any letter he's supposed to have written...well, he didn't give it to me, did he, if it was found in his room? So how could I? He knew I wanted to get away from here because I told him so – I've never denied it – and that I'd always dreamed of being a teacher. He was kind to me. He's a kind man. He was sorry for me, as I was for him," she insisted, dropping her eyes so that Jan would not see her shame at her seeming betrayal. She felt his eyes boring into her heart, and hoped he understood why she denied their love.

"Anyway, Evan was out when I got back; leastways, there were no lights on, and I couldn't be bothered to look. I didn't think he was there, because the range hadn't been banked up. He always does it before he goes to bed and besides he never goes to bed that early. I remember thinking it was odd if he was still out, though, because the dog was chained up in the yard, and he always took him with him. I went to bed. Then I heard him come in about nine o'clock. I know he's told the court he went straight home from the pub, and so he might've done, but he must've gone out again after and dropped the dog off. And I think it's time someone asked him where he was all that time, and what he was doing! Nobody seems to ask the right questions to me. And nobody ever asked how come Jan still had his bicycle when he first got to the *Plas*. If you ask me it's a bit strange he'd go home, shoot someone and then run away, picking up his bike on the way, take it through the woods, and come back with it." There. She'd said it. Finally. She looked over at Mr Davies who was writing furiously in his pad, and passing notes back to his assistant but he didn't seem to have heard what she'd said. Loftily, he informed her when the court adjourned for lunch, that there was enough discrepancy in the evidence there was, without needing to pursue an entirely separate line of inquiry, and her question about the bike could easily be explained.

"How?" she asked, but he turned away to shake the hand of one of the journalists who was waiting, pen poised, for his opinion on the proceedings so far.

As it was, someone in the gallery gasped, and a flurry of outraged shouts peppered the air, 'Shame on you, scape-goating your own cousin.' A babel of voices rose and people stood up, some raising their fists at the defiant figure on the stand. The judge repeatedly banged his gavel, threatening to clear the court as the clerk shouted, 'Order, Order', before the hubbub died down. Gradually a tense silence prevailed.

Annie's rehearsal as a rock stood firm under the intimidating cross-questioning by Mr Cleary, the prosecutor. Although she didn't dare throw suspicion on Evan directly, and it was left to the jury to interpret what she was inferring, the public had already done so, volubly, and clamoured their contempt. The newspapermen, gripped only by the romantic melodrama, and heedless of her innuendo, ran headlines in the Post the next day that shouted,

"ALIBI FOR MURDER
Liverpool evacuee alleges lovers' tryst with Pole"

The judge sat stone-faced and sweating, his mouth a thin line of disapproval, until she left the courtroom.

Dilwyn had been one among several who had laughed as the twins slid and stumbled up the lane from the pub that night, but he alone was called as a witness for the defence. His ears reddened and he shifted guiltily. It was one thing to talk about it casual like in the comfort of his own home or argue the toss at the pub with his mates, but it was a different kettle of fish when you were up here, all eyes on you. And that barrister – all right if you were on his side, but a demon if you weren't, by all accounts. He'd kept his word and spoken up to the police as he'd promised Annie. But he couldn't take how everyone looked at him when he'd tried to throw doubts on Evan's version of events. They were his mates, he'd scrumped apples with them, jumped off the cliffs into the sea with them in a big shouting gang, thrown ink bombs at school with them, gone to war with them... He couldn't imagine life without them, and they'd make his life in the village a misery if he went against them. He panicked at the thought. He'd have to leave. And go where? And perhaps it was this way, perhaps that, hard to tell and likely he'd misunderstood the situation; easily done. True, Evan could be a funny bugger, known him all his life, but harmless, couldn't see him rushing about and shooting people; as for the defendant, well he'd hardly known him, always thought him nice enough, but who could tell really what made someone tick, especially someone who'd been through what he had?

"Well now. Aye indeed, indeed aye, I remember it well." He cleared his throat. He clutched the rail of the stand in front of him to control his hands. Why on earth had he gone and put his oar in about the dog business? This'd teach him to stay out of other folks' business. He took care to keep his glance averted from where Jan was sitting, but Annie's image flashed in front of him, the last time he'd seen her, when she clutched his sleeve and pleaded with him to speak up for Jan. Oh God, he was going to let her down.

"No denying Evan was in a black mood that night – nobody couldn't seem to say anything to him without his lashing out.... I'll admit he carried a bit of a chip on his shoulder and we used to keep well clear of any talk about the war; he was sensitive about that, though no need, no need at all. Sometimes it'd come out without even thinking, though, and then we were for it. This time you mention, I saw him kick the dog as he went out the door. The Polish lad," Dilwyn couldn't say his name, "he'd just turned up, and he said something to him – I couldn't rightly hear what it was – but I saw him push Evan away from the dog. I think Evan thought we'd all rush to help him, but I – I – I pretended I didn't see it happen. We all did. No sense making a fuss about such a little thing, even if we did think less of Evan for how he'd behaved. That was the end of it; never mentioned again. I think the Pole never liked him after that."

He swallowed and stopped. Mr Davies was staring at him in astonishment, and, he thought, with pity, which struck him as worse than contempt.

"Mr Pugh, I have your statement here in front of me. The clerk will give you a copy, so you can refresh your memory about what you said to the police at the time." Dilwyn took the statement and fumbled with it. He didn't need to look at it, he could remember every dratted word.

"Page two, second paragraph." Mr Davies insisted. "I quote: 'You should have seen his face. I don't want to be speaking ill of someone who was a friend since I can remember, but...'" Mr Davies looked Dilwyn straight in the eye,'... if I had been in the Polish feller's shoes I would have kept clear of him from then on, too. Evan was brought down, see, public like, and it was always important to Evan that folk thought well of him, even though he didn't always act in such a way as to deserve their good opinion.' "

Dilwyn dropped his eyes first. He'd never be able to hold his head up again. So much for his own good opinion of himself. He was going to have to live with this for ever. Now he knew what people meant when they said 'between a rock and a hard place'.

"Er… I did say that, yes, but I couldn't hardly see what the truth was at the time. I must've been piss… Er, upset with Evan over something else, and it came out all wrong, like. I reckon it was Jan who was angry at Evan, because Evan being, like, er, Annie's guardian now their grandparents had died, he saw Evan standing in the way of his seeing so much of her. I'm not saying he'd go so far as to want to shoot him, mind, never that…" He trailed off.

He slunk off the stand at the end of it, and went out into the *maes*. To his relief, the square was empty of people. On the other side, a bus for Bangor was coughing fumes, and just pulling out. He waved it down and jumped on; no way was he going to wait for his mates and the thought of going to the pub for a drink after made him feel sick.

Evan darted his eyes round the court. People had their heads together talking, and he could see some of the jury nodding at what Dilwyn had just said. He uncrossed his fingers but didn't dare let his breath out yet, although he knew he'd been let off. Dilwyn had lied, and he wasn't going to have to stand up there, like he'd been frightened of, and try and tell all those lies he'd rehearsed. He would have told them, mind, it was his life on the line. He didn't have a choice. He forced a weak smile as Mavis caught his eye from the end of the row, and gave him a little wave. Wouldn't do to antagonise her right now, but if she reckoned… He didn't complete his thought. And if that bastard Dilwyn Maesgwyn thought he'd get away with what he'd written by changing his mind on the stand, well he had another thought coming.

The last witness of all was Mrs Evans the choir mistress, who strode up onto the stand.

"Oh no. I'm sure that's not right!" she exclaimed, shocked, when asked if Jan and Annie were 'intimate' friends, as others had implied. "There were many who would have liked him for their sweetheart, I daresay, but he was a gallant man, charming to everyone. I won't deny he had an eye for a pretty face, but that's no crime, and he conducted himself with great propriety at all times." She added firmly, "I can only hazard that any accusations of unseemliness between Jan and Annie came out of, shall we say, baser motives? Though I won't deny that they got on very well. But, you see, Annie is a clever girl, thoughtful, a cut above the usual; always curious about things, she likes to talk about the world, and isn't always thinking about what she wears and how she looks. Jan liked that. He liked her. And I, for one, thought it was nice they got on so well together. They both needed a good friend, they were both alone in the world, you might say. But there wasn't anything more to it than that, I'm absolutely positive."

Jan raked the courtroom for sight of Annie, and a light went out in his face when he could not find her. He didn't take the stand himself; to those observers of a cynical or biased inclination, in this way he avoided having to lie through his teeth under oath, probably a lying Catholic anyway, and without the need for a costly professional interpreter. Judge ap Howell read his statement to the court. There were no surprises. He stood proudly to attention as the judge's ringing tones described his love for Annie, but he hardly registered the judge reading out how he had felt too frightened about his future to tell Annie so. Too late, was all he knew, with a shuddering certainty and presentiment. He had left it all too late. Even his Commanding Officer's stirring account of his exemplary record as a pilot failed to penetrate his dazed mind, or sway opinion in the gallery, and his famous courage under fire and on behalf of a country not even his own, withered away under the psychic fire he faced in this hostile and alien courtroom.

Mr Cleary, in his summing up, focused on the pathologist's grim little report which attested to the fact that the shotgun had been fired from no more than ten yards away. "It is therefore difficult to imagine Morris Hughes mistaking the murderer for someone else – despite the defence's histrionic and enjoyable attempt to distract the jury from the truth there," he added. Here the jury chuckled and nodded sagely; they had not, no indeed, been taken in by that piece of sleight of hand. Jan's fingerprints were on the gun, his gun. "And," here he cited an article by an eminent psychiatrist, "wartime experiences tend to erode a person's inhibitions about killing another human being. Ladies and Gentlemen, Jan Zadrzynksi had a reason to hate; he had a motive for murder. With intention to injure or kill, he pulled the trigger that fateful evening. The fact that he shot the wrong person does not change things in the eyes of the law." He finished by telling the jury that they were bound to return a verdict of guilty of murder against the defendant.

Mr Davies took a different tack: "Gentlemen – and Ladies – of the Jury, I ask you only to look squarely at the facts, such as they have been presented to you. Over the past few days you have heard a sorry tale of incompetence, and, which is even more disturbing, one of such out and out prejudice against an erstwhile ally, a gallant member of our armed forces who fought and dared death daily so that we should be free, that I myself feel ashamed, as, I am sure, so do you. We must not allow British justice be tarnished in this way!

"Squalid excuses and stuttering deception dressed up as moral virtues – you are chapel and church goers all, well versed in the ways of human nature. In your time, you have seen it all before. Here in essence we have the romantic story of two young people who found a soul mate in each other and who dreamed of a happy future together. If that future was to be here, in Poland, or South Africa, is irrelevant. We have heard enough to know that far from gazing on their growing friendship with kindly eyes the general response was one of envy and jealousy. Petty sins, you may think. But, in your wisdom, who among you would not agree that such small sins are precisely those that may lead to foul acts of such a magnitude as murder. The pot of rancour boils, froths up and over, and before you know it, an innocent person is dead.

'We cannot but conclude that Emrys Hughes was killed mistakenly for another. The question that faces you is, 'Was Janek Zadrzinski the person who fired that gun'? Or someone as yet unknown, skulking in the wings and allowing Janek to stand trial in his or her place?

'I put it to you that, in accordance with the strict rules of evidence, it has not been possible to prove to the high level required by this criminal court, and I stress – beyond reasonable doubt – that Janek it was who shot and killed Emrys Hughes. And, it is this high standard of proof that is required for you to return, fairly, a verdict of murder.

'Ladies and gentlemen, I ask you to find Janek innocent of that crime.'

All that remained was for Judge ap Howell to instruct the jury, and all could plainly hear his low opinion of the circumstantial evidence that had been the hallmark of the case, and his distaste for its implications on the verdict. He didn't fail to caustically remark on Mr Davies' liking for theatre and drama, very American, and wondered if this was the path that British justice should take in future. He hoped not. Finally, he said, it was Janek Zadrzinski on trial here, and nobody else – all thoughts of some mysterious other person hinted at by certain witnesses for the defence should be seen for the ploy they were, and put firmly aside. It was the innocence or guilt of the defendant alone who stood before them that was to be decided here today.

The jury, all good men and women of the borough, filed out. It remained to be seen if the 'true' could be added.

**

Never say die

From behind a pillar at the very back of the court where she was sitting unseen, Annie watched, a cold numbness overtaking her as Jan was escorted back to the cells.

She'd never see him again. This was it – her worst nightmare. What had happened? It wasn't possible. The truth was on Jan's side! Surely the truth counted for something? Why hadn't it? Because they'd all judged Jan guilty long before he even stepped into the courtroom. That was the only logical explanation. Da always said if something didn't make sense, it meant something secret was lurking in the bushes. What chance did Jan have against such prejudice? And that Judge, pompous old fool. How dared he sneer like that!

There was only one thing for it, there was going to have to be an appeal, a life sentence with hard labour was unimaginable. So he hadn't been found guilty of murder and condemned to hang, but that was only as it should have been, after all. Why should she feel grateful for what was only right? He shouldn't have been found guilty of any part at all in Emrys Hughes' shooting.

Why in heaven's sake had Mr Davies not shown everybody how short-sighted Morris Hughes was – as well as deaf and stupid? – so his evidence should have counted for nothing. Mr Davies was too pleased with himself, that was the problem, and the write-up he knew he'd get in the papers from all that theatrical rigmarole of his with the blackboard, she'd be bound. Well, that ego of his had cost Jan dearly.

So much she didn't understand. But she did know if the jury hadn't agreed on the verdict they did, then he could've been tried somewhere else, where there was no presumption of guilt, by people who had no axes to grind.

Her brain was fizzing so, and the thoughts bouncing round inside it like a game of ping-pong, that she remained fixed in her seat long after the last person had left. It took a court usher shaking her shoulder to bring her out of her reverie and raise her to her feet.

Her first thought was to see Mr Davies, but when she asked for him at the front desk she learned he had already gone, dashing by taxi to catch the next train to London. The duty sergeant refused to give her his home address and she had to be content with his 'Chambers'. The sergeant licked his finger and was so ponderous and slow turning over the pages of the daily ledger which held the details of those attending the court, that she could have snatched it out of his hand. The corners of the pages were grey from his spit and the sweat on his fingers.

He found it finally, tore a page from his notebook and rolled a pencil over for her to write it down. He read it out with so many mispronunciations and so laboriously he hardly appeared literate. If this was the calibre of the officers of the law who had dealt with the case, God help us, Annie thought. Fat chance of that either.

Her next stop had to be the Simpsons. The circumstances of her last meeting with Mrs Simpson were still raw in Annie's mind, but the urgency of her need relegated this to a trifle that was not to be allowed to stand in her way. As she came out into the *maes*, she caught sight of the Simpsons over by the castle talking earnestly and with much finger wagging and head shaking to a plump man who looked somehow familiar.

She pushed her way in their direction through the crowd round the court's entrance, taking no notice of the indignant reproofs as she jostled and shoved. Just as she managed to extricate herself from the crush of onlookers and reporters taking pictures, and waiting for Jan to emerge in the prison van, the Simpsons' new chauffeur drew up in the Bentley, they got in, and the car pulled away. She shouted and waved but they didn't notice. The reporters did, and surrounded her with their salacious insinuations, their horrid familiarity, "Brian – North Wales Chronicle. How are you feeling now, Annie, bit of a shock, eh? Could you just say a few words for our readers?"

"Annie, over here. Daily Post. Will you be going to visit Jan?"

'News of the World. Our readers'd be interested in your romance with Jan; we'll pay more – "

She rounded on them fiercely.

'Sod off the lot of you! I'm never talking to you vultures. Go and pester someone else." She turned her back, refusing to say another word, and gradually they dropped away as she crossed the little foot-bridge over the river.

She looked back and saw the man the Simpsons had just been talking to disappearing round a corner. Some intuition urged her to find out who he was. She crossed back over the bridge, and walking as fast as she could in her smart smooth-soled shoes so as not to slip and strain an ankle on the slippery cobbles, she pursued him down a narrow street heading for the dock, where a launch was tied up. She caught him as he was about to walk up the gangplank.

"Excuse me, sir?"

He turned, "Yes, what is it?" As he saw who had accosted him his eyes hardened. "I'm sorry, Miss Williams, but it is highly inappropriate that we engage in conversation," he said, his voice cold.

'How –? Oh!" Annie's hand flew to her mouth as she recognised him as His Honour Judge ap Howell. "Well, I don't see why not," she rallied. "I just saw you talking to Mr and Mrs Simpson. What's the difference?"

"The difference is, my dear young lady, that I know Mr Simpson personally. He is a friend of mine. You are not. Good day." He raised his hat, turned and boarded, leaving Annie standing open-mouthed on the edge of the harbour wall.

As she watched the captain release the mooring ropes and the launch purred out into the strait, she felt the stirrings of despair. This was how it would always be, how it had always been. How could she expect to alter anything, her, a common working class girl, without powerful friends or influence? It wasn't bloody likely, that's what. And on top of that, viewed with mistrust by everyone, judge and jury, because she wasn't from round here, they didn't even respect her enough to believe she could be telling the truth, never mind her relationship with Jan. We hadn't come a long way from primitive tribes, whatever anyone said about how civilised we were. But never say die –'

Her breath caught in her throat at the unwitting solecism. No, never ever give up. She knew she had to fight as she never had in her life before, marshal all her considerable energy and wits and use them as best she knew how. She might not be clever but she had the truth on her side and that was worth everything. If she could just persuade the Simpsons to act on her and Jan's behalf, maybe there was a slight chance.

She walked back to the square and boarded the first of the buses which would take her home. Evan and the rest of the village lads had retired to the Black Boy for a pint, thank goodness, she didn't want to contend with those lying louts this afternoon. As she sat and the mountains jolted past, she jotted down in the small notebook in the Nain's handbag what she would say to Mr Simpson, using the sergeant's pencil which she'd walked out with in her dudgeon. She had to get this right. Satisfied, she got off the last bus and determined to call in at the Plas on the walk home... recoiled at the word 'home' in conjunction with 'Bron Felen'.

As she approached the Plas she felt the familiar pull to go round the back to the stable block, but resolutely marched up the steps and pulled the bell handle next to the imposing front door. The new maid answered, one of the young girls from the village, and was flustered on seeing who it was.

'Oh, it's you. I'll go and get Madam now. Wait here,' she ordered, leaving Annie on the steps and shutting the door behind her.

Annie heard the click-clack of high-heeled shoes over the tiled floor, then Mrs Simpson opened the door. Her face softened, 'Oh Annie, my dear. Come in, do. I'm so glad you've come, we were just talking about you.'

Did this augur well? Annie hardly dared hope. Mrs Simpson led Annie into the drawing room where Mr Simpson, head buried in his newspaper, was smoking a pipe – the smoke drifting in the draught towards the fireplace in which a bright fire burned. Annie sat down stiffly on the edge of the seat Mrs Simpson indicated, but shook her head at the offer of a cup of tea.

'We're having one anyway, aren't we, Edward?' she addressed Mr Simpson.

'We'll get the maid to put out an extra cup and cakes, just in case.' Annie capitulated, suddenly hungry. Mr Simpson nodded at Annie, folded his paper and put it down on the small table beside his chair.

As they waited for the tea in the quiet of the room, time stretched out thin as chewing gum. Even as Annie replied to Mrs Simpson's small talk about the weather and her health, she was uncomfortably conscious of the loud tick-tock of the long-case clock in the corner. Mrs Simpson crossed her legs and the silk of her dress slithered against the velvet of the chair. Mr Simpson's phuk-phuk-phuk as he drew on his pipe overlaid the sputter and shift of the logs in the fireplace.

'The conductor's the only thing missing,' she thought. Then, 'Perhaps it's me who's the conductor,' and any movement she made would send the whole fragile edifice of comfortable sounds crashing down around them in a melancholy cacophony, a sort of Trio for the End of Time, an aural version of the fireworks that by their earthly brilliance brought out the deep blackness of space. All three jumped as the door was flung open and the maid wheeled in a trolley, parking it next to Mrs Simpson.

"Get Banks to fix the squeak on that trolley later, will you, Doris?" barked Mr Simpson. Doris looked puzzled, then did a funny little curtsey, "Yes, sir."

Etiquette performed its miracle and by the time all three were holding a cup of tea and a plate with an iced bun they were considerably more relaxed. 'They're as nervous as me,' thought Annie, surprised. This emboldened her to be the first to voice what was on everyone's minds.

"I wanted to thank you for sticking up for Jan and giving him that character reference. But it wasn't enough. I don't want you feeling sorry for me or apologizing. What I want is an appeal. I don't know how to go about it, so I want you to have a word with some of your friends."

She held up her hand to stop them interrupting. "I know I'm out of order, but I'm desperate. You both know I wouldn't lie, and Jan was with me that night. There was no reason for him to shoot anyone, and I think anyone who had the ears to hear what was said would realise it was more likely to be Evan that shot Emrys Hughes, though I can't prove it. But everyone wanted it to be Jan. It suited them that way." She turned to Mr Simpson.

"If Jan's father really is a good friend of Lord Marchant, as you told the Judge, I want you to speak to him and see if he can do anything to help. Anything at all. Anything to stop him going to prison for the rest –" she broke off and sat rigidly, clenching her jaw, her hands gripping whitely round the fragile tea-cup till they feared it would crack. Mr and Mrs Simpson tore their gaze away and looked uncomfortably at each other. She nodded and Mr Simpson said, "We were just talking about Jan before you arrived, Annie. We both think from the evidence that the verdict was – well – hasty and ill thought-out, and I incline from what we heard on the witness stand to believe that you're correct about the prejudice displayed towards Jan. It's true that his father is a friend of Lord Marchant, and Lord Marchant does have influence in significant quarters, including the judiciary. Whether that will be enough I cannot know, but I do promise you I'll do all I can." He tamped his pipe.

"Thank you," Annie said, simply. Slowly and with great care she set the scarcely tasted cup of tea down in its saucer, returning them to the trolley along with the plate. She brushed the crumbs from her skirt onto the floor, hoping no-one had noticed, but caring very little if they had.

'Don't worry too much, and look after yourself, dear, you don't look at all well." Mrs Simpson saw Annie to the door. She touched her hand lightly on Annie's shoulder. 'I'll let you know how Mr Simpson gets on, but I don't expect it will be for a while – these things take time. I don't know whether to encourage you to hope for best, but I think it would be wiser to expect the worst. God be with you, Annie."

*

After Annie left, Mr Simpson stood for some time in the library looking out across the lawns to the ha-ha, idly noting the big old beech tree that needed to come down, rotting inside from honey fungus, the mare in the little paddock with the cut on her neck from the stallion, best keep them apart... knowing he was putting off what had to be done. Unpleasant, but what other recourse was there? Life was bloody unfair. What a circus the trial had turned out! And old Powell, the utter snob, cringing like a cur when he rebuked him for that lacklustre summing up. Should be reported for dereliction of duty. Damned good mind to do so. That poor girl; his heart went out to her. Smart as a whip. Pretty little thing, too... better not say so to Dotty, though, broad minded as she is, there's only so much praise a woman can take about another.

He turned and sat down at the writing bureau, took out his pen and ink, and set his mind to the letter he was going to write.

*

When Mrs Simpson called to say she was going up to bed, he was just blotting the last of the sentences he had carefully crafted.

"Won't be a mo, darling. I'll just read this through and put it out for the postie in the morning."

He sighed as he sealed the flap. Done. Let what will be, be. Off your conscience now, old man. He poured himself a generous malt and poked the fire before ringing the servants' bell, forgetting for a moment that there was no butler any more, and the maid didn't live in. Gracious, times were changing, the war had certainly hastened in a new era. But it hadn't changed how the old machinery worked, remained to be seen if anything ever would – still depended on who you knew. Old Hanley-Green was right, the time for heroes was past, and it was over to the grey, sober, suited men, whose footsteps would now echo down the halls of Westminster – sensible, liberal men, carrying forward

Winston's vision for a new society that took care of its own 'from the cradle to the grave'. What was it the Manchester Guardian had called the Beveridge Report? Ah yes, 'a big and fine thing'. Now that was a rallying call, if ever there was – social security and health care for all – about time. Sorry to have to go off so soon, really. Would have been interesting to stay around and have a hand in things. Ah well. He drained the last of his single malt, turned off the lamp, and dropped the letter on the hall table for posting the next morning.

Dear Robbie,

Hope the old leg's not too painful. I hear you're gallivanting as usual with the family over in Nice. Lucky beggar. And how's that son of yours, up to his pranks as usual I'll bet? Dotty and I are being sent out East, leaving next week. Spot of bother up country needs a firm hand. Don't know why they asked me, never got on with stuff like that. Anyway, we're shutting up the old heap for a couple of years, and Dotty'll go and stay with her aunt Sophie in Simla. I'll leave a poste restante *if you need to get in touch, or you can always go via the office; Harry Burns'll give you what you need.*

That barrister you found by the way – pretty sharp operator, and I thought he'd actually get Janek off the charge. Had the jury eating out of his hand for a while. But I'm sad to say that isn't how it turned out, and all down to that dolt William Powell. Do you remember him from Cambridge? – a cringer, as ever. I had a stiff word or two with him after the trial finished. If he'd been a bit sterner with the jury and explained the law of circumstantial evidence better, we might even now be celebrating Janek's release, and looking for the real murderer. As it is, they brought in a verdict of manslaughter, and sentenced him to hard labour for life. Marginally better than hanging...

So it's over to you, old sport. I wouldn't ask, but that travesty of a trial beggared belief. British justice? I'm ashamed to be associated with it. As pretty a picture of bone-headed prejudice as you'd ever hope to witness. You could almost see the jurors squaring their self-righteous shoulders as the trial proceeded; and I imagine it rather suited their smug provincial opinions to demonise Janek, to type-cast him as an example of all the hundreds of displaced persons, loitering on our shores with evil intent, only waiting to bite the hand that feeds them. Seem to have forgotten most of 'em fought with us, and we were all of us fighting to liberate most of the others!

The fact of the matter was, still is – if Janek didn't shoot the man, who the blazes did? That's what stuck in their craw. And that is the single question that most definitely demanded to be begged. And I can assure you, answer came there none, resoundingly.

Janek's young 'friend' came visiting this afternoon. She impressed me, no side to her, a down to earth Liverpool lass. Straight to the point. And I believe her. I thought at the start it was just possible that Janek had shot the man. It looked deuced bad – the gun from the stables, the killer running down the drive. The brother was an idiot, though, and Davies made short work of him alright. The more I heard, the more I became convinced it was someone from the village. Someone with a grudge. You know how it is, these grudges can last generations, yet you ask them about it and it's all smiles and how my great grand-uncle knew his grandmother and no, there were never any bad feelings, no sir, whoever told you that pack of lies?

Long and the short – would you have a quiet word with Teddy Huntington? He's got the PM's ear. At the least we should argue for an appeal to be heard at the Old Bailey, and failing that, perhaps a quiet dispensation or whatever a few months from now when the furor's died down. The lad wanted to go to South Africa I hear, but that may not be possible. See what you can do, old chap, won't you?

Yours truly,
Eds

**

Two pies

Over the months, that became a year and more, following what I briefly thought of as my hard won 'victory' at the inquest, the triumph of vindication trickled away and a flatness set in. Looking out was impossible, so I looked inwards, only to confront a featureless steppe across which, as in a dream, I slowly journeyed. On the horizon not one, but many, pyrotechnic storms danced and burnt their complex patterns on my retinas. Opposites hugged, likes repelled, particles collided and electrons zapped. Seeking equilibrium. The flicker of colossal voltages, those weapons of the gods, lit chartless pathways which flirted and beckoned me on until the tension grew so great that 'ping', the fragile air parted. Released, I did not know which way I faced, which way to take, they all looked the same. It stretched to breaking point my sanity, my marriage, my home, and I was forced to reach out for help.

Eva had long gone the way of all my other friends, repulsed by my obsession and offended by my curt reception of their overtures. Harry was shut to me; I had tried his patience too far. I made an appointment to see Julia Lockley, the analyst recommended by my General Practitioner.

Julia received patients at home, a village chapel converted in modernist style. The small courtyard sported Astro turf and large terracotta pots with colourful acers and azaleas, haphazardly placed yet with an eye for effect. She escorted me to the room she used for her analysis at the top of the building: leather sofas, glass shelving, black glazed pottery, elegant white furniture, spotlights strung unobtrusively among the contemporary black beams. A water feature tinkled in one corner. No place for superfluity or subterfuge.

She left me while she made coffee downstairs. I was so shut into myself, that my anxiety impelled me to open the French windows and step out onto the parapet, to look over at the mountains in their evening pink. One quick glance was all I could bear; I returned to the sofa, in case she found me outside.

That first session was a blur of tears and balled-up soggy paper handkerchiefs while my coffee got cold. I didn't find it especially hard to confess to the guilt, revenge or anger- they lived on the surface. The real problem ran beneath. Ditches, I thought. I need to dig some ditches.

*

"These storms you see, Sarah. Can you tell me more about them?"
"They're – they're just – storms. Always getting closer but never reaching me."
"Describe them to me."
"I see them coming from a long way off. They head straight at me. They destroy everything in their path. I see houses burning, the earth melting."
"What do you feel when you look at them?"

The sofa squeaked with sweat from the back of my thighs as I shifted my behind. I shrugged. "I'm not afraid. It's as though they're mocking me, they're not any real threat. Sort of daring me... No, it's too impersonal for that. They make me feel – inconsequential. I don't know..." I shook my head, tried a different way. "One day in the summer I saw a field mouse scurrying through the grass. She knew she was the buzzard's breakfast. She kept stopping and peering at the sky, listening for the beat of wings, her heart whumping as she dashed from cover to cover –"

I stopped. Why couldn't I just say it simply as it was?

I want it all to stop! I want some peace and quiet! I want to be able to be in this beautiful place where I live, and feel happy again. I want to be able to go back and visit the first place I thought of as home, and remember Fleur when she was little, playing in the fields, going to school. I want to tell her what a beautiful talented person she is, how proud of her I am. I want to listen to her play the guitar, the guitar I've hidden in the barn with the wear marks on the frets from her fingers. I want to look at photos of her, not hide them along with the guitar in boxes in a barn. And I can't, I can't, I can't.

*

After that first session, and at Julia's suggestion to help me connect with the person I was, I retrieve the few photos I possess from their hiding place and spread them over the kitchen table. Maybe they can help me understand – if I can bear to look at them. I feel distinctly dubious. I never owned a camera; I thought taking photos was artificial, and I wanted to just remember what stuck in the mind naturally. I regret that as time goes on and my memories wear thinner. There is a photo I want to find of my children in front of the house in Mid-Wales where we lived – when we were still what passed as a family. Before it all fell apart.

I look at it, and wonder if every family looks as normal on the outside. Three generations of Wilsons – except for Tony of course. We seem a jolly lot. We are all smiling for the camera, in t-shirts and shorts – except for my father, who is wearing a full-sleeved shirt and slacks. I never saw him in anything else. Holidays at the seaside, he would sit on the shingle in a deckchair and roll up his trouser legs to the knees, while my mother and I went swimming. And it's not until now I realize the only memory I have of his body, apart from his bare hands and face, is his white shins which every year went a fiery red and blistered so badly that, added to the visual memory, is the smell of calamine lotion.

The photo I have found was taken one summer when my parents were on one of their rare visits. They had driven down the evening before from Grange-over-Sands in Cumbria, in my father's Ford Capri, his pride and joy. They drove all the way back the next day, my mother having taken umbrage when I retorted that I'd had enough of her carping criticisms – of me, my husband, and my children. My father stood outside in the dusty yard and washed the car while my mother packed. I hovered between them, wanting to say sorry yet determined not to. Reduced again to the defiant child who would never amount to much. I went over to my father hoping for some small reconciliation but he forestalled me, saying, 'Your mother needs me, Sarah, and...' Here, his courage failed him and his voice trailed away. He could only look down and drop the cloth into the water. I nodded. That was all I was going to get. We were not to speak so much as ten words on the telephone over the next four years. And it would be yet another two before I saw them again in the flesh. By that time I had completed his sentence over and over again, and finally found the version I like to think was the sad reality behind his words.

*

Our shadows are long and slanting across the yard, our bodies thinning towards our pea-sized heads, and to the side I can just make out the white muzzle of our old donkey, Paddy, whose delight was to trot around the orchard under the low boughs of the apple trees and knock the children off into the grass.

My mother is on the left, a swarthy nut brown woman with jet black hair in a bun. Everyone used to ask if her family came from Pakistan, which made her cross. 'If India's the other side of the Pennines,' she'd answer tartly. Her origins are a mystery. Beside her we all look like English roses, with our creamy skin and long blonde hair. My mother's hand is a frozen blur halfway up holding a tissue, and Tim, my son, in front of her, is scowling. I know she has just rubbed a smudge off his face because it is clean, while his hands and bare feet are muddy from playing in the small brook that flowed past the house, down into the little hamlet, where it ran under a small stone bridge and joined a bigger stream, to become the Wye. Bernie and Ro, his older sisters are behind him left to right in ascending order of size. Bernie is holding her favourite doll up to the camera, and is red faced from crying because Tim said it was stupid. Ro is already displaying the budding model's instinct for the most flattering pose. I am kneeling down next to Tim, holding Fleur in my arms. I remember she wouldn't look at the camera, her face is hidden in my neck and she is sucking her thumb. At the time, I remember, the only place I could find any peace from her for a couple of minutes was in the toilet.

My father stands on the far right, his hands in his pockets, head turned to glance across at Bernie, so all we see of him is his profile with his Roman nose. Next to him there is Tony, barely in the picture at all – which, knowing him as I do, is probably what he wanted. You can tell it is the seventies from his tie-die loons and hair in a ponytail. He is squinting in the late sunshine. He will rush into our bedroom and roll a spliff in a minute. My parents will determinedly ignore the funny smell. There is one thing that puzzles me – who took the photo?

*

I pick up another photo. It is a black and white one taken in one of the public gardens in Blackpool. I am standing next to a statue of a huge painted plaster gnome, a grotesque rendition of Big Ears. I am carrying a shiny black plastic handbag, my hair in a bunch each side of my head. I'm smiling. I look happy. But I know I'm fearful and timorous, and deep down angry, and someone is going to have to pay. The gnome isn't there any more.

It is the summer of 1956 and I am six. We are on our first family holiday, me, my mother and my father. Dad had been into Dunnerdale to see an old friend of his from the war who rented out a flat in Blackpool for holiday lets. We lived in a tied cottage on a large estate where Dad was the head gardener-chauffeur. An aunt and uncle were respectively the cook and butler at another estate a few miles away, and another uncle was a farm manager over by Settle. Mum used to take in ironing and do local cleaning jobs. We were, as history portrayed us later, the last bastions of the servant class. So a holiday was quite an event.

"What d'you think, Marge?" I heard him ask Mum, when they thought I wasn't listening. Mum's reply was sharp, as she always was.

"Well, it's about time we managed a holiday, Bill. The last one was our honeymoon..."

I hunched my shoulders and raised the book I was reading until my face was hidden behind it. I hated the hectoring tone in my mother's voice, and could never understand why my father put up with it. I think she was embarrassed at his 'weakness' as she called it, and what embarrassed her became a focus for her hatred, even though most of the time it meant she had her own way about things. When I helped her make the beds I could feel her resentment in the abrupt snapping of the sheet over the mattress, the jerky tucking in, hard, and hostile. I listened to her over the strains of Uncle Mac playing 'The Runaway Train'.

"Your father just will not stand up for himself." This was the acme of her disapproval, when he became my 'father' and was no longer my 'dad'. 'I could wring his neck. He stands there like a rabbit in the headlights, and takes everything they throw at him. Why he doesn't leave this dead-end job and do something with himself, I'll never know. As though they're any better than us really. They think they are, but you should see the muck in their bathrooms." 'They' being the gentry Dad worked for. She frightened me when she spoke like this, and then, close behind the fear, came the dislike, for her being so angry all the time, for making me feel scared of her, for being envious of other people. For making me want more.

Mum always claimed she had a winning streak and it was true; almost to the day she died she won at cards, raffles, and lotteries. So we went to the arcade on the pier every afternoon and played Housey-Housey for a couple of hours. Bingo. She came away with cutlery sets, mugs, scarves, a coaster set, a necklace. When Dad won, he always let her choose a prize for herself.

I never won, until one afternoon. I knew exactly what I wanted. I'd set my heart on a big bouncy ball. I remember crying while my mother chose a set of doilies. I can still hear the other players booing, the shouts of 'Shame' and 'Let the kid have it'. Through my tears I pointed to the ball, and it was thrust into my arms. Victory over my mother was sweet, but it was scary too.

"Come on, Marge, let's get a bit of fresh air," whispered my father, without looking at me. Grim faced we walked back to the flat. We never went back to the arcade. I can't remember if I played with the ball, but it definitely did not come home on the coach with us.

*

Another photo. I must be about ten. It is a school photo and I am wearing the pretty dress my mother had just made for me. Cream with pink roses and little puff sleeves and a lacy collar. After the photo session we took our chairs out into the playground and sat in a circle for our story book lesson. My best friend put her chair close to mine and when she stood up it caught and tore my dress, a big tear right through the skirt. At dinner time I went home and told my mother what had happened. She was angry and shouted and wouldn't listen to me, and through my tears I saw her bang her dinner down on the table. When she pulled her chair back to sit down she pulled the table cloth with it, and her plate fell off the table and spilt her dinner all over the floor. She wept and cried, and put her head in her hands, and would not be consoled. I remember I couldn't stop trembling.

Those times were when I learned to stay very still and make myself very small and invisible; when I concluded I was a bad girl who would come to no good end; who made awful things happen for other people. It was only years later that I saw maybe it wasn't my fault she was so angry; that there was much to oppress the working class and knock the spirit and dreams out of them. Marriage in war time, I realised, just can't be easy and my father had been captured at Dunkirk, a mere six months after getting married – he had got drunk and signed up for the army one evening with a couple of mates – and spent the remaining years quarrying stone in a prisoner of war camp on the Polish border.

Who was it who came home? Not the same person as went away. The man who returned was a man who had seen violent death, experienced gratuitous brutality. What did he come home to? A society grown hard and selfish. Where material wealth was the measure of the man. Unemployment and scarcity of food, the lot of most. A new Jerusalem in the offing maybe, but not enough room in it for the thousands in need. And a woman spurned and abandoned.

My child's point of view didn't recognise the broken dreams, and the anger they gave birth to. I thought she was angry at me, me, me. And it made me frightened. And sad. So sad that when I graduated from the Infants' to Junior School I would put my head on my arms on the double-seater desk and weep until the motherly girl next to me put her arms round me and asked me what the matter was, and stroked my hair. I never told her what the matter was, and her sympathy was so wonderful that I deliberately cried every morning just to get her to hug me. Until one morning when she said crossly, 'You're always crying. I wish I could sit next to someone else." The shock was enormous. I never cried in class again. I learnt to choose when I cried with care.

*

Another memory. When I was a child you could buy a simple game which consisted of a small plastic 'box' with a see-through top, containing a large drop of mercury. You shook it and the mercury split into tiny silver balls, which scattered and rolled through the box's maze-like runnels. By skilful manipulation you had to gather them all together again in their 'home', a hollow in the middle of the box, where they merged to make one large 'blob'.

Fear is like that. My fear rolled through the runnels of my life like those blobs of quicksilver. I felt it in the shortness of breath, the taut belly, the high shoulders, the voice that strained from the throat only. Fleur's death worked on this fear like a miner who daily opened up new seams, bringing the precious ore to the surface. It made me cross the road rather than talk to an acquaintance I spied coming towards me; it made me scowl at strangers who brushed roughly by me in the street; swear at traffic lights and stupid pedestrians; it made shop-girls sulky and waitresses downright hostile; it permeated the fabric of my life in a myriad small ways that I could never have imagined, and I no longer recognised it, or myself. Envy, jealousy, pig-headedness, bossiness, defiance, anger. The mean and sordid sins. Fear has many aliases.

*

The following week, after the obligatory coffee ritual, Julia drew a circle on a piece of paper. "This is a pie you're going to share," she said. I frowned.

'It's a 'blame' pie," she added, "a piece for everyone you think is to blame for what happened to Fleur."

I cut myself a big slice.

"How about Fleur's father? The same size slice?"

"Yes. No... oh, I don't know, I suppose so."

"What about Johnny?"

"A small slice," my small voice said. How did I dare?

"Okay, let's cut a slice for the hospital next."

Yes, that was easy. A big, big slice. So big, I needed two pies.

"Anyone else?" I shook my head. There was no one else.

Eva hesitated, "We mustn't forget Fleur, though, must we?"

She slipped the knife in deftly and watched as the thin white line blossomed red. My heart slammed, I sweated and my mind froze. As it unfroze with an almost audible 'plock' I couldn't stop it, I really couldn't; I howled with laughter. She'd got me; I had been check-mated by a genius.

But however clever she was, still I could not confess to her what I knew was the darkest truth for me – that I could exonerate everyone else but me. And the hospital. I still wanted to take a shotgun and blast everyone in it to pieces, a riot of killing and blood and shattered flesh. The fantasy gave me satisfaction; but to utter such thoughts aloud would be an act almost of transmogrification. I couldn't take the chance; I didn't know any longer who I was and what I was capable of. I felt nauseated at the rancorous, vindictive hag I saw I was becoming. My hands shook and rattled the coffee cup in its saucer until I put it down and all I could think to do was reach for the box of tissues and cry to stop the session.

That night I had a dream. An 'other' I, from whom I have long since divided, is seated opposite me in, curiously, a tea shop with waitresses in caps and aprons, and twittering housewives who regard each other with secret envy. An image seared into my synapses from this earlier time. I regard this other, older, 'I' with interest, this 'I' who carried on into the future seamlessly, who didn't veer off recklessly at a tangent at every opportunity. She gives off an aura of solidity, of success, whereas the 'newer' I feels loose and – manufactured out of failure. She returns my look with something akin to distaste, and I decide she is a prig. I thought I might regret I didn't take the path she obviously did, but now I'm glad. She is here tonight for another reason. She is here to provide the answer. All I have to do is find the right question, the one single question that will brighten the colours of the universe, shift them like a giant kaleidoscope into a pattern that answers every question that ever begged to be asked. I search my brain, but it's useless, and before I can think of what it is I have to ask, she fades and is gone.

Each time I left Julia's house I was wrung out, and kidded myself I was healing. Yet every midnight saw me hunched and shivering by the little woodstove in the caravan, silent tears dripping on the dog curled in my lap. Those desert nights were two, or even three, large hairy dog nights, not nights that one small smooth-haired terrier could warm.

Exhaustion overwhelmed me. Several times I found myself nodding off at the table in the canteen after lunch, and just managed to catch my book before it fell on the floor, looking round hoping no-one had noticed.

'I'm swimming so hard against the current," I told Julia, when I went for a session in the evening after one day at work where I made mistake after mistake, my head so fugged I couldn't think, 'sometimes I think I must be insane – if I accept everyone else is sane, that is. But I don't. Most of the time I think I'm living in a totally insane world... so I guess I must be the sane one! "

She smiled.

'Years ago," I continued, 'I was struck with the idea of being the river, from its source to its ending in the sea. Not a leaf whirling along on the surface of the water, at the mercy of the currents. Now I want just the opposite – I want to float wherever the water takes me, lie there with my hands behind my head, looking up at fluffy clouds in a blue sky –"

'Sarah, Sarah – " But I would not be stopped.

"– to drift out to sea, among the corals, in and out of the reefs. Roll over and over in the surge on a sandy bottom and look up at the belly of a basking shark; scrape over the barnacled keel of a hulk, and look through the portholes at the verdigris on the pewter tankards in the galley; peer down the periscope of a submarine at the dead..." I paused, frightened by the images that sprang into my head.

In short – abdicate, hand it all over!

'Sarah," gently, 'you still haven't told me how you – you – feel. It's all very well to dress things up in metaphors and poetic images –"

'I can't. I just can't! It hurts. If I make it into a symbol I can find a symbolic release! It stops being unique to me, and becomes part of what we all have to come to terms with. All that weeping for loved ones. Some of them murdered by psychopaths in cold blood – think how unbearable that must be. Some killed in indifferent wars over oil or gold or some other 'commodity', by smart bombs ordered up by men in shirtsleeves sucking their teeth in a high rise office block half way round the world. In some macabre way it helps me, don't you see? Even if it's not exactly the world I ever envisaged belonging to. So I play act, over and over again until I find an image, an allegory I can accept. It's an alchemy of the mind.

"The one thing I won't let go of is the anger. Not yet. It's more manageable than it was, I'm not repelling people quite as much as I used to. But it's the anger that motivates me to get what happened out in the open, to force changes in how the mentally ill are looked at and looked after – too late for Fleur, but not too late perhaps for some other poor sods. I know the power anger offers is an illusion, but just now everything in my life seems illusory. Some sort of natural 'end' will come, I'm sure – I'll know it when it does. This is the only way I can express myself without falling to pieces..."

"Fine. In that case, let's see what we can do with what you're able to give me."

*

In the ensuing weeks with Julia's help I came to better understand the nature of grief. But although I nodded and agreed, I knew the whole package – sorrow, guilt, blame, regret, anger, retribution – was one I'd be lugging around for the rest of my life. Even while I smiled. Even if I got used to its weight. OK, repression maybe, but no matter, I thought. There was much I failed to understand. And there was one final act in the drama, before the curtain could come down.

I gave it my best shot; I braved the talons, stood on my back legs and squeaked my fury, my right to know; my hopes for a human side to the corporation, a clasp of hands across the table.

What a laugh. What a fool. Meet the Health and Safety men.

**

Call me Charlie

'Nobody wanted to open this Pandora's Box because who knew what would spill out at the wake. And among the acronymic viruses that stalked our twenty-first century hospital corridors, viruses like MRSA and C-difficile, the virus called LPC, or 'loss of public confidence', might have been discerned. This was NOT to be allowed.'

- Anon

2005

"Mr and Mrs Blake, ah, nice to meet you, if under such sad circumstances." I forced a smile and shook their soft hands. "My name is Charles, Charles Rowse, but please call me Charlie – and this is my colleague, Carl – Carl Fenniman."

We had arranged to meet conveniently at a friend's house in Chester. I later vowed if there was ever to be a next time (there wasn't) I would insist on their coming to Bron Felen just to watch them struggle through the mud in their nice polished shoes, and fend off Harold the gander's territorial attack with their briefcases, to arrive breathless and daunted on my doorstep. Charitable I was not.

'Call-me-Charlie', was a small leathery man with a quick look in his eyes, which I had hoped meant he was intelligent. He was. Carl on the other hand seemed lethargic, almost stupid. He looked at us as though weighing us up for dinner, but with the heavy lidded look of a lizard in the sun, too lazy to bother. He wasn't. Charlie was the chatty one – 'No sugar thanks love I gave it up when I stopped smoking I was doing nearly forty a day and coughing fit to bust but then all the lads I worked with smoked in those days. I must have put on about a stone when I stopped and talk about puffing and panting up stairs I wasn't seeing the benefit so the wife said 'Cut out the sugar and starch, Charlie, or it's a heart attack for you if not lung cancer.' She was right of course and I did. I haven't smoked for nigh on twenty years now thanks love" – as I handed him a cup of coffee.

Having dispensed with the small talk, we got to the nitty-gritty. It all sounded cheerily optimistic with fulsome promises to look at the damning information it had taken me painstaking years to unearth, information I was so eager to pass on to someone who could, and would, do something about it. I felt suddenly rather better.

'I've got a report here, dated July 2000." I shoved it across the table to them. 'I don't know if you've seen it. There should be a copy in the police documentation. It was commissioned by the Board following an attempted suicide at *Llanfair* six months before Fleur's, from a shower rail. The summary clearly mentions the necessity to remove all non-collapsible rails in the Unit. Yet nothing, nothing, in that action plan was ever implemented. As you'll know, the Coroner's Rules prevented her from looking at any other incident at the hospital in detail, although she did read this document – thanks to me and my barrister. The hospital was very keen to prevent it being disclosed at the inquest."

Call-me-Charlie took it and flicked through it. 'Well, it certainly looks like the police didn't give us all the documents. We'll get onto them, eh Carl? Make a note." Fenniman made a face, whether or not it showed a disapproving surprise at the police incompetence, or my unwelcome paperwork, I couldn't tell. But there was no mistaking the disapproval.

'Nothing had changed, you see." I continued. 'That's what's so damning. The rails were still all there. As you know only too well, because you were there when they took them down after Fleur's death.

"And then again," I forged on, ignoring the quick looks darted at each other, 'that manager Stodden from the Works Department had the sheer effrontery to claim he had tested the rails to make sure they were collapsible and the Unit was safe. But there's no mention of which rails he tested, where they were located, and not a hint of anything in writing; the only evidence to confirm any 'testing', if you can call it that, was a member of the ward staff who said at the inquest that he vaguely remembered someone, some time or other, coming round and 'yanking' on the rails. 'Yanking' on the rails? How could anyone take seriously a large man yanking on a rail as an acceptable test that it would collapse under the weight of a small woman?

"The Crown Prosecution Service, as you know, said the evidence didn't pass the test for prosecution for corporate manslaughter, because it wasn't the rail that was the 'cause' of Fleur's death. Bizarre. And the reason they came to this conclusion? Simple – someone was lying. This same person, the one who gave the Unit such a clean bill of health, claimed Fleur was sitting on the floor, not hanging – so the cause of death was asphyxiation by her belt, not the rail. 'Not our fault, luv.' My God, is this what the law comes down to?

"It was only under oath in court that Sharon Evans, the nurse who found Fleur, finally told the truth, and admitted she was hanging from the rail. Why didn't she say so before, to the police? Simple – if she'd admitted it before she would have been put under pressure to change her story, and face the prospect of losing her job if she didn't. I hear she left anyway, and I'm not surprised.

"Over to you, now, anyway. But because of this bit of sophistry from a person who held a high position in a public organisation, a person we could reasonably expect to have some integrity, nobody bothered to think it through! I had to. I've got a research article here by a Russian professor," I riffled through the papers in my briefcase and brought it out, slid it over the table to join the action plan. "Please read it. It tables the percentage of a person's weight taken by a ligature point if fully suspended, sitting, kneeling, or lying down. In all cases except lying down, Fleur's weight on the rail would have been over the permitted limit. The police ignored this article. Why? Another imponderable."

I caught their look. "And if you think I must be bloody weird to go so far, think how you'd be if it was your daughter and everyone was determined to ignore you, make you feel useless and crazy, so you'd creep away and stop bothering everyone, so that the simple fact of the hospital's criminal negligence could be swept conveniently under the carpet. You'd do anything. Anything. Like I've had to."

Call-me-Charlie made a gesture I chose to ignore; let them take my voice ringing in their ears away with them. I selected another couple of papers from the sheaf I'd brought.

"Llanfair claimed at first that they didn't get any of the Safety Alerts about ligature points that had been distributed. And when they were forced to concede they did get them, they claimed they must have 'mislaid' them. How very convenient!" I was foolish enough to risk the sarcasm, confident I had them on my side by now. 'What does that say about the truthfulness of the senior managers? Are you surprised we don't believe them? Especially as here are the minutes of two ward meetings where these 'mislaid' alerts were actually tabled and discussed. So someone must have had them, even if they didn't action them. Who? Who is it pulling the wool over everyone's eyes? It shouldn't be left to me and my family to find out! You and the police –"

Fenniman cut me off, 'Thanks Sarah. Good work. We'll put it in the hands of our legal advisors; see what they make of it.'

'There's a lot more here I've –"

'Great. Send it to us. Are you on email? Although we can't guarantee we'll look under every last stone, we probably won't need to anyway,' 'Call-me-Charlie' interrupted again. Good old Charlie. 'We'll do all we can; but it's best to be forewarned that no matter how much we investigate there're going to be things we may never know – you may never know – and we wouldn't want you to be too disappointed.'

'But you will take a tilt at the hospital's working practices? The senior managers?' I asked. 'It was never just a matter of bad nursing, however much they tried to shift the blame –"

'Oh yes sure sure. What I mean is there's only a team of four of us to cover the whole of a huge geographical area and what with sickness and our budget put through the wringer this last year and all these targets, well you know how it is anyway not to worry we'll look at the evidence and see where our best prospect for prosecution lies.'

Fenniman cut in, oil in his voice, 'I expect you're wanting all this to be over as quickly as possible so you can find closure. It's been a long time now, people are starting to forget things –"

It was my turn to interrupt, 'Well, I'd rather your investigation take longer and be more rigorous than hurry it up at the expense of the truth. Will how long it's taken jeopardise the outcome?' I asked.

'Nnh-hnn. Shouldn't. The hospital's keen to get on with things without too much more fuss. They don't want their services disrupted any more than necessary – which seems the proper way of thinking to me.'

Fuss? Fuss!? 'But you are going to interview staff again, aren't you? The police interviews were pretty useless; they didn't know enough to even ask the right questions, let alone get the right answers, and –"

"Ah, we'll look at all the evidence and go on from there – unfortunately, as you know, a lot of the witnesses have left *Llanfair* now and some of them moved away, so the time and effort needed for us to chase them up could be considered disproportionate – on a cost benefit analysis. Not that that's the only consideration of course," as he saw the flood of red across my face. 'Unfortunately, I have to tell you, the collection of witness evidence wasn't done properly – by the police not us, mind – so we can't use some of the original statements. We may not need them, of course; we may be able to prosecute on other evidence."

I felt suddenly much much worse.

'But – what didn't they do properly?"

'I'm sorry, I can't tell you exactly. It was a question of protocols not being adhered to."

'Does this mean you might not be able to prosecute at all? I thought it was certain. That's what the detective inspector told us. If they couldn't, you would? Two bites at the cherry? You were there."

'That's right. Like I said, we'll put it all together and hand it over to our legal team. It's a sad fact, though, that it's very rare we're able to prosecute an individual. In big organisations it's almost impossible to link an individual senior manager directly to the incident, most decisions are taken in committee; but I can say it looks at the moment as though we might be able to prosecute the hospital for a breach of the Health and Safety at Work Act."

'Might? A breach?" I frowned. 'But there wasn't just one breach, there were several; the Coroner identified them in his verdict. And as far as I'm concerned it's quite clear there were one or two individuals who were completely incompetent."

"Ah, but it isn't a crime to be incompetent, you know," said Fenniman, watching me sideways. He thought he'd bowled me out. But he was wrong. It was a crime, no matter what they said. It was, it was.

Afterwards, as we shook hands outside, I could barely bring myself to say a word, knowing that if I opened my mouth and gave them an unexpurgated version of what I thought any residual chance they just might decide to re-investigate would instantly evaporate. Harry attempted gallantly to fill the uncomfortable silence with inconsequential chatter. Everything he had predicted seemed now not so much cynicism as harsh realism.

They got in their car and motored off back to wherever they came from, and I knew I'd missed something important. I couldn't quite put my finger on it; I couldn't understand the reason for all this ducking and diving. Why wouldn't they listen to me?

Could I ever have imagined that at the heart of it was their determination to tidy up the tragedy that was my daughter, with the least possible fuss for the public authorities? Never mind us.

**

Poison berries

'O I fear you are poisoned, Lord Randal, my son!
I fear you are poisoned, my handsome young man!
O yes, I am poisoned; mother, make my bed soon,
For I'm sick at the heart, and I fain wad lie down.'

- Trad. Folk 'Lord Randall'

Winter 2005

Before winter was well on and crept into his knees and slowed him down with the pain, Dilwyn took his tractor, an old Massey Ferguson TEA20, or 'little grey Fergie' as it was popularly known, and they both panted and wheezed their way up the hillside that stretched behind the village, to gather sacks of the sphagnum moss that he sold to the local greengrocer and florist for wreaths and hanging baskets. The old cattle and sheep market had closed down long ago and been converted into a block of flats for the elderly, 'I always used to think I lived in that old market I spent so much time in it, and I'm darned sure I'll be going back to live in it again one of these days," he joked whenever he had the chance.

"Scratching moss off the hill. That's all my poor old bones are up to these days. Keeps me out of trouble," he grinned at me. 'I like it on the hill. You get above things." Until, that is, he got stopped by the traffic police one evening on his way home from *The Bell*, on his tractor, and was done for Driving Under the Influence – of cider, his favourite tipple. The story made it to the local paper along with a photograph of a beaming Dilwyn on the tractor, his old jacket tied round with a bit of red bailer twine, and for a brief moment he knew what it was to be famous. Or rather, infamous.

"What were you thinking of, Dilwyn?" I scolded him. "What are you going to do now?"

"Oh, I 'spect you can handle that old engine all right, can't you? You can take me up the hill until this all gets sorted out, it's only a couple of months," Dilwyn answered airily, and inaccurately.

So, for the length of time it took for his ban to be over, I trundled him on the old tractor up the hillside, perched in the transport box behind, shouting me through the gears and waving madly at anyone who saw us. I learnt to rake the moss with the short-handled wooden-tined rakes that Dilwyn made himself and pack it dripping in the sacks on the back of the tractor. Then we'd haul it off into town to Mrs Evans the florist, and stack it in her back room, with the buckets of daffodils and all the other flowers she carried in there for the night, and from where a brown peaty trickle would gradually emerge and run across the floor and out the door.

Being out on the hill encouraged Dilwyn to reminisce, and I made sure to always steer him towards Annie. And he wanted to talk about her, I know. He might look askance at me, but the urge was there, long held in and needing to be given rein.

The young Annie started to emerge, just a few spectral lines as yet and as though seen through a dark glass. I sensed her peering back at me, and wasn't sure if she welcomed my curiosity. "It's like developing a photo," I thought. "but it's as though I've forgotten what I took a picture of in the first place, it was so long ago. It's all latent, only potential." The light reflected off things and events in the past only here and there – the roses, the snowdrops, the door handle, the Pole, the village, Evan. These were the clearest. The photons crowded their way to these images, but elsewhere the lattice was too unstable. What was it that had been exposed? What was waiting to be developed? A delicate process, a question of intuition really, I thought. Too much or too little and I might as well forget the whole thing.

Was I equal to the task? Did I really want to expose something that had been hidden for so long? And, moreover, perhaps it had been hidden by the adamantine will of the very person I wanted to reveal... No. Who can it harm now? Everyone's dead now except Dilwyn and George. I just have a feeling she's been waiting for me.' It didn't occur to me that I had been waiting for Annie.

I asked Dilwyn where she was buried, and one bright afternoon we walked together down to the little church by the beach.

'She was brought up by her mam as a Catholic, you know," he told me. 'But she never went to Church; well, there wasn't a proper Catholic church round here. The Church in Wales did as well, I suppose." He tapped a newish looking headstone with his stick. 'Here she is. The only time I ever saw her in church was at Blod's and Huw's funerals," he pondered, 'that was just after the end of the war. Never since. Gave up her singing too, for good. Shame."

Her gravestone was at the back, under a yew tree, with the poison berries dropping on the soil all around. It was a stark plain stone, just her name and date of her death.

'How odd. No date of birth."

'None of us knew it, and we never knew her celebrate a birthday in all the years she lived at Bron Felen." Dilwyn explained. 'The only papers we found after were letters from the Evacuation Board, and the damp had got to them so they were just about illegible."

Quite how someone could exist so outside the petty bureaucratic entanglement of modern life was almost unbelievable. No social security number, no bank account, no bills? Annie was a relic of a bygone era.

'I reckon she deliberately destroyed it all." Dilwyn shook his head. 'I never knew such a stubborn woman. She didn't want to belong. She didn't want anyone knowing anything about her. I think she just wanted to disappear into the earth and be forgotten."

This, more than anything else I'd heard about her, saddened me, and I felt a surge of pity for the Annie of my imaginings. Forget her, I could not.

*

The weather turned vicious, a hard sleet in an easterly wind, and out of regard for his rheumatism – 'Brought on by the cold, doll, that's all. Right as rain rest of the year' – we left the Fergie in its shed for the day, and sat in front of the fire in his living room. Dilwyn, wincing whenever he moved his legs, sat upright on a kitchen chair, and planted his blackthorn stick between his legs, leant both hands on the intricately fashioned handle polished to a sheen by constant use.

'How did Annie come to be living down here in the first place, Dil?"

'You don't give up, do you, doll?" he chuckled, though his face was sad. 'Oh well, what's the harm, now? It was like this, see. Annie was evacuated from Liverpool during the war. Her mam, Moire, an Irishwoman from somewhere over on the West of Ireland she was, married the Williams' younger son. Then both Annie's parents died, see, and she had no-one else. Maybe there was an aunt or uncle somewhere out there, but she didn't know who and it wasn't easy in those days to find such things out. I'm distantly related to her Nain, Blod, on my mother's side, but way, way back."

"Mm. There're quite a few old people in the home with my Mum who came from Liverpool as kids during the war," I mused.

"Yes, Manchester too. Old George was from there originally."

"Well at least she came to family, not like most of them. I've read stories of how some evacuees were so badly treated you'd call it child abuse these days. Sleeping in barns, fed on bread and dripping. I've always wondered how it must have affected them. They were casualties of the war as much as the men who died or the women who were left widows."

"Well, Old Huw, her Taid, I heard he kicked up a bit of a fuss about her coming here, but Blod wouldn't have her going anywhere else. She stayed on at Bron Felen after the old folks passed on, through all the troubles after too. Lived there till the day she died. She saw Evan into his grave. She wouldn't have anything to do with the village if she could help it – kept herself to herself after the Polish feller's trial. Still, it was the village's Christian duty to look out for her when she got old and sick and couldn't manage on her own. That's just how it was."

"Why didn't Huw want her to come? That's a bit strange – his own grand-daughter."

"Ah, *nachdi*. It's not for me to say, but between you and me he saw trouble. Evan was their grand-son by a daughter who died when he was but a babi, the father gone off who knew where, and he was always... well, he never had a girl friend, awkward sort of feller he was. But he'd follow Annie round when she used to come down to visit before the war even. Obsessed with her, like. We all noticed. She didn't have time for him at all. It didn't feel right, and Huw knew it. Anyway, when old Huw and Blod passed away quick, one after the other, and there was just the two of them... well, let's say things didn't get any easier."

"So there was just Annie and Evan living together at Bron Felen after the war? That sounds like a recipe for disaster. Why on earth did she stay?"

"Maybe so. I daresay you're right. I don't really know why she stayed. Times weren't the same as now, mind. Prob'ly wouldn't be allowed today, given her age, but we all had difficulties to deal with. We all knew each other, there weren't many from away; people didn't move about like they do now. And if someone acted a bit queer, well we knew them, see, so nothing much ever happened that we couldn't take care of between ourselves."

I knew this was not entirely true, though; that a village couldn't always take care of its own, especially the weak and vulnerable. When I was growing up we all knew, as children, who to avoid. Our parents never said anything directly, all that was needed was a look and a raised eyebrow. We didn't ask why or what, we just accepted the unspoken judgement. Anyone who happened along would intervene if something got nasty; the day had not yet come when passers-by turned their heads and walked on. It wasn't true, of course. But I could not imagine how it must be to live day after day with somebody like Evan. Where anything that happened, happened behind closed doors, in private. Especially a young girl like Annie.

'Oh, Evan was harmless enough,' said Dilwyn. 'There was nothing really, nothing you could put your finger on; if you happened by him in the street or casual like in the pub you would think he was an okay lad, a bit morose maybe, introspective. But he was bad with the animals. You could see it at market, the way he hit the beasts to drive them in the pens. Unnecessary. We didn't like it, but we kept quiet. We all respected Huw and Blod, see, and didn't want to upset them. He was quiet enough apart from that.'

*

I thought about Gordon. Everyone knew Gordon too, or thought they did, his cycling round the roads, whistling and whispering obscenities if he passed you. Everyone scoffed at the thought of his doing anything really bad. Until one night, when he stuffed a wad of his parents' Watchtower magazines doused in petrol through an old couple's letter box, and threw a match in after. Two people died in that fire, and everyone went round shaking their heads saying how it was plain to see he was a bad 'un, and sooner or later something like this was bound to happen, didn't they always say so?

*

Once I breached Dilwyn's defences, the barriers came tumbling down. I can't pretend I wasn't shocked at what I heard. I was. But I was fascinated. There was a strange sense of the pieces of a jigsaw puzzle locking into place.

'You couldn't talk to her anymore,' he said. 'She just looked through you and walked away as though the only reality she could see was what was the inside of her eyeballs. If she ever grunted anything it would be to curse us for betraying her and the Pole.'

He pursed his lips. 'Strange how things change. Hard to imagine. So fast. One night everything was as it always was, and the next all hell broke loose. I'd stayed in the Bell a bit longer, but everyone else had gone home. It was powerful cold and the Hughes brothers had a long way to walk in those conditions, so they left earlier than they might've usually. They only had the feeble little lights on their bikes and though it was full moon there were a lot of clouds flying over it, bringing in the snow. Seems this apparition came screaming and yelling down the Simpsons' driveway and shot poor old Em point blank in the heart with the double barrelled shotgun the gamekeeper always used on the estate.'

'My God! Murder...' In this quiet little village?

'Aye. Anyway, when Morris stood up from Em the murderer, whoever he was, had disappeared back up the driveway. Morris went and raised the hue at the Simpsons'. Got the Mrs up and she called the police and the ambulance, but it was too late by then. Em was past caring, and the feller who'd shot him long gone by the time the bloody police got there. Mind you, it was only old Brian Bryn Bela on his bike. Not much he was good for at the best of times.'

'Who done it, I mean did it, then?' I asked.

'Well they reckoned the Pole. It was him they arrested anyhow. Never really looked for anyone else. He lived at the Simpson's, see, and came back from choir practice after they'd taped the place off, cool as a cucumber, wanting to know what was going on. Just walked up the drive with his bike like nothing had happened.'

'That seems a strange thing to do if you'd just shot someone and then run off,' I observed.

'Mm. But don't forget he was one of them fighter pilots in the war. Nerves of steel. If he hadn't gone back it would've looked worse, wouldn't it? And where could he've run anyway? I s'pose he'd be good at hiding in the woods and living wild, like, but this was Britain, it wasn't the same as Poland. He'd stood out like a sore thumb.'

I was silent, considering what he said. It still sounded an odd thing to do.

'But why did he do it? What was his motive? Had he fallen out with – Em? – or something?' I persisted.

'Nope. Not Emrys. But Evan.' Dilwyn shot me a look I didn't quite catch, and took a puff on his roll-up. 'Everyone knew Evan was 'protective', let's say, of Annie, see; he didn't like this foreign bloke 'messing' with her, as he thought it. He told us he reckoned he'd go back to Poland as soon as it was safe, and leave her. Either that or he'd marry her and they'd all end up living on the farm. He couldn't ever see further than his own backside... What I mean is, he was –

what'd you call it? – parochial, that's the word, and that's what would usually have happened round here. If that happened, he used to say, he Evan was off to Yankee-doodle land, and good riddance to Wales. Good excuse to go. But I thought that was all a bit of a fancy bluff, like."

'Looks like Evan thought there was more to it than their being friends, then? Even if you didn't."

"Well, jealous, he was. Doesn't need rhyme or reason, jealousy, does it? That's why he tried to turn everyone against the Pole, especially since the incident with the dog. Let me tell you, by the time he finished telling it, everyone believed it was him who'd been wronged, and the Pole it was who hated him, not the other way round. It was only me who remembered different. Well, it was only me and old Mrs Evans the Choir mistress who told the judge that – "

"The Pole was tried for the murder, then?"

"Oh, aye. Forgot to say. The others might have thought Evan had it wrong, but they weren't saying. Funny lot – don't mind saying it now they're mostly dead and gone. They didn't like Evan, but they didn't know the Pole. So they prob'ly stood up for Evan by default, like, 'cos they had to live with him the rest of their lives. Leastways, that's all I can think of. I tell you, it fair broke this village apart, this murder. And there's still families who won't speak to each other to this day because of it. Though not so many now…"

I remembered the buggery in the woods that had obsessed me at the start of Fleur's inquest, and how that village in South Wales had been destroyed from the backlash. I recognised the possibility that Dilwyn was right in how he read the situation.

I had to ask. Bron Felen and Annie were exerting a fascination on me I couldn't ignore. "What was Annie like in those days, Dilwyn?" Why was I so fixated with ferreting about for what passed as the truth in a story half a century old? As if I haven't enough to worry about.

'Oh she was a bit shy until she knew you, didn't say much, but she was a good listener and sharp as a tack. Sang like a bird. She used always to be laughing when the Pole was around. We all felt sorry for her when she first came here. She'd lost everything," he sighed, "and then she lost everything all over again. Always wanted to do everything proper. A hard worker, she knocked spots off Evan, the lazy bugger. He wasn't a very nice person, really, even if he was sort of my mate, and I really took against him after what happened. At the trial he played on the fact that she was sweet on the Pole, so it meant nobody listened to what she had to say. Thought she was lying to protect him. Hypocrites, all of 'em. As if they weren't twisting the truth themselves, and for much worse reasons. I still had a fancy for Annie then, myself, see, and I noticed things. Still reckoned I had a chance. Never had the courage to say, and by the time I did it was too late. She'd got spiteful and nasty, so I never spoke to her 'bout how I felt. Looked in now and again. The wife wouldn't've liked it if I'd spent too much of my time down there, but after she died, and Annie was getting on and couldn't go about, me and George used to go and see her near every day. Nobody else from the village bothered – can't be wondered at."

'No, I suppose not. The lady at the post office told me that everyone was scared of her. She said she thought Annie didn't like people and they didn't like her."

"That's about it, aye. She was rude and ungrateful and you'd wait a fortnight of Sundays for her to say thank you for any kindness shown. The kids all took to calling her the Bron Felen witch."

I tried to picture the rosy round face of my own drawing, scowling and furrowed with suspicion and hostility. 'I'm amazed the village still brought electricity, telephone and coal into the place, then. They must've cared something."

"Ah well, you know how folks are. Could happily dance on your grave once you're gone, but while you're still alive can't stand for being told they're acting un-charitable, like..."

Dilwyn stopped suddenly and I looked at him in surprise. With an effort he went on. 'It's no good, I've got to put the story right, doll. It isn't nice, what I've got to say, but it's the truth. It was me, not the village, that got the telephone people to put a phone in, though the Council paid for it, and it was me that got my nephew to dig the ditch for the water pipe from the spring to the house with his new-fangled machinery. I was past doing it myself by then. Believe me, nobody from this village would lift a finger to help her, to this day. Evan the Wern, the milkman, would help with the coal – I couldn't go heaving sacks about like that at my age, and he was a youngster; but only when I asked him, mind. Youngsters don't think about us old ones when they're chasing girls. He never knew Annie, nor cared, so what went before and all the stories about her made no difference to him. You know, she never came out to thank him, not once in all the time he did it. Now I think on it, his family wasn't from round here, they moved over in the eighties sometime from Cwm Nant near Moel Famau. But he married Mavis Thomas from town, and her folk had the dairy. In Church Street it was in those days..."

Dilwyn rumbled on about how he couldn't have let Annie down, the families in the village and who'd married who, and the children that had moved away to live in the cities or go to University. And how he had to stand by Annie. Why was he so exercised about that, I thought. I nodded and made a few encouraging noises, then stopped listening, let the noise flow round. I thought about the old Annie. The pariah. The witch. A plastic bowl under the single brass tap to serve as sink and bathtub. A milkman who had to be asked to bring in buckets of coal and tip them into the big wooden box by the tiny grate to keep her warm, and save her falling over on the icy slope to the coal shed. Something still didn't fit. A piece was missing.

*

"Did I tell you it was me and George that found her?" Dilwyn broke into my thoughts. "We used to have a bit of a walk every day along the old foot-path that went through Bron Felen and see how she was doing. Take care of things. Nobody else much used it and it was never a public right of way, not like it is now. It used to be the path the postman took before they got vans, to get from the fishermen's cottages along Beach Road up to the village."

"I heard she died of hypothermia." I said.

"That's right. Broke a leg she did and stuck outside. We never could figure out why she was out at that time of night in the bitter cold. She had coal in, enough to last a couple of days. It was foolhardy, in that ice, her legs were bad even at the best of times."

I thought about the shed where the coal was kept, and the rusty old oil-drum on its side, built into the shed wall where the gate opened into the garden. Part of a ploughshare with a chain attached was driven into the ground close to its mouth, and I'd tripped over it only yesterday.

"Aye. That's where Evan used to tie up old Pabi; he was a border collie Blod rescued from the last litter his mother had. She was a grand animal, the mother. Obedient? I've never seen any bitch as clever. Old Huw only had to move his head or his arm and she knew just what to do. Pabi was the same, but even more so if you know what I mean. You could almost imagine he could hear what you were thinking. He was like one of the family. But when old Huw died..." Dilwyn shook his head.

"That dog became so vicious he had to be chained up all the time when he wasn't out working with Evan. Many's the time I'd come down, and he'd be skulking in that oil-drum. His kennel. Waiting for you, he was. And when you passed by in a bit of dream maybe, that dog would leap out like a wolf, snarling and foam flying from his mouth, so strong I feared he'd choke himself on that chain. I've had to move pretty fast an' all at times to get out of his way, and Evan used to laugh fit to bust. Lord knows what he did to that dog but he ruined him. Just for that, I found myself starting to dislike him. We'd sat next to each other at school and up till then I'd given him the benefit of the doubt, it's not even as though he needed the dog to guard the place. We were all neighbours and friends and looked out for each other. We had no secrets, and we had nothing anyone would want to steal. What was the dog meant to be protecting?"

No secrets? Who was Dilwyn kidding?

"Was it after the murder, perhaps?" I suggested.

Still I didn't want to let go of the young girl who skipped along the lanes and splashed through the surf, throwing sand dollars and spoot for a dog; the apple-cheeked smiling little round woman of my garden, who would offer a passing walker a cup of tea and a scone. Despite all I'd heard, I knew something else had to have happened. What was it? I had to know. When you're sixteen or seventeen your whole future beckons. You couldn't hold on to things that happened so early, and let them blight your entire life. Could you? I felt sick.

The lurching recognition of my own heart held the possibility of an answer, and I looked in the mirror of my desperation and whispered Annie.

**

185

Like rain on rock

Annie spent the next weeks in a fever of impatience. Her hatred of Evan had by now congealed to a cold contempt, so that he flinched in anticipation of her cold stare when she came into the room, and made a show of being busy at all times. Annie sifted through all the options open to her. To flee was not an option – there was nowhere to go, she was penniless, and there was nobody she trusted to help. She decided the best revenge she could have would be to stay, to endure, and by her very existence and contempt to irritate and grate on Evan's every moment. This decision afforded her some malicious comfort.

It became a rare occasion on which they spent more than a few minutes in each other's presence, and their exchanges were limited to practical remarks about the ewes or the cattle, which ditches needed work, and housekeeping money. Annie's dependence on money from the farm's activity and so, vicariously, on Evan, became almost insupportable, adding to the strain, often bringing it to snapping point. Evan lost no time in escaping Annie's vindictiveness; he found solace of a sort in the company of his old mates in

The Bell of an evening, ensuring he only came back when he knew Annie would have retired to bed.

*

In contrast to its inhabitants, the farm prospered, which was not as strange as might first be thought, as Evan put in extra time and effort outside in his attempts to avoid Annie in and round the house. He undertook repairs and maintenance to buildings that had been falling apart since Taid's death – slates missing, guttering broken or full of debris, and damp percolating through the old walls. Ditches long filled in and overgrown that had caused the lower fields to flood in the winter he cleaned out, filled with stones from the beach, rebuilt stone walls, and cut terraces out of the hillside, which he cleared of the encroaching bracken, and planted with potatoes. Annie, flushed with the energy of mid-term pregnancy, dug and weeded, grafted and pruned, edged and planted in her garden. As the summer drew on the garden burgeoned with lettuces, spinach, peas and beans, marrows and tomatoes.

But for all the work expended in growing the food, by the time late August approached Annie's spirit was drooping and the considerable effort needed to harvest, eat and preserve the glut proved too much. She stubbornly refused to ask Evan for help: the tomatoes split and dropped from the vine to broadcast their pheromones to the wasps; the pigeons took up their positions in the ash trees, beadily eyeing the cabbages the caterpillars left; and the blackbirds scuttled around the feet of the raspberries. Annie's neglect was their good fortune, for she gathered only a fraction, just enough for her alone; what Evan did for food was a matter of indifference to her, and had he starved she would no more have stirred to his succour than she did to the pests' deterrence. More and more often he could be found visiting neighbours when mealtimes came around.

Annie's feelings about her body during this time were ambivalent. She wanted to bear Jan's baby and hoped by some miracle he would be restored to her, but she could not completely quash the lurking despair at the unlikelihood of such a happy outcome. She entered on the ninth month of her pregnancy and it was getting more and more difficult to hide her fattening, no matter how many layers she wore, how tightly she strapped her stomach. The child in her womb kicked for its freedom, and she was fearful the unnatural constraints would harm it. She stayed on the farm, occasionally walking on the beach at dawn or dusk, seeing no-one; Mrs Evans Tyddyn Bach, the choir mistress, accosted Evan in the road one evening and asked why she hadn't been to sing with them for so long, surely she was over the shock of the trial of that young man by now, and singing was bound to lift her spirits. He mumbled,

'She's not well."

When, full of solicitude, she expressed an intention to call on Annie, he rudely put her off, 'She doesn't want interfering busybodies hanging round. She'll do all right if she's left alone."

Steadily, the isolation wrought a permanent change in Annie's personality. Other people, who threatened to break into her soliloquies, she felt as irritations, disturbing the soliloquies in which she talked variously to Jan, a fictitiously sympathetic High Court Judge, and a god-like Lord Marchant. These monologues always naturally tended to the negative, so that Annie was forced to replay them over and over again, altering this fact and that supposition, expanding that and retracting this, until she was satisfied it reeled off the press exactly as she wanted it written. It became forged in her brain so that the words scrolled across the sky in fiery letters, and she could repeat each line like those from a well-rehearsed play. Distractions sent her into a fury; she strode across the field shaking her fists at the sky, or sat sobbing and cursing, screaming at the clods of soil or a startled cow, her voice hoarser and hoarser till nothing emerged but a scratchy cough. Then she became scared at what such paroxysms would do to her unborn child, and clapped her hands to her mouth, the sounds stillborn. A few solitary walkers witnessed these episodes from a distance, and the talk of the village was of her madness. On other occasions, when she spied a person in the distance something verging on panic assaulted her, so that she swivelled her bulk and ran.

She could not forget the villagers' attitudes to Jan and their assumption of his guilt, Dilwyn included, who no longer called in on his way past up the hill, seldom even came that way any more, and she had no energy left for the confrontation she was bound to force if she did not flee. Soon, she stopped even her short excursions on the beach and kept within the boundaries of the farm, then restricted her activities to the house and yard as she grew heavier and the swaddling she tied tight round her to hide her belly made her breathless. Still not a word passed between her and Evan about her being with child.

*

After some weeks and having heard nothing from Mr Simpson, she gave in. She waited one evening until it was dark and braved the walk to the *Plas*, up the drive, to knock on their front door again. Would they notice her condition?

Even if they did it was unimportant, and besides they were not part of local village life. What was it to them? But when she got to the house it was dark, shuttered and locked, and it was clear their absence was for some time to come. Frantic in her need to hear what, if anything, they were doing to help Jan, she waited up for Evan later that night, then burst out, "What's happened up at the Simpsons? I was walking by and the place is all shut up."

Surprised into talking he told her Mr Simpson had been posted abroad for a couple of years. "They laid off the housekeeper and put it all under dust sheets, and old Nobby Penrhos' keeping the garden tidy. Word has it they're thinking of selling up. They never had much to do with the village so it won't be much skin off our noses."

He saw the hopeless crumple of her face at the news and was shocked by an unexpected surge of pity. For Evan, the world revolved round himself and his perception of how things were; other people, if forced to factor them into his plans, he accepted or rejected on the basis of their usefulness, and once that was sucked dry he cast them aside. He couldn't do that with Annie. No idea why.

During the past months, the horror of what his jealousy and hatred had driven him to, and the shame and guilt that little by little lit up his nascent conscience at the barefaced lies he felt forced to sustain in order to preserve his own life, had worried away at him like rain on rock until he was forced to think about Annie's plight. Another person's plight! It had wrought a change, almost imperceptible but growing hidden as the radicles and shoots of a seed underground. He was a childish man, people always said, who had always before reacted by growing smaller in mental stature at the blows life had dealt him, without the insight that would allow him any choices. By dint of the forced relationship he now had with Annie, tied to her psychologically as he was by the nature of the dreadful events that had rolled over them both with the force of an avalanche, he found himself unable to hold at bay the emptiness left by the destruction of something he believed he had once loved. The Annie who had so entranced him with her lively wit and merry ways when she had first come to Bron Felen had retreated into the shadows as if she had never existed. She had been revolted by him and his behaviour and he had struck out with all the negativity at his disposal, reaping her resentment in turn.

The flash of unaccustomed empathy lodged under his ribs, he turned and bolted out into the night where the tears sprang down his cheeks and the well from which they were drawn was bottomless.

**

189

So many answers

Annie wrote to Mr Davies, Jan's barrister. It was a plaintive letter in parts, angry and bewildered in others. Despite all odds she'd believed the truth would hold the day, and couldn't understand why the jury returned the verdict it did. In her eyes, the truth had been betrayed. She spent time composing this so important letter, searching for the right words to enlist his aid, not wanting to alienate him or cast a slur on his professional skills. She wrote her letter in pencil on Basildon Bond economy stationery. It took her several nights of labouring over it with a candle guttering in the holder by her bed.

'Thank you very much for representing Jan. I am of course happy that Jan was not found guilty of murder, but the result is just about the same for me; it has deprived me of the person I loved, for ever,' (and the father of her child – she did not, of course, tell Mr Davies this last) 'and I don't know how I will hold out.'

'The law seems to have thrown common sense out of the window, when one man's biased opinion is taken up as truth by the jury, mostly because it neatly absolves one of their own from possible guilt, and its effect was to feed the prejudices and fears of most of the people who were there. I have lost hope, and all faith in the laws of the land.'

She asked, 'Are there no grounds for appeal to a higher court?' She mentioned Lord Marchant and her request to Mr Simpson, and begged Mr Davies to 'Please enquire on my behalf. You are my last hope.'

To post it she waylaid the postman on the road and handed him the price of a first class stamp.

*

'Dil! Dil! Wait!" He heard her calling, he'd been long expecting it. He wouldn't have come past this way if he'd thought she would see him, except he was in a hurry to get home. He turned to meet her, his face hunted, shocked at her gaunt face, how she'd let herself go, overweight. 'Let's go on a bit, shall we?" She took his arm and gave him a quick look, nodded back to the house. Dilwyn saw a curtain move and Evan's red face retreat inside the gloom.

'You're a stranger. Why haven't you been by?" As if she couldn't guess.

'I – I – didn't want to stir things up with you and Evan, Annie. I've been hearing him going on about it all at the pub, and he's a bitter man. He hasn't forgiven me for what I said in my statement about the dog incident, either."

'You didn't yourself any favours with that. And you betrayed my Jan too, on the stand. Dil, how could you do that? Nobody knew what to believe. I was so angry."

He seemed to shrink, and the look on his face made her say, 'I can't say I blame you, not really. I know you liked him, and it takes someone strong to stand up against folk. You just didn't have it in you. I misjudged. Anyway," briskly, 'the fact I haven't seen you must mean you haven't had any letters for me from Jan, then?"

'Na. Not a one. But it's early days yet..." He trailed off as her face crumpled. She faltered to a halt.

'I can't believe he'd forget me, Dil. He was going to ask me to go to South Africa with him. You heard the letter they read out. He loved me. I don't understand."

She rubbed a hand over her eyes. Dilwyn looked round at the sound of footsteps coming along the path.

'What are you doing here?" a rough voice said. 'You're not welcome. Get where you're going, you nosy bastard, and stop bothering folk."

Evan stood there, his stance threatening. From behind him came a low growl as Pabi, alert to his every mood, heard the aggression and sought to ingratiate himself. "Ah get away with you, you stupid fucker," Evan swung his stick at him and he slunk back a few paces, his growl giving way to a soft whine.

'Now you look here, Evan Williams, I can come and go wherever and whenever I want, and it's not for you to stop me. Besides, I'm talking with Annie, not you, so it's none of your business."

'Stop it, stop it, I can't stand it. As if there hasn't been enough happen without you two squaring up to each other." Annie rounded on them both, silencing them with her ferocity. 'Best say 'bye, Dil'. And you – you just stay out of my way," she hurled at Evan, then turned away and ran off down the path into the wood, leaving the two men standing there, looking uncomfortable, until,

"Aye. Best be off, then."

"Aye. And make sure you shut that gate behind you."

*

She heard nothing from Mr Davies until late September when the post man walked the track up to the farm and popped a letter inside the door when she didn't answer his knock. She hid in the scullery until he had gone. The letter had the address of a London Chambers printed on the flap. She took out a single sheet of expensive watermarked paper.

'Dear Miss Williams,' she read. 'Thank you for your letter regarding Mr Janek Zadzinski.'

She noted the mis-spelling of Jan's name.

It went on, 'I fully appreciate your anxieties, but must advise you that I can find no legal grounds for lodging an appeal. I am gratified that you feel that Mr Zadzynski was ably represented. The letter of the law was adhered to, and the evidence, circumstantial though it may have been, substantial enough to permit the conclusion reached by the jury. This would, I feel, be seen as convincing, and an appeal disallowed. You are of course at liberty to disagree with my opinion and take the matter further personally should you so wish.

'I do not see how I can be of help regarding your suggestions about Lord Marchant, as I feel sure that, with due deference to any political influence he may have, his conscience would not permit him on the basis of a purely personal relationship to interfere with the due processes of the law of this country.

'I am sorry if you find my reply unsatisfactory, but I feel there is nothing further I can do. Please accept my deepest sympathy in your position as a good friend to Mr Zadrinki. I am sure the last few months have been very difficult.

Best wishes for the future. Yours sincerely, Mr Samuel Davies.'

Annie tore the letter into small pieces and burned them on the range, thrusting them deep into the coals with the poker.

**

Watcher and worker

Summer 2004

Two years after that first meeting I confront the Health and Safety men again in the person of their legal advisor. He by now thoroughly dislikes me for not keeping quiet and going away. I stand in a station car-park and listen to him. He can't wait to rub salt in our wounds,

"Of course, everyone involved in the case knows the hospital cocked up on a massive scale," He shrugs with a 'What can I do?' gesture – one that said, to me at any rate, 'What do I care?' "but we have to proceed strictly in accordance with the law, and, as sorry as I am, it is not, in my opinion, in the public interest to prosecute a senior manager," and with that, walks off to get a cup of tea. Well, thanks a bunch! I think.

We sit in the Courtroom and listen to the hospital's guilty plea. Pre-negotiated. Guilty of just one small breach of Health and Safety. Not guilty of negligence, not guilty of the catastrophic failures as per the Coroner's narrative. Of course not. Targets for successful prosecution met, costs kept to a minimum, effort expended negligible, rap on knuckles duly administered. No possibility that the judgment given would force any improvement to standards, or encourage a change in attitude and behaviour in those responsible for the delivery of mental health services. All shake hands, good friends and jolly good company. There is a rustling of papers being put away. All make to leave.

Tony has had enough. He stands up and begs the Court's indulgence.

'It's astounding I have to even ask, but we'd like a public apology from the Board. We'd like to hear them say they're sorry for what happened to our daughter in their care."

An apology? An admission of guilt? More work for the lawyers? The judge turns to Toady, acting for the Board yet again.

'Has the hospital not apologised to Fleur's family yet, Mr Titmarsh?" he asks with a small but definite hint of acerbity. Consternation, mild, breaks out, with much snapping of briefcase locks and coughing. Quick exchanges.

'Er. Hmm. No, it seems not, Your Honour. Although my clients tell me a letter of condolence was sent to the family after Fleur's death."

'Then I think you should discuss with your clients now whether or not they are prepared to offer an apology to the family, here in court today."

After some brief conferring, 'Toady' grinds out, successfully hiding his satisfaction at the prospect of even more litigation, "The board has authorised me to offer an apology to the family, Your Honour," while the row of senior managers blow their noses and rummage in handbags – anything to avoid looking us in the eye.

As we leave the courtroom the bottom feeders descend. We thought we were getting better at this, but how wrong we were. Newspaper editors and television producers have their own agendas, and they rarely coincide with the expectations of those being interviewed. Out of a forty-five minute interview during which we poor mutts were happy we had said exactly what we wanted, the sixty second clip on telly just shows a shot of us blowing our noses and wanly saying we feel 'let down'. A big banner hangs from the sky behind us and says, 'You've been had!' Banana skins litter the pavements.

People say again how happy I must be (that tired old refrain), how I can at long last let go of my anger, my outrage and my frustration. But my heart knew there hadn't been an apology worth a damn, and justice had not been served. Yet again I feel diddled and duped, but this time I know I've run out of others' sympathy. What happens next is solely down to me; the rest of my life hangs in the balance. Can this really be the end of the road?

*

"Here you are, then, *bach*. Not feeling so good?"

A month or so after the court case, and a depression still hangs over me – like the weather, which hasn't helped, continual winds from the North bringing a fine drizzle, and the sky low and overcast. I am pruning Annie's roses but, lethargy overtaking me, have sat down on the old seat under the plum tree. I start out of my reverie, and look up to see Dilwyn, his green cardigan done up wrong so that one edge hangs down, leaning on his stick and gazing at me. It is the first time I've seen him for what seems like the whole summer. His voice is so sympathetic that the tears prick the back of my eyes despite my willing them away.

"Nope. Nothing makes much sense to me any more, Dil."

"Aye, it's a funny thing, the law. You think it's there to winkle out the truth. You think that's what justice is. And then you find out it isn't that at all."

Dilwyn proved to be a sensitive and intelligent friend, and often surprises me with his grasp of the ways of the world. Although he knows I've been away at an important court case, I have never been able to bring myself to tell him about Fleur. It is a relief to be around people who don't know, and who accept me as they find me. Added to that, what I'd suffered was too much for most people to handle – if I told them. So I don't any more. I hate the look that steals into their eyes, the false note that creeps into their voices. The sense of hidden judgment. Dilwyn never pries, and we're able to while away many comfortable hours in this way, silence as he watches me at work, punctured by occasional bursts of conversation. We both understand the flow of wordless dialogue between watcher and worker, and it comforts me. I had spent a childhood sat on the path, watching my father intent at his gardening – each forkful, each toss onto the wheelbarrow, each pruning and planting – we both did them.

Although I find it easier this way, the impulse to blurt out the ugly truth that lurks inside wells up like the urge to be sick, the pain almost tangible. I find if I wait, it sinks back down; and the distraction that comes over me, and that my listener sometimes notices, but not invariably, I can laugh away, 'Thought a sneeze was coming.'

*

"Aye, I know how it is. I've had a couple of brushes with the law myself." He chuckles as I say "What? You, Dil?" in surprise.

"The first time was out in Burma. I told you I was stationed in Burma, did I? A sergeant, I was. One of the lieutenants in my regiment was up in front of a

Court Marshall charged with assaulting the wife of one of the local bigwigs. He was a right bitch, begging your pardon, and we were all hoping he'd be found guilty and thrown in the glasshouse, or worse. Not a chance; rigged from start to finish, just 'cos he was on hand-shake terms with the powers that be. I thought then how the law was a dead loss. Nobody listened to us, the little men. The men who knew.

"The second time – well that was a different kettle of fish. Talk about a farce. And this time it was someone I thought should prob'ly be found innocent. But the verdict, well…" he shakes his head and his mouth draws a grim line. I know who he is talking about.

"Even after all these years when I think on it, it gets my dander up. That's why I still don't have much truck with some folks in the village, it downright disgusted me the way some of them I grew up with behaved. And me too, for that matter," he falters.

As I look enquiringly at him: "The Polish lad as I might've mentioned before." He is not going to relinquish things easily. He turns it aside, indignation colouring his voice.

"What happened in that court fair destroyed her, I can tell you. I still can't forget how they shut her out after. Blamed her for the whole business. Never even lifted a finger to help her when she got ill."

"What happened then, Dil?"

He ponders for a while. Can he trust me? Then in a rush,

"He was accused of murdering one of the Hughes boys on their way home from the pub. Did I already tell you? Aye, can't remember what I've said to who these days. His brother Morris moved away a bit after, went back to Bala where the family came from. None of them round here any more. So I don't s'pose it hurts to say now. It was only by the skin of his teeth the Pole didn't get sent to the gallows, neither. Tore the village apart, it did. That's what I mean – the problem with the truth, see: some folk'll insist it was one way, and some the other. You'll never get 'em to agree. They get so wound up with what's in their head they can't distinguish. And, more like, what they want the truth to be. And me, I never really knew. Depending on what axes're being ground. I reckon the truth's a slippery, twisting thing. You think you've got the big fish you've been after catching in your net and then you look – and all you've got's a bit of a tiddler."

I nod; I couldn't agree more.

"The judge, I remember," Dilwyn continues, my encouragement oil, "was the Right Honorable Gwilym Ap Howell, in his early sixties back then, died not long after I'm told, heart attack. Not surprised. Had his eye fixed on a seat in Parliament. Everyone laughed at him behind his back 'cos he insisted on using the Welsh version of his given name, Powell. Some said, to curry favour with the nationalists round here who hated the English. He didn't speak a word of Welsh though." He pursed his lips. 'I mind he was a short, fat man; had to keep wiping that great red cushiony face of his sweating away under his wig, and the usher, old Tudur Pant, was kept proper busy bringing him glasses of water."

I move to sit on the grass, my back against the knobby trunk of the old apple tree, and Dilwyn lowers himself onto the seat. The tale is underway.

"The whole thing hinged round Morris Hughes. He swore as it was 'the bastard Pole', as he called him, had done it, he'd seen him with his own eyes – and everyone wanted to believe him. Like I said. I told you about the Pole, did I? Aye well, apart from being a foreigner, most of the opinion-makers in the village had him down for a labourer, a servant, proper working class; but when they heard about his father's connections with Lord Marchant – they'd both been industrial designers from before the war and met at some exhibition or other in London – Crystal Palace, I reckon it was – now that's a place I'd like to see, all that glass..." The momentary wistfulness of the frustrated traveler lights his eyes before he resumes his story.

"... there were some red faces, I can tell you, and as how he was a friend of Marchant's son Ronald, being his pal during the war, instructing over at Montford Bridge. Well, the jolt to that notion proper disgruntled 'em. The Cofi civic worthies – them from Caernarfon, that is –" he added for my benefit, 'all in their pride of place in the front rows of the public gallery, I reckon they shuffled their bottoms a fair bit too, when they heard who he really was. I knew, 'cos I'd had a fair few chats with him in the Bell of an evening, but I kept it to myself, like. They said it was old Marchant who paid for the hot shot lawyer he had, down from London – or Mr Simpson up at the *Plas* – we never knew for sure. Though I know old Simpson did get involved, 'cos Nobby – the gardener as was – heard him talking to his missis about it after the trial.

"Anyway, try as the lawyer might to shake his story, old Morris, he wouldn't be moved, and everyone could see he was cutting a dash with the jury. It was a proper drama followed after that, though; made everybody sit up straight. They say the Pole's lawyer strode up the aisle to the back of the court, everyone's head following like a flock of chickens watching a fox, then turned and bellowed right at Morris and asked him to repeat back what he'd said. Well, that was the first crack in the edifice, all right. Morris must have sensed a trap, 'cos all he said was it sounded foreign, and he couldn't say if it was Polish or some other language. He thought he was being clever, see. Then the lawyer wrote on a bit of slate and held it up for everyone to see, and I heard as there were titters springing up round the court like meadow larks from the grass as they took it in, and then everyone starting roaring. He'd only written '*Rech mewn potal* '!"

"Why? What's it mean?" I ask. Dilwyn is cackling loudly and I can't see why.

"It's a bit vulgar, like, but basically, it means a person who's proper useless. Well, who could believe Morris after? All that insisting the murderer was shouting in Polish, and he couldn't even tell Welsh when he heard it! Or couldn't hear more like. Deaf as a post he became later on. Well, the old edifice collapsed with a loud rumble after that, what with one thing and another. But not enough for the jury to find the Pole innocent. That's the point I was trying to make. They all had it in their heads it was the Pole before the poor bloke even stepped into court. 'Cos if it wasn't him, who was it? Easy – it had to be one of us. So no matter what they heard after, he was going to be the one done for it. And for all I know it was him. And the Judge, pompous old fool! Moithering on about circumstantial evidence. He should have kicked the case out of court, or referred it on. But he didn't. Got his own agenda. You can imagine, the reporters had a field day. Not quite as polite as the lawyer – 'cos the headlines the next day read:

Barrister accuses witness in Polish murder case of being 'FART IN A BOTTLE.'

"Begging your pardon..."

After we've both finished laughing and Dilwyn's coughing fit subsides, I suggest a cuppa. We settle ourselves at the kitchen table, and Dilwyn takes up where he left off.

"The worst, or p'raps the best, was when Brian Bryn Bela, the local copper, made a proper pig's trotter of himself, him and his well thumbed notebook. He couldn't hardly read nor write, we knew that from school. He said –" Dilwyn chortles again, and I have to wait for another fit of coughing to subside, "– he said as how he'd only picked up the gun he'd found on the muck heap up by the stables and smudged all the fingerprints! Daft old bugger – well he wasn't that old, but he was old enough to've known better. So that was the end of that, really; the lawyer feller was down that hole so fast, like a ferret after a rabbit; made him out to be proper incompetent. Which he damn well was.

'Same with the footprints. Oh, he had a field day with them. Brian'd followed these footprints he saw coming down the drive in the snow, spaced out like whoever it was had been running, so they were the murderer that's for sure, he thought, and he swore they were the same footprints going back up and out round the back and into the woods. *Nefi blw* – that man was never meant to be a policeman; in the time it took for the plain clothes lot to get there, it fair snowed a blizzard so you couldn't see them no more! And it didn't matter how much he huffed and puffed about them, could've been anybody's! We never found out whose, though I suppose, if you put two and two together, or wanted to more like, it wasn't hard to guess who might've been a likely candidate," he adds. 'Course, the police weren't interested and the court neither, they'd found the perpetrator and packed him off where he couldn't upset anyone round here for a long long time. And that was the end of that."

"Who do you think?"

"Aye well," he gets up stiffly, forestalling any awkward questions with the thump of his stick on the floor. He won't be drawn in. 'Better be off, places to go, things to do."

**

The plum

The garden was at last taking shape. Hours of labour went into it, as I struggled with my grip on reality. I dug over what had been an old vegetable patch and put in more apple trees and perennials. I cleaned and enlarged the little pond in the corner which drained the top of the garden for the frogs and was absurdly pleased to find we had some great crested newts. I replenished what had obviously been a herb garden, and planted rosemary, bay, pennyroyal, ginger and pineapple mint, coltsfoot, hyssop, thyme, marjoram and oregano, rue and meadowsweet, dill and fennel and angelica. I tried to keep the garden's character as far as I could detect it had been in Annie's lifetime; I wanted the garden to be a memorial, as all gardens are to those that labour in them. I wanted to add to her influence, even if her death diminished it.

Surrounding the dilapidated garden shed and lining the path to the house in Spring were the narcissi – jonquils and daffodils. All sizes and hues of cream and yellow, with the beautiful double variety predominant. I never understood why daffodils, along with the leek, were the emblem of Wales until Dilwyn explained, 'Leek in Welsh is '*cenhinen*', doll, and daffodil's the same, *'cenhinen Pedr'* – Peter's leek. Never knew why the 'Peter'. When I was a lad, I used to go and visit an aunt over in the Conwy valley at a place called Llanbedr y Cennin. But I reckon it was the English who wanted the daff to be the symbol for Wales; they didn't like the leek, see, after Saint David told the Welsh to wear leeks on their jerkins into battle and we defeated the Saxons. Smacked a bit too much of the rebel for them, maybe." He peeped at me teasingly. I refused to be drawn.

When the peonies sprang back into life, and the astilbe waved its pink feathery heads, I conceded that Annie had more of a feel for a pretty landscape than I did, and my appreciation of her fleshed and clothed itself in the beauty of 'our' garden. Each revelation set me to wondering anew about what had happened during those long years between the imprisonment of the Pole and her death, for it seemed not to matter how much beauty she cultivated outside, all she showed to others was a mean crabbing spirit and ugly countenance. I was sure the Pole had been her lover despite Dilwyn; this made more sense and helped explain why she'd been so badly affected. Yet, was it possible for that alone to wreak such destruction in a once sunny personality?

Annie's roses, as I thought of them, blossomed from late June well into December that year so balmy was the weather, and perhaps my efforts at pruning helped prolong their flowering. I was surprised when someone in my gardening group told me the oldest living rose was thought to be a thousand years old, and still grew round the Hildesheim Cathedral in Germany. That gave me pause to think. How old were the roses in my garden, then? Perhaps it wasn't Annie who planted them? But it didn't matter because, however old they were, and whoever planted them, they were redolent of Annie's tending and pruning, and she had smelt their perfume and picked them for over half a century. I had been doing the same for only a few months, and already they were becoming 'mine' too. And it was the rose garden that in some large measure initially helped reconcile the stories I was hearing about an Annie who was hating and bitter, to that laughing young woman of my imagination.

The old farmsteads always had an elder, or bore, tree planted nearby and Bron Felen was no exception. I took cuttings and planted a hedge of it on the eastern boundary, looking over at the mountains. Elder was reputed to keep witches away, I knew. Although I couldn't vouch for this, the leaves of an elder are so highly aromatic they are said to make a very effective insect repellant. When my children were little I used to cut and hollow out the soft pith of the smaller branches to make the best whistle pipes of all. The old stories warn against sleeping under an elder tree in case the faery folk enchanted you, but I thought it was more likely that the strong smell of the elder had narcotic properties. But you never know.

No matter how I looked at it, though, the wild plum was a monster. It sent out hard stringy runners in all directions which emerged as gangs of small, tough tree-lets every couple of feet or so – a miniature thuggy forest. We declared war on each other. The more I chopped or strimmed, the more determined it became. When we first opened up the garden, Harry took down one of its offspring that had grown large enough to shade the smaller apple trees and left it as a bare catapult-shaped sculpture to carve as a totem, but for years after it drove out its stubborn pioneering roots and sprouted its defiant leaves.

On the plus side, there were so many plums in the autumn that we couldn't pick them fast enough and the orchard ended up smelling like a brewery. We invited friends and neighbours, and they arrived with baskets and boxes, and still we couldn't keep up. I had damson jam, jelly, chutney and wine enough for three years from one year's worth of harvest. It solved the problem of Christmas presents.

My earlier spooky experience with the plum had faded by now, and the old seat under it, covered now in a thick blanket of ivy had become a dappled resting place on a hot summer's day. I hung six two-inch diameter stainless steel pipes on one of the bigger branches, so a modal melancholy of bells rang out on windy days. Just in front of the seat were the snowdrops, so thick you couldn't see the ground between them. Not that I sat out there much in January. Even though I knew they represented the passing of sorrow, to me they more forcefully represented its coming. I had come across the snowdrops during our first year in the caravan when I walked into the garden and thought at first it had snowed under the old plum, so thickly were they growing. Drifts, carpets, blankets of them. I gasped in shock. I knelt on the ground and ran my hands over their waxy heads. So perfect they were, but I did not pick a single bloom.

"What am I going to do about this plum tree?" I asked Dilwyn. "I can't leave it; I want to put up a swing on the Bramley for my grandchildren, but the plum's killing it."

"Only thing for it is to chop it back a bit, and take out the roots in between."

"I suppose I could. It shouldn't be too hard to returf it, and rescue the snowdrops – I wouldn't want to sacrifice them, they're a feature."

"That's a lot of hard work on your hands there, doll," he said looking at it. "Shall I get that young tackle of a nephew of mine to come and give you a hand?"

"No thanks, Dilwyn. If I take it easy, it'll be OK. I quite like the idea of doing it myself."

Dilwyn decided to come and supervise. The next morning I sat him down on the seat with a mug of tea and set to. "You've got this place looking real nice, fair do's," he said. "Annie was always out here fussing around too, liked sitting on this old seat. She kept it nice in her younger days, but it went to wrack and ruin these last years. Well, I don't feel up to gardening much myself either. I let the youngsters do it these days, they're my knees."

A robin came and eyed me beadily from the hedge, hoping for worms. "Territorial little buggers, robins are. They'll fight to the death, you know," said Dilwyn, noticing. "I've seen 'em rolling over and over on the ground, holding on with their little legs, and trying to blind each other, pecking at their eyes."

"Yes, I know. My Dad was a head gardener. I always remember the robins sitting on his spade. I saw one once dive-bombing a rival, trying to knock him off his perch. I used to spend hours as a kid watching the birds. That's why I won't have a cat here. I never minded mice, and Molly seems to keep the rats away."

"Aye. Jack Russells're champion ratters. Mice're dirty things in the house though. They never stop weeing – make you ill enough if you're not careful."

"When I was little I used to follow our cat about, and when she caught a mouse I'd rush over with a cardboard box and put the mouse in it. I remember one we called Nelson because the cat had clawed out one of its eyes. I kept it in a cage on the living room windowsill for a couple of days, then one morning I came down and it'd gone. Mum and Dad said it had escaped. They told me years later they'd actually killed it and thrown it out. I've always had a soft spot for the little things."

"I didn't know you were brought up in the country, doll. I sort of thought you were a townie."

"I've never lived in a town, except on the edge of one when I was a student. I don't like towns; I can just about handle them for a long weekend. I like not seeing any other houses, and hearing birds, not roaring traffic. I like seeing the stars at night. I didn't have brothers or sisters and spent a lot of time on my own so it doesn't worry me if I don't see other people. Our house wasn't the sort of open house that had kids running round and visitors dropping in at all times. But if I wanted company there were always the two old under-gardeners around who worked with my Dad. I'm surprised they didn't get fed up with me, I used to pester them something awful. Maybe that's why I get on with you, Dil," I joshed.

"I'd time it so I went out round about eleven to catch them in the shed having their tea break. One of them was called Chalky – Chalky White – and he must have been about seventy. Had a bad limp from being in the trenches and a cough you wouldn't believe; he said he'd had a dose of mustard gas, but he was full of all sorts of stories and Dad said you never knew if he was making it up or not. I loved listening to him. He used to bring a thermos of black tea with him, the thermos was stained black as the tea, and so was the enamel mug he kept on a hook in the shed – he never washed it. He always tried to make me drink some, but it was so bitter I spat it out and everyone laughed.

'He had this big pocket knife with a curved blade and he'd get that out and a packet of chaw from his coat pocket, and cut off a wodge of baccy. He'd put it in his mouth straight off the knife, chew away, and then squirt a jet of brown liquid out the door of the shed. He tried to get me to have a go at that too, but Dad stepped in pretty quick.

'He died at home in his sleep, they said, when he was about seventy two, and I was really upset. These days he would have gone to hospital and be told he was dying of cancer of the oesophagus or something just as dreadful."

"Well, they reckon those were the days," said Dilwyn, detecting my disapproving tone, 'but I think it's much better today. We had to be hard, we used ourselves up, and people died a lot younger than they do now with all this new medicine."

"Yes, but what's the point of keeping people alive if all they can do is sit in a nursing home and don't even know what day of the week it is, and can't recognise their own children or grand-children?" I asked.

"Ah, it's all very well for you to think that. We didn't used to have the National Health Service when I was a boy, and it was the old back-cracker over a bale of straw in a barn, or the vet, often enough. We couldn't afford the doctor or the dentist. I remember my da used to take out his own rotten teeth by tying a string round the tooth and the other end to the door handle and then getting one of us kids to slam the door shut. You can't tell me you'd like to go back to those days."

'I think you're having me on, Dilwyn," I laughed.

'No, no, it's true. You ask old George, he'll tell you."

"Well, I do believe everyone should have free healthcare, otherwise I couldn't work in a hospital. And of course I see what a godsend it was for everyone after the war. Care for everyone from the cradle to the grave and all that. But I think it's got now so people just hand responsibility wholesale over to the doctors for every little twinge. And the waiting rooms are chock full of people who've smoked all their lives, or who've just got a bit of a cold. Everyone's scared to death of getting hurt, or getting cold, or wet, or walking more than ten yards from their car. I've seen people on the hills here who can't walk over rough ground any more. And they go down with everything that's going because they sit around all day and eat a load of stodge and wipe every surface with Dettol to kill all the germs – their immune systems are packing up and –"

"You're right there, *bach*," Dilwyn interrupted. "That great-grand-nevvy of mine, young Gwynant, he's only two and he's always ill with something. If you ask me it's the fault of television and all that food out of tins."

"– and what's more the doctors like it that way, that way they're in control – the so-called experts. We're not allowed to be in charge of our own bodies anymore."

"Fair do's, fair do's. Sounds as if you've got something personal happening there, *bach*. I don't want to argue with you."

As we were talking I had been cutting a deep ditch into which I now stood a length of corrugated iron, leaving an inch or two proud. I threw the soil back in around it and stamped it down. I was fed up with myself too for always ranting on and on, and my dissatisfaction with myself was compounded by the vague sense of bodily unease that had been creeping up on me over the last year or so, the difficulty I had in bending down to put my socks on, my reluctance to wear a bikini (not that I ever had, but I wanted to think I could) and the tiredness that would sweep over me in the afternoons. I put it down to middle-age but that didn't help, rather it made me feel more depressed. I avoided scales like the plague, frightened of what they might tell me, and was still able to delude myself, so powerful is denial, that the mirrors that showed my increasing girth were cheap nasty products from a cut-price store, prone to image distortion. Worst of all, although I had given up smoking for a couple of years now, my lungs still felt stuffed with phlegm so that my shortness of breath shouted 'emphysema', and every ache and pain in my upper back I now ascribed to incipient lung cancer. That all too familiar feeling of about to be crushed by some titanic force I couldn't foresee and couldn't avoid.

"Fancy another cuppa, Dil? Let's go in and have it in the kitchen."

While I was making the tea Dilwyn pottered about the kitchen looking at this and that. "Well, look at that! That's the handle Annie had on her bedroom door," he said. "I remember her buying that from old Murph, the tinker at the market."

"Oh, so it was her! I was wondering." I exclaimed. "I just can't seem to get the measure of Annie; it's like there were two of her. The one that sang like an angel and grew flowers and had an eye for nice things – the sensitive young one; and the other one that everybody hated, the nasty old woman. How could someone change so much and for ever?"

"Mm. I know what you mean. I never could make proper sense of it, not really. But like I said, she went a bit peculiar after the Pole got sent to prison for shooting the Hughes boy. I didn't see much of her for months after that, years even, she mostly just sat in the house and Evan would stand in the doorway and shake his head when we asked after her. There's some who thought he should've have had her put in the loony bin but he wasn't hearing any of it, and it wasn't up to us to be interfering. Times were pretty hard for us all. My da was sick and took to his bed about that time, and I was working all the hours God gave me for practically nothing, then going home and taking up the slack. My sisters were pretty good, but I was the only man in the house." He shook his head, remembering.

"We used to talk about it between us at first, but as time went on our own lives took over. Evan would come to The Bell for his pint, ignore me totally, and just say '*Iawn, iawn*', and that was it as far as we were concerned."

We spoke no more of Annie that day as the sun went behind a cloud and the afternoon degenerated into a rain-swept unpleasantness. I drove Dilwyn home and invited him to come to supper one day the next week. He looked apprehensive at the idea, so I thought it might be he was wary of being given something he'd feel bound to eat for politeness' sake, but would hate.

"*Nac ydw*, I'm not at all," he said, "It's just my old tum isn't up to much in the way of meat these days."

"That's OK. We hardly ever eat meat anyway. What do you fancy?"

"I know you'll think it's funny, but I've heard Harry say you do a good curry. I haven't had a good curry since I left the army. I fought in Burma you know, I don't know if I told you."

I had to smile. "You mentioned it a couple of times, Dil. That's great though. Why don't I do a vegetarian curry and you can come and tell us about your Burmese days? It won't be a Burmese curry though. Indian OK?"

"That sounds good. Friday's a good day for me."

"Friday it is. I'll come and pick you up."

**

The devil you know

After work on the Thursday I went shopping in town. I loved the little shops –
Davies the Baker, who made round walnut loaves to order, and whose ovens
infused the shop with warmth and the fragrance of freshly baked bread, which
wafted out onto the street outside; Hughes the Butcher at the farm shop, who
made his own sausages to a family recipe and who could get you mutton, goat
and hare if you asked; the little tailor's shop with old-fashioned suits and jackets
hanging in the dusty window; the hardware shop, whose rails of custom-made
leather belts catered for up to fifty-inch waists these days. And now there was a
sprinkling of family run Indian and Chinese businesses to leaven them, included
Mr Singh's Indian grocery store. I didn't want our characterful high street to
transmogrify into a street full of posh over-priced antique shops and estate
agents; or, worse, gift shops full of plastic rubbish. I'd seen it happen where I'd
grown up – the busy housewives with their baskets, chatting and exchanging
news, who'd wave and ask after your auntie or your old dad – all gone; the
cricket club become the fashionable out-of-town haunt of city commuters with
names like Featherstonehaugh and girlfriends called Jasmine, driving Jags and

MGs, who drank martinis instead of light ale or stout, and who bought their Tudor style second homes from the estate agent on the high street but that was as far as their local patronage went. The council estate at the top of the road still housed families with whom I'd gone to school, but as my mother hadn't let me play with them – the one word 'diddicoys' rendering them unfit for my august company – I really had no friends there, and as soon as I left to go to college it ceased to be home for me.

*

I determined to do Dilwyn proud. I bought okra and cashew nuts, a huge head of cauliflower, asafoetida grains or 'hing', brown cardamoms, fresh ginger, rose water, paneer, butter ghee, and khoa. I had potatoes and onions in store, and spinach still grew in profusion. The poppy and mustard seeds were saved from my own garden, likewise chilies, coriander and flat leaved parsley in the freezer. Haricot beans substituted for the more esoteric pulses for the dhal. Hereford cider, in deference to Dilwyn's favourite tipple, and Anglesey ale for us. This, I vowed, would be a feast to remember.

'I'll go and pick Dil up; he won't want to eat too late at his age," Harry said, and I finished off the khautluma bread, put out the chutneys and pickles, and added the garnishes to the gobi pillau keeping warm in the pressure cooker.

'Now that takes me back a few years," said Dil, sniffing appreciatively as he took his coat off. 'I haven't tasted spicy food like that since I was out in Burma. Ellie wasn't a very adventurous cook, though she was champion at the basics."

'Let's hope it doesn't play havoc with your digestion then, if you're not used to it," said Harry.

'It ought to be okay; if it's not too hot. I was never keen on lots of chili."

I hastened to reassure him. The kitchen smelled wonderful, pervaded by a multitude of aromas, which, had they been colours, would have been a rainbow stretching from the cooker to the nostrils. When I thought of the women in the villages pounding their spices and husking the rice, setting out the paneer to drip, tending the fires, day after day, year after year, I was ashamed of the mod-cons in my modern kitchen that reduced food to almost an afterthought, hunger satiated at the flick of a switch – but not so ashamed that I refused the blenders and grinders that made cooking so easy; in fact I had a penchant for kitchen gadgets.

To my immense satisfaction, Dilwyn ate everything put in front of him with relish and when we were ensconced in arm chairs round the fireplace the talk naturally turned to Bron Felen in the old days, and Annie. Dilwyn had left the story off after her Pole got sent to prison, and although I knew of his assiduous attendance on her in the latter part of her life I knew nothing about the intervening years.

"I saw her out and about again one day in the spring of 1948," he picked up the thread. "I remember that because my da had just died and we'd had his funeral down at the church. Lovely, it was; full of daffs. She was walking along the beach picking up pebbles and shells and stuff when we came out of the church yard. I was about to shout and ask how she was, but she took one look, then turned her back and scurried off. Scuttled, she did. I tell you, the words just froze in my throat and I stood there like I was paralysed until someone shook my arm. So thin – like a skeleton – and she'd been pretty stocky before. It felt as though someone'd poured a bucket of cold water over me, the hairs stood up on the back of my neck and I had the goose bumps. Something about the way she looked, all hunched up and shifty, and that quick little scuffling walk. She was only eighteen or nineteen, yet you would've thought she was in her sixties."

The image of Annie in my mind stirred like a creature poked with a stick from a deep sleep in a hedge bottom. I didn't know if it was friendly or hostile, but I held on. There was something here; it pricked the edges of my remembering. I hunted for it. I saw a shy quirky smile; then a white face and hunched shoulders on the edge of a seat. I threw the memory away as if bitten. My heart thumped and my stomach clenched and it was all I could do to sit there, holding my drink. Roughly I seized the memory and shoved it deep in a drawer, ramming 'Would you like another drink, Dil?' and 'Ooh, it's getting chilly, I'll stick some wood on the fire' on top. Filling the moment with distraction; or maybe returning to the moment, the here and now. Until my breath slowed and my heart returned to normal. I thought of Aldous Huxley's 'Island' again, with those infuriating birds cawing 'Here and now! Here and now!' all over the place. Perhaps I'd missed something when I'd read it as a teenager.

Dilwyn carried on oblivious.

"Well, after that, I took to avoiding the path through Bron Felen. My job changed and I didn't need to go that way any more, besides I'd had enough of her to tell the truth. Too peculiar like, and any thoughts I might have had of asking her to marry me went right out of my head. No use crying over spilt milk: selfish little sods youngsters are. And anyway this other girl was catching my eye by then, though nothing came of that either. Then I met Ellie. She was

George's sister-in-law from Manchester and we had a good marriage till she died. Twenty years back now." He shook his head in wonder, paused to take a draught from his glass, and I caught a dampness in his eye.

'Do you have any children, Dil?" I asked. I had never heard him refer to any.

'Na. Can't say I really wanted any. Ellie didn't mind – she came from a big Catholic family, see, and I reckon she just wanted a bit of peace and quiet. I'd seen the trouble kids always seemed to bring folk, and I couldn't stand the bawling racket they made. I can't now either and I've to get up and leave wherever I am if one of 'em starts up."

'Oh well, they're not everybody's cup of tea," I remarked lightly.

'What must it've been like for Evan and Annie all those years here together?" I wondered. 'I still can't get a grip on why she stayed, when she must've hated Evan so much."

"Aye. Doesn't make sense, I know. You know she'd this bee in her bonnet that he'd had something to do with Em Hughes' shooting? Maybe he did at that, and I think she was right – but there was no proof. I reckon straight after the trial Annie was too upset to even notice him. He used to grumble to us he had to fend for himself, Annie did nothing for him at home. Besides, in those days folk used to accommodate strange ways of living more easily, seems to me. People didn't used to go barging into folk's homes and telling them they couldn't do this or that like they do now. There's tales I could tell you about folk up in the valleys round Caernarfon that'd fair shock you."

'I suppose so –" I said doubtfully.

"Anyway the world'd changed by then and we were heading for the fifties. There wasn't so much work out there for the girls, what with the lads coming back from all over the shop. I remember there was quite a fuss with the land-girls and factory girls who were laid off; they'd got used to earning a bob or two. Perhaps she didn't feel up to starting off new somewhere else. Better the devil you know."

Dilwyn paused to take another swallow of his cider. Once the alcohol loosened his tongue he was difficult to stop.

"Talking about queer folk, there was a lad round here, back about thirty years; when he went to school all he did was bark. Grown up with the farm dogs for company all day. His parents never spoke to each other, nor him, and if you called in, like I had to from time to time selling feedstuff as I was, the wife, Myf, would hide in another room. Old Selwyn'd shout, 'Tea' and she'd come out and put the kettle on but always kept her back turned. He never said anything else to her ever, over all the years I called there, and she never answered if I spoke to her. Selwyn could speak, monosyllabic, but I often wondered if she was a mute. They just treated the lad like he was one of the dogs, didn't know any better. Shocking, but none of us would've dreamt of interfering in other folk's lives."

"What happened to the son?" I asked.

"Oh, the school brought in all sorts of busybodies so I heard – Social Services and the like – and he learnt to talk OK in the end. He was always 'different', but last I heard he'd joined the army and was off in Northern Ireland."

*

We were out in the garden the next day, finishing the area under the Bramley where the swing would go.

"Oh, by the way, I meant to tell you last night about this old guy who turned up here when we'd just moved into the caravan." I said. The penny had finally dropped. "What you said about the trial the other day reminded me. He was about your age and had a foreign accent – said he'd worked at the Simpsons just after the war –"

"*Diawl* –"

"Mm! I think it was Annie's Polish friend. I never thought to ask his name though."

"I forget his name now –"

"What happened to him, then, Dil? You said he got sent to prison, why didn't he and Annie keep in touch? It can't have been that hard. And for him to come back looking for her after all these years... She obviously meant a lot to him."

Dilwyn shuffled his feet in the loose soil and reddened. "I've never told anyone this. And I can't hardly bear to tell you, doll, but you seem to... I don't know... feel kindly to her. Annie, I mean." He sighed. "Maybe you'll understand me too. Before he was taken away, Annie asked me to arrange through my cousin who was one of the prison officers in the local nick, for him to write to her care of my address. No good letters going direct to Annie, and Evan blowing his top."

He looked up and I swear I saw tears in his eyes. "I only wanted to protect her, so when I got the letters from the prison in Manchester and later on down south, well I – I – I burnt them... I told her none ever came, and after a while they stopped."

He appealed to me. "She was hurting so badly and he was sent down for life. What sort of chance would that've given her? I would never've done anything to hurt her. I'd've married her myself, I told you, but she went all peculiar... Oh it's no good. The truth is, I knew they were lovers. And it explained everything.

Evan was right. But I was still sweet on Annie and thought I might have a chance yet. I didn't do it from noble motives or anything like that. It was just plain jealousy, no better'n Evan, and hoping to get something for myself."

'Oh, Dil –"

'I've lived with that all my life, and it's gnawed away inside of me like a rat. Wondering if she'd've been happy if I hadn't been so selfish. A guilty conscience isn't something to live with for too long, it poisons something in you. I don't know if it'll be any better now I've told you. I left it all too late. I could never bring myself to tell Annie..."

I sat down next to him and patted his knee. All those years. I wondered if the rest of my life too would pass in regretting, full of guilt, rancorous and hating; such a thought had never really clothed itself in such colours and paraded itself in front of me before.

'I don't think you can ever know what's going on in someone else's head." I tried to comfort us both. "They construct their own prison out of their own fears, and you can't rescue them from it. They don't even think they're in a prison, it's what they call 'normality'. Don't be too hard on yourself, Dil. Pointless now. You don't want to die a sad old man, do you?"

He shrugged. 'I wanted to die when she did, you know. Annie, I mean."

I nodded; I, of all people, did know. He was, after all, one of that global company. I felt the droop of him as I put my arm round his shoulders, then he rallied, pulled them back, looked at me with his rheumy sad eyes, forced a small smile, 'But life goes on, doesn't it? And we've got this swing to put up, haven't we, cariad?"

*

I had intended to double dig the whole patch where the plum babies grew and pull out all the severed roots – I didn't know if they would have enough vigour to root once detached from their parent, but was not going to take any chances. Because I hadn't been feeling too good for the past few weeks, I took care to rest in between every few spadefuls, leaning on the handle to catch my breath and watching the horses prance in the field. A chattering sounded in the apple tree above me and Dilwyn, my self-appointed and ever faithful gardening consultant, gripped my arm and whispered,

'Shh. Look up slowly."

On a branch perched a little squirrel, tawny and tatty-tailed, staring down at us. When she saw us looking she jumped up and down and stamped her feet with a cross chitter. She was telling us off for trespassing in her back yard;

I could see her quivering with indignation. We both burst out laughing and she fled along the branch and disappeared in a flicker into the ash tree in the hedge.

I went back to my digging and suddenly my spade clinked against something hard. I got under it and levered it out, and found myself staring at fragments of rotting wood – and a tiny human skull. The ivory was discoloured and pitted, the nasal cartilage a fragile echo of flower buds. I slowly reached down and picked it up. It fitted into the palm of my hand, and I could see from the open posterior fontanels it was the skull of a newly born infant. Dilwyn was chatting away about something, he hadn't looked down yet, was still looking up for the vanished squirrel, and his voice receded into the distance. As I felt my legs start to give, I sank down on my knees and started scrabbling around in the partially loosened soil for whatever else was buried there. The soil was as cold and clammy as I suddenly was; I tore at it with my fingernails and unearthed what remained of a tiny skeleton, shreds of some material-like substance adhering to it, with the plum rootlets wound round and through the bones forcing me to pull and tear.

'*Iesu mawr!* What in God's name is that?" Dilwyn croaked.

'Shh." A breeze passed through the orchard and the tubular bells hanging from the plum shivered and sent forth a soft silver melody. I wrapped my arms round my own shivering body and sat back on my heels on the wet earth, staring at the bones. We didn't say a word to each other. At length I got up and fetched a hand-fork and garden sieve, and excavated further afield. The earth here was compacted, and composed of a smooth grey clay, and the medusa-like roots from the plum had drunk all the moisture. I put aside all I found – the tiny bones of the hands and feet, the small bones in the neck, and the vertebrae, were mostly missing – arranged them carefully until we were staring at the skeleton of a tiny infant, not forty centimetres long.

I hoisted myself to my feet, understanding dawning at what I had unearthed, an uncomfortable feeling of sacrilege at the accidental exhumation. Rummaging through the containers in my shed I came across a stout metal box with a lid that would do the trick, and lining it with sacking I carefully placed the bones inside. We both heaved a sigh as I shut the lid.

'So that's what it was all about," Dilwyn said slowly, his thoughts on the same track as mine. "A *babi*. That would explain a lot." He turned to me, "The only people who lived here in the last eighty, no, ninety years, was the Williams. It can't have been old Blod's, she was already in her seventies when Annie was evacuated here, past child-bearing by more than twenty years. If it was her, those bones'd have to be a hundred years old now. Could they be as old as that, the bones, d'you think?"

I shook my head in ignorance. I'd have to do some finding out. For the time being I didn't want our discovery to be common knowledge. Someone had buried the infant here not wanting anyone to know about it, and there would be time enough to think further when we knew more.

'I'll go and see the pathologist at the hospital and pick her brains, she ought to know about decomposition of human remains. I can say I'm doing some research. I'm sure it depends on all sorts of things. I'll look on the internet too... I don't think it's a good idea to tell anyone else about this though, Dil. For the moment. What do you think?"

Dilwyn was staring at the box as though it held his doom. He shook his head. 'Not if it's what I think it is, I won't tell a soul. Poor thing, poor, poor thing."

**

Scarlet as her hair

It was difficult to ascertain anything for certain about the age of the bones without subjecting them to forensic scrutiny, which we decided was too difficult, and moreover too disrespectful given what we suspected. More to the point, although we didn't say this, we didn't want to get involved with any authorities; neither of us had reason to trust them. And who knew what hoo-ha they'd stir up. By dint of much careful research on the internet, however, into such arcane subjects as 'taphonomy' (the study of decomposition), and involving soil types, depth, temperature and humidity, I established to my and Dilwyn's satisfaction that the interval between interment and our finding the skeleton had to be within fifty to seventy-five years, taking us back to the thirties or forties, and far too late for Blod. The scraps of material with the body I knew were hessian and Harry said the rotten wood was oak.

What to do next? Harry was no use. He just threw his hands up when I told him what Dilwyn and I thought. 'I'm not getting involved, Sarah. I'm sure it's breaking the law. If you want to, fine. Go ahead,' and turned back to his sawing and hammering.

Everything I had learned about Annie led me to feel strongly protective of her, and as the tragedy of her life unfolded, what I wanted was to lay her ghost to rest, above all to let her secret lie. I went up to Dilwyn's house.

'She suffered enough, Dil, and to have strangers pawing through it all, shaking their heads with sanctimonious disapproval, invoking laws that have nothing to do with anyone still living, and disturbing the dead... Well, I don't know what you think but it's anathema to me."

I took his agreement as given. He hadn't come down since the unearthing of the bones, but he'd told me enough to guess at a strong element of guilt, or shame, within any grief and shock he might also have felt, and I worried he would go downhill to his own grave as a result of our discovery.

As I leant on the gate in the evenings looking at the breath-taking sunsets of the high pressure weather pattern we were enjoying, watching the blood red spread over the wet sands below, I became convinced the laying to rest of the bones would be synchronous with my own recovery – and Dilwyn's. I thought it might bring some peace – to everyone. Over the years, Annie and I had morphed, in spirit at least. I was the guardian of the well-being of her soul, even though, pragmatically, I scoffed at such a notion.

There remained one more ritual to perform. I went and banged on Dilwyn's door again, and had another word with him.

*

Tylluan came as soon as summoned, reminding me again of a perky little sparrow with the tilt of her head and her shiny black eyes, and the way she chirruped when she spoke. She nodded furiously when I told her about the bones – without doubt, the spirit needed to be put to rest. She did not say whose. She was pleased when I asked her to conduct a small ceremony.

The three of us stood round the small deep hole Dilwyn had dug. He had insisted he perform this last act even though I feared he might collapse from the exertion. In a story the snowflakes would be gently falling, a robin would be hopping nearby, and we would smile sadly as the little box was laid to rest in the cold earth. Reality had its own way of dealing with romanticism, I thought, as the icy wind threw hard spicules of sleet in our faces, and the ground became mud. The anti-cyclone that had persisted for nearly two weeks had suddenly given way to polar weather conditions of vicious intensity. It was difficult to move without slipping and sliding. I went to get some sacking to stand on.

My atheism prevented me from countenancing any rites that assumed a belief in an afterlife or a god of the Judeo-Christian-Islamic variety. Dilwyn didn't care one way or the other. The ground we were standing on was saturated with the animistic Celts, with their beliefs in the gods of nature, especially streams and trees. The apple and plum in the orchard would be now, I felt, benevolent guardians. We had appeased them. I had wrapped the bones carefully in a blue linen tablecloth, and packed them into a rough-glazed pottery urn my son had brought back from one of his travels. Into the folds of the cloth I slipped a poem I had written, and a sprig of rosemary, then sealed the top with beeswax from my hives.

Tylluan took the pot and placed it in the hole. I shovelled soil on top and we each planted handfuls of the little bulbs that would be snowdrops next winter. Tylluan invoked the four cardinal points, the Earth, Air, Fire and Water that comprised the stuff of the universe and persisted in burning aromatic herbs as purification although it was pretty pointless, the wind snatched it all away in an instant. The circle was closed.

I cast an anxious eye towards Dilwyn, but I needn't have worried – he stood there his eyes glued on Tylluan as her bright red hair, the colour of rowan berries, whipped in all directions, and her flowerpot tossed, and she skipped about like a young thing. I caught his eye, and his cheeks went scarlet as her hair.

**

Path of least horror

Autumn 1947

That first Friday of October 1947 is a date forever emblazoned in Evan's mind. He returns home from his stint at The Bell to find Annie still in the kitchen, which is unusual for she tends to go to bed by dark. The fire is blazing away and a flare of apprehension passes through him. He keeps to the doorway while he looks around warily for what might be wrong. It could be anything – she is beyond him these days. At her feet he sees a heap of rags she is dropping onto the coals one by one with the laundry tongs. She does not turn round at his startled exclamation, continues to sit in Nain's old wooden chair rocking backwards and forwards, while the rags burn. His nostrils flare as he smells the burning reminiscent of slaughterhouse waste, the iron stench of blood. It is a few seconds before he takes in that it is Annie herself who is 'wrong'. She is strangely withered, a deflated balloon, disheveled, her hair matted and stuck damply to her head. He peers around but can't find what he looks for.

He whispers, "You've had the *babi*? Where is it?" Apart from a slight hunching of her neck into her shoulders, she shows no sign of having heard him. "Where's the *babi*, damn you, Annie?" he shouts now, fearful of her unhearing emptiness.

For answer, she raises an arm and points towards a corner, her gaze rapt on the flames dancing in the grate. He looks over to where she points, and sees an old Hessian sack. He steps across the space between, and pokes it gingerly, fearfully, with his foot. There is something small and yielding inside. He pulls it open. The baby stares blankly at him, unblinking. He staggers backwards in his surprise, tripping over the fire irons, which fall with a shattering crash in the hearth, and cracks his head on the range. Annie feeds another rag onto the fire. Evan pulls himself shakily to his feet, rubs his head, his eyes, stares at the tiny form, and slowly his numbed brain registers the unnatural stillness, the angle of the fragile stalk of a neck.

"*Iesu grist!* What have you done? What have you done?!" he shrieks. He turns and grabs Annie by the shoulder, shakes her. His voice comes high and loud, a childish falsetto in his horror, the breath rasping through the stricture in his throat, "You've *blŵdi* killed it! You've gone and *blŵdi* killed it! You must be mad! Hasn't there been enough madness for us all? What do we do now? You'll have us all in jail..."

Annie shrinks away at this, shrugs his hand off. She still hasn't looked away from the fire. He falls silent, his hands fall nerveless to his sides, the only sound his hammering heart in his ears. No! She wouldn't, she couldn't. Surely not.

Now she slowly raises her head, straightens, and looks straight at him. Is that triumph he sees flickering in her eyes, or the flames? Then it is gone, and she slumps again. Turns back to what she is doing.

"Nothing. There is nothing to be done. Bury it," she says simply.

She stands and watches, her face cold and hard, the bones stretching the soft ivory overlay of her skin, the freckles a sickly yellow spray across her nose, as Evan lays the little wooden box in the hole he has dug where she pointed, and throws the earth on top. He wallops the soil flat with the back of the spade, once, twice, then walks away. Not a word is spoken.

She plants snowdrops taken from the woods. Stooped and intent beneath the plum tree, she places each delicate bulb, scores and scores of them, carefully in the prepared holes made with a dibber and rakes the soil over. She stands there as a shower of hard little dessicated damsons falls to the ground in a sudden gust of wind. A buzzard circles silently high above, its sharp eyes searching; the old horse crops the grass in the field with his broken teeth.

Evan knows himself to be a broken man. He looks through the eyes of others, to see the years of carping, whining, the little man he has been. That he has brought another being to this pass, that his treachery, his jealousy, his hatred gave rise to such a horror – it is hardly to be borne.

They are down-to-earth people, they go about the daily chores as usual – the cow must be milked, the ewes tailed, the hedges trimmed and hay cut and carted. Annie does not speak a word, and Evan weeps silently when no-one is looking. He is smaller, softer somehow, the bitterness slowly draining out through the holes the events of the past year have pierced in the fabric of his being.

Gradually the ripples calm and die away until there is nothing on the surface to mark the thrown stone.

*

As the weeks, then months passed, the killing of the baby – the sole act she considered to have the power to steer her life down a path of least horror – created a void which sucked in the fluttering remnants of her energy and spirit, until the slightest attempt at gardening, even walking, left her breathless and tearful. As the years turned, so she turned her head dispiritedly away from the land with its demands. The onions bolted and threw up flower stems, becoming hard and inedible; and the potatoes, carelessly exposed to light, became little crucibles of green poison. Spring came and the peas and beans that Evan sowed became the scalloped prey of the busy weevils. Summer brought the carrot flies swarming in, clouds of minuscule locusts, leaving red blotches on the leaves and runnels through the roots, which rotted and turned to orange slush. With early autumn the cabbages were larder for hordes of bright green caterpillars and their dark green droppings of masticated chlorophyll, all they left were lacework veins; and no matter what the season, the slugs and snails that lurked in the damp dark recesses of the garden during the day glided out at night and mowed the lettuces and other tiny green shoots before they did more than show their primary leaves, the only evidence the silvery trails that wove their patterns over the black tilth.

'I'm sure I saw some of that copper mix in the shed. Better to spray the spuds before we get blight, isn't it?' Evan would blurt, forced into speaking by his vexation at seeing his own labour going to waste – he had ploughed the terraces in the bank behind and sown them with potatoes to feed themselves along with the cattle and sheep.

'I'll do it tomorrow, plenty of time, don't rush me," she'd answer testily, annoyed at being pulled from her state of trance-like apathy by such quotidian demands.

"The carrots need something put round before the fly gets in 'em," he would persist.

'I told you! I'll do it when I've got time, what with the chicks and the milking and everything in the house. You do it if it bothers you," was her sharp riposte.

Somehow the days went by and every time she thought to rouse herself to go out to do one of the jobs in the garden, something equally strong inside of her resisted, rendered her either cross and impatient with the futility of it all, or full of dismay and a sinking reluctance. She hated the garden – smug, taunting, knowing the rightfulness of what it gave birth to – the new life in the setting of fruits and seeds, the swelling and then the collapsing – job done. And what it held under the earth. The garden would go on into the future, but she had no future without Jan and the baby.

The sight of the great wild plum with its heavy secret bending under its crop with their misty bloom, and the sense of waste in their drop, waste that had not even registered on the outer margins of his radar before, so infuriated Evan that he dared ask the women from the village to come down and gather the purple fruit for jam and chutney, his excuse being Annie's 'wasting sickness'. And, their curiosity getting the better of them, for a few hours the orchard was full of chattering and sharp glances. At the end of the day they flounced off with their buckets declaring their intention never to return in the face of Annie's cold disdain Such rudeness!

Annie thought, Well, bugger off. No loss to me.

The Bramley, that co-conspirator, let its apples fall and rot prematurely on the ground as canker and other diseases gained a hold; the buddleia puffed up like a prideful king on his throne, so round, so magnificent it completely overwhelmed the small pig-snouted apple below the shed where they kept the tools, and which Evan maintained, refelting the roof boards to keep out the worst of the weather. The snowberry crept out across the lawn; the wild cherry and hazel hedge so clogged the ditch with their roots that the southern uphill end of the garden became waterlogged most of the year round. The ash heap grew and sank, grew and sank. The privet hedge threw itself into an unrestrained middle-aged spread so that even standing on a ladder with long handled shears it was impossible to reach the middle, the end result being a strange leafy Mohican-style hair cut; rabbit, hare and pheasant trails wound through its base on secret paths.

Evan added the gardening to his growing list of tasks, and nobody in the village recognised, in the figure that worked on in the failing light until it was impossible to see, the old Evan, who would drop his work like a shot to go ferreting, stand gossiping at the gate for hours with a passer-by, prop up the bar in the Bell with his pint, and cuss the animals to perdition with their ever-present need of his attention.

The following winter was mild and wet, which was a relief to all. But in February a cold spell set in as bone-cracking as that of the previous year. Annie took long solitary walks along the beach, picking amongst the icy flotsam and jetsam that the tide deposited high up in the dunes for the pale, smooth drift wood in myriad shapes and sizes – spoons, snakes, clubs, and, once, the curious elongated head of a melancholy greyhound with the wind of his passage blowing his ears behind and his yearning jaws reaching for the tape.

When Evan was finally driven inside by the cold or the dark he found the cottage strewn with this strange collection – hanging from picture hooks, swinging in the inglenook, inserted into gaps between the stones of the walls, nailed above the doors and windows, on ledges and steps. He would lower himself into the high-backed wooden settle, placed so as to protect him from the chill draughts the range sucked in from the nether regions of the building, and stare about with frightened fascination. He half expected to find bones hidden in the rafters, a thing he had heard tell the witch doctors in Africa did.

As suddenly as the thaw, her obsession with driftwood disappeared, to be replaced by jars, pots, tins and vases, all manner of receptacles, filled to bursting with fragmites' stately seedheads, paper thin honesty, and bulrushes, that rustled as they passed, on the steps and stairs, on the windowsills blotting out the meagre light through the dusty panes. Annie had to bring the dead outside, inside.

The house accumulated dust and the cobwebs gathered and hung in the eaves, the mice dared to venture across the floors to nibble crumbs, and woodlice rolled into grey metallic balls in the cracks of the window frames.

Evan felled trees, chopped the wood and piled it in stacks in the fireplace; he oiled and sharpened the blades on the lawn mower and gardening shears; he carted muck for the vegetable patch; raked leaves and stored them in wire cages. He made cups of tea and placed them on the table by Annie's elbow as she sewed, or in the hearth before bedtime. Although his heart was withered from the evil he knew he'd done, by his actions he sought to repair and mend, in the timid rough duty he showed his cousin.

The only conversation he enjoyed was on market days and the rare night he now ventured into The Bell. Even The Bell's charms waned as the new publican remodelled the bars and introduced gassy mass-produced beers that kept him awake, farting and burping into the night, and the time came when he hardly bothered unless pestered by one of his erstwhile mates to make a four for a game of dominoes.

He at least slept well, being exhausted in both body and mind, while Annie, impaled by her dawning sense of the terrible wrong she had done, spent the nights frightened of sleep and the dreams it brought. She grew thin and feverish. Her eyes were puffy and ringed with blue bruises.

After tossing and turning hotly one night, she fell into a restless tossing sleep, in which she dreamt she was sitting on a bench in a public gardens, holding the leash of a velvety beige puppy she had just bought and named Maya, laughing at its foolish attempts to catch its own tail which it could see twitching out of the corner of its eye. An old stooped man with a Malacca cane crossed over the grass and lowered himself carefully onto the bench next to her, insensitive to her body language to ward off his approach. After some minutes, he turned towards her and asked the name of the puppy.

'I used to have a dog after my wife died. Long, long ago now, but I still miss it. A dog's company's like nothing else," he reminisced in a soft, shy voice.

'I miss my wife too, of course –" His smile was sad.

'She's called Maya," she told him, ashamed at her shrinking from this lonely old man.

"Ah, Maia, the goddess of spring and of growth. The loveliest star in the constellation of Pleiades. When I was in Egypt with my family, I studied the stars – such clear nights in the desert, you could see every twinkle. Not like here in the West of Wales, where it is a rare good day when you can see the sky at night – if you take my meaning," he smiled at his own unintended humour.

'Egypt?" Despite her deep-felt reluctance, she was caught by the snare he set so cunningly.

'My mother was married to a naval officer posted in Alexandria after the Khedive was put in power, and I spent most of my younger years in a villa on the Mediterranean coast. So beautiful. The desert is so clean and pure, the wind blows and all the ugliness is hidden beneath the sands. That's where I met my wife, she was Egyptian – " He broke off and stared across the town at the hills in the distance. Annie turned and looked too, and the hills were misty, dream-like.

"Ever since she was killed, I've been looking for the answer. You know how it is, I can tell – the answer to life and death, the only question worth thinking about. I became obsessed; I studied all the magic and religions of the world for I believed the answer lay there. I learned to charm snakes in Egypt, to climb a rope in India, the potions which turn people into the undead in Haiti, I visited Dracula's castle in Rumania. I joined up with the Great Beast, believing him to be the greatest magician there ever was –"

"What's – who's – the Great Beast?" Annie interrupted.

"A man called Crowley, Aleister Crowley. Perhaps you have not heard of him even. He died, just last year. But he couldn't help either, living or dead. I'm too old and tired now, and I retired to this part of the world where I was born, my roots. We tend to dismiss the importance of our roots when we are younger." He sighed and turned his rheumy eyes to her.

"What a fool I was. All those years, dashing from pillar to post, here and there, this guru or teacher, that cult, those rituals, the dark and the light, the good and the bad. Oh, I learned many, many answers. So many answers I've forgotten most of them now. But never did I learn the right answer. The answer, the only answer I wanted. I wanted to bring her back you see, to restore her to me, to break the boundary between life and death." He shook his head and fell silent.

"Oh well, time for me to go home. It's been nice talking to you. I hope I've not bored you. Good day, my dear, and don't forget – we cannot be given the answer however much we wish for it."

He hoisted himself to his feet with his stick and raised his hat to Annie, who sat there in the sunshine feeling the chill run through her veins. His smile was kindly as he nodded goodbye and made his way slowly back across the grass, until he passed behind a big elm and was gone.

The dream settled in her soul. Although she lost fragments and details over time, the feeling of wisdom imparted comforted her during the times of anguish when she relived her loss.

*

One day in the summer they are trotting past the Simpsons' as a white Jaguar sports saloon turns in and roars up the driveway. Out climbs Mrs Simpson, gay in a striped dress and large sunhat. She waves to Annie who does not wave back, does not even turn her head.

Annie is sweeping the floor the next morning when there is a knock on the door, and on opening it Mrs Simpson is standing there.

"Annie, my dear. I thought I'd call in and see how you were. We just got back last week from Mr Simpson's posting. How are you?" When Annie frowns a grudging "All right," and keeps her standing on the step, she falters.

'I was wondering if you heard from Janek?' Annie still stands there silently, one hand on the latch, the other gripping the door jamb, and Mrs Simpson rushes on, 'Mr Simpson did write as he promised to ask Lord Marchant to help, before we left. It took a long time, but we heard he was going to be repatriated back home to Poland. We thought you would have heard from him by now – oh, my dear –' as Annie's face slowly crumpled, 'we thought –' She steps back as Annie straightens up, her face working with disbelief and anger,

'You thought? You thought?" she spits. 'No-one never thought, that's the trouble. Repatriated? That's the last thing that should've happened. Sent to his death, more like. You must've known what happened to those who went back? As if he hadn't suffered enough, his family all murdered, treated like a traitor and murderer himself by the ruddy Welsh, and then to get sent back to the Russians –" She stopped, choking on her fury. 'I suppose you want me to thank you. Well, I don't. And no, I haven't heard from him, nor I wouldn't expect to now, dear God in heaven!" Her voice rises as the unaccustomed blasphemy trips off her tongue. 'I don't believe in no God,' she thought, 'and never will.' She steps back inside and slams the door – hard – stands there panting. After a few minutes when her breath has slowed she cracks the door open an inch or two. There is nobody there.

**

A shoal of gargantuan proportions

'Ideas come to us as the successors to griefs, and griefs, at the moment when they change into ideas, lose some part of their power to injure our heart'

- Proust, A la Recherche du Temps Perdu

I knew I had been storing up trouble. What I didn't foresee was how this trouble would manifest. I had to get away. I took leave, and for a month I escaped to the Middle East, alone, a last minute jet to the sun, where I didn't so much celebrate my sixtieth birthday, as give a brief nod in its direction, a solitary celebrant amid the bubbling of hookahs and the clack of backgammon counters. For my last week I took a ferry across to the Sinai and stayed in a small Bedouin encampment which bordered the Gulf of Aqaba. My fellow guests were mostly historians, and their thoughtful academic discussions were an enjoyable diversion. With my return home looming, I declined their offer of a taxi to go to Mount Sinai and watch the sunrise – although I quite fancied the visit to a village of carpet sellers on the way back – and spent the next morning alternately snorkeling and reclining on the beach with my book. I picked at my lunch of *shakshouka* and *laban*, a kind of yoghurt cheese, and finally allowed myself to think about Harry. I was missing him. I wished he'd come with me, but knew he'd have hated it. He'd said he was too busy, but I suspected I was the last person he wanted to be with on holiday, and I had left in a sulk, impotent to do anything to change his mind. Determined not to allow myself to get dejected, I leapt up and decided to do some exploring on foot.

I followed a narrow goat track out of the village, which headed inland. The desert here was unlike any desert I'd ever imagined before, and more suggestive of builder's rubble than anything else, untidy and cluttered, and a vague sense of being cheated accompanied my steps. Eventually I came to where a series of low hills rose up, and picked my way along the bottom of a small valley. The wadi was narrow and the colours of the sand were muted in the shade. As I walked deeper into it, a vast quiet fell and enfolded me, thick as a woollen blanket. Then, deep inside the silence, like counterpoint, welled the dry scratching of the grains of sand against each other, the enraged shrieks of minuscule silicate creatures protesting my sandals. The few clumps of dusty grey vegetation that survived the aridity shook in the tiny whirlwinds that from time to time raced along the floor of the wadi, and their spines and thorns rattled and clacked a dismal disjointed rhythm. The bellows of my lungs soughed in my ears. Nothing else, no other sound. Just me and the desert. My mood of a sudden turned to unease, I slowed and stopped. My inner world had already shrunk to a barren ditch; nothing in this one was going to brighten my spirit.

I retraced my steps to the sea, if it hadn't been so hot I would have run, but the water in the oppressive heat was thick and treacly and there was no surf. It deadened my spirits rather than soothed them. Time seemed to slow. In the distance I saw a farmer standing motionless in a patch of shallowly cultivated desert, his iron grey galabiya covering him from head to toe, protection from the harshness of the sun. I watched his shadow imperceptibly move round. He could have been a sundial. After a while, another man passed close by, his sandals making a 'shhhhh, shhhh' sound. He paused to make a salaam before walking on, wordless, leaving ghostly tracks that the wind soon erased.

The hubbub of goats being herded back to their enclosures, and the thin soprano calls of the shepherd boys broke the spell. The Hilux roared up to camp and disgorged my fellow travellers in a noisy, carpet-laden horde, with tales of warp and weft, and extravagant prices and bargains made and lost. A coffee pot gurgled and I re-emerged into the land of the living from the twilit crystalline world I had fallen into. Enough was enough, it was time to stop fighting, pick up the pieces and reconstruct the mirror.

*

I returned to a cold, wet and miserable Wales. While Harry went in to do some last-minute shopping, I sat huddled in the car in the supermarket car park, watching pallid, bloated people scurrying hunched-up and grim-faced round the puddles, the soft drizzle a deadly poison. I had to struggle against the impulse to get back on the plane, any plane, jet off somewhere else, New Zealand, Thailand, South Africa, it really didn't matter, just not the desert, and leave them to their gruesome wet fate, as though by so doing I could avert my own.

*

We pulled up at the cottage, I got out of the car avoiding the worst of the mud, and went and stood in the garden. I yearned for the softness of green. But instead I was surrounded by the arid rustlings and rattlings of the crispy heads of the *Hydrangea macrophylla*, the translucent papery discs of *Lunaria annua*, the desiccated spiny whorls of *Dipsacus fullonum*, which resembled nothing so much as the sounds of the dead. Or those mineral groanings and shiftlings of the desert sands, of silica and carbon, those hard atoms with their infinity of choices and options for becoming, not yet become, the unborn. The crystalline deserts, the skeletons of winter... Suddenly I thought of Tylluan, her warnings, and my heart contracted. Tongue tied landscapes, these. They did not permit me to speak to them and their harsh voices only spoke of things which I could not bear to hear. I thought of Annie. Did she find the long wintry grasses, the brittle brown bracken stooping over the walls, the dehydrated husks of fruit bored out by wasps and other parasites, as dispiriting as I did that day? Did it shake her to the core?

*

My nemesis when it came was shocking in its intensity. It was as though the last five years had carefully saved up all the shreds and shards of anger and anguish, to pack them into a pulsing agony deep in my abdomen. While I writhed on the floor and later in the ambulance, I could do nothing but beg for something to kill the pain. Please, please, please, stop it! Please, anything, just stop it!

Alcoholic cocktails always sent me into a pleasant stupor, but, believe me, pharmacological cocktails knocked the spots off them. I got down with the world of Burroughs and the frenzied be-bop of Davies. A sort of package-holiday to narco-land. Emigrate there in my retirement I would not, but a grateful two weeks later I emerged, minus a few parts I could do without.

What scared me most about the whole episode was the not-knowing, the waiting – for blood tests, biopsies, scans. I suppose it made sense, I had not-known and waited enough to last me a lifetime. Time, exacerbated by my propensity to expect the worst, uncoiled like a cobra on a winter's day, but, sluggish as he was, his fangs still packed a punch. What scared me equally was the fear all the knowing, available at the click of a mouse, right now this very minute, also brought with it.

The cyst had been growing undetected on my ovary slowly for months, maybe years – no-one could tell me. My ovary, that communicator of my DNA through the generations, had twisted 360 degrees upon itself, and had become a full technicolour, no-holds-barred, bloody embodiment of the poisonous warp and twist I had nurtured since Fleur's death, my daughter's death. In some small part, I suppose, the experience did serve to reconcile me to the positive side of the National Health Service. For this I should be grateful?

*

The New Year came and went, and the early bulbs were pushing their first tentative leaves above the soil when I came home. When I was able pull myself into a sitting position, and then to stand up and walk, I mooched around the garden pulling a stray weed here and there, inspecting the disintegration of the shed roof, and the algae on the polytunnel. As my strength returned I realised I felt better than I had for years. Something foul had gone, leaving me bright and clean and enthusiastic. My body felt airier, I walked up hills easily, without becoming breathless, my lungs more able to expand as though my kidneys were tugging my breath down, anchoring it in my belly. I looked in a mirror and saw the corrugations between my eyes were smoothing out. I stepped out lightly, gaily almost. I had had a reprieve, and I didn't intend to waste it on futile recriminations any longer. It was time to move on.

The decision made to move on and away from futile fights I could never win, released from the chains of my obsession, I had space to look around and see what I had wrought closer to home. The psychic mirror was taking shape, yet the sense of something still remaining to be done bugged me. The taint I had carried with me during the years of anger and righteous seeking clung to me still, like the whiff of decay. I had risen to start a new day, but the imprint of my head on the pillow remained.

Harry was also clearly wondering where he found himself now the house was more or less finished.

'I've been offered a job in Dublin,' he said one evening, after I returned home from work and threw myself down, drained, on the sofa. He never did know how to pick the moment.

His words floated towards me, camouflaged in nonchalance. It took time for them to penetrate my sluggard of a brain and deal the blow. When they did, I jolted out of my weariness.

'What sort of job?' I asked, once I got my tongue in order.

'I'm not sure yet. It could all come to nothing, but if it's confirmed it's a year's contract with Howden and Sons.' He named a company that managed large industrial projects. 'It pays well. Very well in fact, and I thought I'd like to use some of it to go and do that trip to the Himalayas I've always wanted to do.'

'But, what about here? Us?' I wished I hadn't asked because I wasn't fast enough to duck the answer.

'I don't know, Sarah. I'm sorry, I just don't know. This place has become too much for me. I've got no life, or at least not a life I recognise, and certainly not one I would have ever chosen. All I do now is chop wood and fix things. In the summer all I seem to have time for is mowing, and –'

'But we don't have to... We can let the field go wild, you don't have to keep mowing it if you don't want to. I know wood's a problem,' I gabbled, 'but we could buy a few loads in and give ourselves breathing space. I can help much more now...'

He shook his head. 'It's more than that, Sarah. Something's eroded. I just don't feel about us like I did. Up to a year or so ago I was absolutely certain I was your man and I'd never leave you. I wanted to support you, and I really admired, still admire, your tenacity and your fight for the truth. But you shut me out all those years. I'd try and talk to you sometimes and it was as though I didn't exist, you didn't even raise your head, even if I asked if you wanted a cup of tea. That's done something to me. I just don't know what's left.'

Something big crashed down on me, rendering me small and helpless. No, worse than that, I was a bug smeared on a windshield – or that old road-kill again, flattened and bloody. No, the train was still coming on down the line and I hadn't stepped back. I had left it too late.

Although I tried to persuade Harry away from his position it was clear that the damage was deeper than just my mere wanting to repair it being enough to change his mind.

'Look, I'm not saying it's over. I think we need – both of us, not just me – some space to sort of regroup, and see where we are. All we do is bicker these days. We don't listen to each other, we don't seem to have any joy in each other.

I find it hard to see where we have anything in common. I'm constantly feeling I don't live up to your expectations, and I can't carry on like that."

I put my head in my hands and tried to blot out the ugly words.

'I don't think I can cope on my own, here," was all I could find to say, feebly side-stepping.

'No. I understand that if anyone can – it's a hard place to handle. Look, it's only in Dublin and I'll try to get back and do anything major that needs sorting. I won't just abandon the place. Till we know...' He stopped and drew a breath.

This wasn't what I had meant. Even so, it was something to cling onto. It hadn't all gone down the plughole, wasn't completely finito, he still cared something. Even if only for Bron Felen. And wasn't I part of Bron Felen, too? But was that 'something' enough? All these years of thinking I was independent and strong and there I was on the floor, a boneless jelly. I hadn't realised the extent of my reliance on him to support my fight, comfort my despair. Now they had gone, but so had he. And I had to let him. I couldn't even hold, let alone grasp him; he was water through my fingers.

I could feel his tensing to say more. I didn't want him to say any more.

'Look, Sarah. I don't want to meddle in your feelings; Lord knows you've needed to get over everything in your own time and in your own way. But I'm going to be absolutely honest here, OK?"

I put my hands over my ears, and hummed a tune that flew into my head. 'Oh, my name is MacNamara, I'm the leader of the band...' Where the hell did that come from? Oh yes, Patterdale 1967, Outdoor Pursuits school trip...

'Well, I'm going to say it anyway, and it's up to you to take it on board or not. The distance between us – it's not just between us, it's between you and Fleur too, and I think that's the problem. It's as though you've transferred all your feelings away from Fleur, and into Annie. You seem obsessed by events that happened sixty years in the past and to someone else – not recently, and to you. What's it all about?"

Good question. He came over and sat next to me on the sofa and pulled my hands gently down. The water was falling, falling, a downpour that would never stop, a flood to drown me, and I couldn't find the tap to turn it off. Angrily I wrenched away, and jumped up. He dropped his hands and sat there, and the look in his eyes made me rush out of the house. I went and sat on the big wooden swing I'd put under the apple tree, and shivered in the frosty air, the snowdrops a white lake at my feet. I swung and I hummed. Wraiths of mist curled off the grass and paraded across the lawn. I stilled and sat in silence. The stooped shoulders of – it could only be Evan; the young curly head of Dilwyn turned away in rejection; Taid with his fists in his eyes; Nain a feathery wisp; then, when I thought it ended, Annie. I knew it was Annie, I had seen that defiant shape in the mirror too many times, the warrior stance – shoulders squared, jaw jutting, feet spread – alone. Alone. As heavy as the earth even though everything that threatened to hold her down had been shucked off. Slowly she drifted towards me until at the last moment she lifted and was gone into the boughs above my head. I didn't come in until I could see the light go out in the bedroom.

After he went I had many solitary hours in which to think. I didn't mind solitude – as long as I chose it and could choose when to end it. This time I had no such choice. Slowly it unravelled. I sat there in my sofa-boat and bobbed along on the sofa-sea. My thoughts slipped, a net, through my fingers, and in their skein I caught many a juicy fish, primitive, ugly, coelacanths of my own making.

Anger, a good catch – I grabbed its barbed tail and hauled it in; I would feast on that for a long time. Fear – gotcha! I tossed it in to squirm around with anger. I wasn't finished yet. I held my hand over my eyes to shield them from the glare of the glassy sea, and saw them – sprats, tiddlings, krill – tiny mouthfuls too small to bother with, as I first thought. I hauled them in hand over hand, made greedy by their weight, their numbers, and then threw back in horror as I saw them for what they were. A whole shoal of them, a shoal of gargantuan proportions, so large that as far around me as I could see tiny silver fins flapped and splashed on the surface, twinkled in the last rays of the sun.

Hopes, expectations. Never met. My mother's, her mother's, mine... Fleur's. Dreams that hovered on the edge of night. A daughter and a mother. I cursed myself for the fool I was, so blindly had I looked but not seen.

**

Tangled wires

As the turbid days rolled by, unbidden images rose to the surface, and flickered past like a badly loaded reel of film, a home movie from the sixties. Nonsensical and uncomfortable, nevertheless they formed an integral part of the stream of consciousness that was 'myself'. A story that insinuated itself across the generations, and mocked my attempts to write a different one, for my children. It held an answer of sorts, but it was an answer that forced me to recognise that I could not escape the past. I could only accept it, and allow the alchemy of understanding and kindliness to soften and transmute it.

*

As a child I was always prey to strange ideas and fancies, and used to secretly imagine I was on the verge of unravelling the secret of the universe. There was a period around the age of eight or nine when I'd spend an hour at a time looking in the mirror. I'd stare without blinking, one inch away from the glass, pupils meeting pupils. Feelings of drowning, and vertigo, shivery vertigo, would start to overwhelm me. I wanted to pull away, but the pull towards was too great. Questions like 'Who am I? Who is it in there? If I was born in a different body, would I be the same 'me'?' would drift upwards like bubbles in lemonade. At this propinquity, the pupils of my eyes seemed to go back forever, but I could not penetrate their darkness. Could not see the synapses flaring behind them; didn't meet any angels.

*

One day when I was out shopping, the image of a woman surfaced. I think she reminded me of my mother, but the mother for whom I now had some feelings of fondness, not the one against whom I had raged and refused to love. Whoever she was she held a strange fascination for me.

An unremarkable person, someone you wouldn't stop to look at twice, hundreds of them hurrying around the towns and villages and getting on buses and trains or into cars, bustling in and out of grocers and bakeries. She is carefully coiffed – in my memory it was always a permanent wave; lipstick of a subtle shade carefully chosen to complement her complexion which is protected with foundation and a dusting of powder; her perfume is light mid-range, probably by Coty or Yardley – no heavy oils that might linger in the curtains and cushions; jewellery is confined to discreet earrings, a wedding ring, and a watch inevitably correct to the second. She usually wears a fitted coat or jacket with narrow shoulders with a smart patterned or colourful scarf in rayon. On her nylon encased feet she wears polished court shoes with a little heel for comfort. She may or may not have gloves. She is accompanied by her handbag, always leather and nicely buffed, containing handkerchief, lipstick, key ring, purse, tickets, diary, safety pins, and whatever her husband doesn't want to carry in his jacket pockets. There's something peculiarly comforting about her, although you probably have to have been born in the forties or fifties to appreciate this. You expect her to reach into her handbag and whip out, at the speed of lightning so you can't duck or move away, the spotless handkerchief with a wild flower motif in one corner, spit and dab at some speck on your face. Ugh. I never did understand why the smell of spit on a handkerchief is so repugnant, but it's true. Even the smell of my own spit repels me.

But anyway, quite ordinary, the acme of British respectability. What was remarkable was that such women still exist. They've come through the decades seamlessly, moulded by their own mothers, respectful of themselves and others, as you can discern in their grooming and domestic habits. A whole era summed up. It beat me... ordinary was something I imagined I had eradicated ever since adolescence and my 'eviction from paradise', when I learnt my parents weren't my parents. When I learnt at the same time that I was not 'me', or at least not the 'me' I thought I was.

The shards were on the floor before I fully registered it, although I couldn't see the pieces and wouldn't cut my finger picking them up.

What changed? Nothing organic that's for sure, for when I looked in the mirror I did at some point reconstruct I still recognised myself. Something behind my retinas had changed, not in front of them.

*

'You're adopted aren't you?" the horrible little girl said who lived down by the recreation ground. 'My mum said so." I looked at her and nodded, Oh. Yes. The information seemed at once so disturbing and yet so familiar.

I think that might've been the first time I consciously donned my carapace for dealing with the unexpected, the blow, the shock to the core. I don't run, or fight (not initially at least); I freeze much as the proverbial rabbit in the headlights, but only emotionally – if you were looking you wouldn't see me stop dead in mid-stride or in mid-pour from the teapot. You'd have to be very alert to notice the infinitesimal pause in my physicality, the millisecond's hiatus in my breathing. Instead, I place the danger securely in a boxed-in little corner of my mind to which only I have the key, to be opened and pored over when I'm feeling stronger. I do not show my wounds to those who hurt me, intentionally or not. But inside something is starting to fracture, like the mirror is crazed, like the glazing is crackled on Egyptian ceramics.

'Mum, Sandra Gillet said I'm adopted. Am I? Does that mean you and Dad aren't my parents?" Mum is looking at me and I can see dread reflected in her eyes.

'Oh dear." Her hands fly to her heart. 'Dad'll be home in a minute and we can talk about it then," She is looking at the clock on the mantelpiece and I can hear her 'Help! I can't deal with this myself'.

It's like, at that moment, inside me, a darkness started to grow. It must have been more corporeal than that though because it felt heavy and seemed to jostle my innards to shove over, make room, like a fledgling cuckoo in the nest. Shove over kidneys, make way liver, womb shift yourself, guts slither off, I'm here! It's still here. Sometimes it sits on my perineum, sometimes it pushes up my diaphragm, but it's found an 'in' and, with as much tenacity as an economic migrant, it's made its home inside me.

Something bad got into my recipe at that moment; some contaminant curdled the soup, some bacteria turned the meat 'off', and soured the pudding. It cut a groove in my psyche for rivers to flood through. It brought me to this place I find myself in, right now. My old friend anger. The humiliation of deception. The freeze of fear. The 'I thought it was like this, and now I find it's like that' feeling; the realization that all along I had a flaw built in like a Japanese pot; was vulnerable to attack from out of a cloudless blue sky and against which no-one gave me the means to defend myself.

Fifty years later. Another mirror, another universe, more shards on the floor. I heave myself off the sofa and unerringly find the old gas-mask box in which I kept all the old family photographs and certificates. And here she is, my mother, beaming proudly with the huge cream-coloured perambulator, and my baby face dimly visible inside. If anything should have poured balm on my hurt all those years ago it was that smile of hers. Behind it, banished for ever as she thought, lay who knows what pain and sorrow. All those years and they never once talked about why, about how they felt.

*

Towards the end of mum's life, when they came to stay on their annual visit from South Africa, I drove Bernie, my middle daughter, and thirteen-year old grand-daughter, Tanya, over to see Mum-Granny-Great-Granny. Mum wasn't at her best by then, beset with cruel arthritis that curled her fingers and relegated her to a painful wheelchair, and fairly deep in dementia; but she was still mostly able to be present in the moment.

We loaded her wheelchair into the back of the car, manoeuvred her gasping with pain into the passenger seat, and set off to a garden centre. This was the jaunt out she loved best, being wheeled round the benches and trestles loaded with flowers and shrubs, and alpines and herbs, up and down the aisles past the fruit trees and roses of all kinds, the clematis and ivies and honeysuckles. The pots, glazed and unglazed, the plaster gnomes and garden furniture. When I was a kid and Dad was head gardener at some posh National Trust place in Lancashire, Mum worked in the nursery. So it always reminded her of times past. Happier times, hopefully, but that's something I can only conjecture. Tiring of walking around, we went to have a cream tea in the centre's café. 'Just tea for me,' said Mum.
Once we'd sat down, though, and were buttering our scones, Mum began to eye them greedily.

"Do you want some scone after all, Granny?" Bernie asked her.

"Yes, I might as well. They do look nice. Just a taste though."

"That's OK. We'll cut them up and all have some. Granny can manage them if they're cut into finger pieces, can't she?"

"Yes, she'll be fine."

Bernie cut the buttered scones into small pieces and laid two or three on a small plate in front of Mum, who picked one up and slowly placed it in her mouth. She chewed with contentment. After a minute or two we noticed an expression of discomfort cross her face, strange contortions succeeding one another in an effort to dislodge with her tongue something that was apparently stuck between her teeth. As we watched without seeming to, not wanting to embarrass her, she reached up, took out her false teeth, upper and lower, and banged them down on the table, sighing with satisfaction. There they sat, covered in scone and butter and jam, in full view of everyone walking by. My grand-daughter, Tanya, and I were mesmerised at the sight, and I can still recall the confusion of crossed wires in my own head as I looked at Mum sitting there without a care, then at the teeth on the table.

Saving the day, as always, Bernie jumped up and bounded over to the hatchery where all the condiments and cutlery were laid out, picked up a couple of paper serviettes, swooped on the teeth and wrapped them up, saying,

"I'll put these in my bag, Granny, for when you get back home."

"Thank you, darling," said Mum sweetly, oblivious to any problem.

My grand-daughter, released from the freeze, turned her head slightly towards me and mouthed sotto voce, "It's embarrassing, isn't it?"

I nodded, trying to suppress an awful urge to giggle. But one look at my daughter set me off and we laughed. God, how we roared with laughter.

"Don't! Everyone's looking at us!" said Tanya, in a paroxysm of teenage self-consciousness.

"What are you all laughing at?" Mum asked grinning gummily in empathy.

"Nothing Mum. If you've finished your scone I think it's time we went back."

Mum's dementia worsened quickly after she went to live in the old folks' home, and I never knew what, or who, I'd find when I called in. I dimly remember someone telling me that if you change the present you change the past, and it didn't make any sense to me at the time. But over those last couple of years or so something did change between us – perhaps she just didn't have the energy to keep up her defences any more – she let me help her, do things for her. She relaxed. And it was just that small thing and suddenly a crowd of forgotten feelings and memories came flooding through me, and when they receded my perception of the past and who she was had completely altered. I understood what it meant to feel compassion... It opened the door to kindliness, affection, and – good humour. I found I could laugh with her.

*

One afternoon Mum was sobbing in her chair, and when I asked what the matter was, said,

'Isn't it awful, that little baby dead in its pram, just like that? The mother never knew what happened, she was inside the butchers, and when she came out it was dead. Just like that."

I frowned. Mum never read the newspapers and was quite unable to concentrate on the TV. She clammed up after that one sentence.

Another time she said sotto voce, 'Don't look at her," nodding meaningfully behind me. 'Her. Over there, trying to attract our attention. She'll just come over and pester us."

'What's wrong with her then, Mum? Don't you like her?" I asked. I was used to Mum's rather anti-social ways and the sudden likings and dislikings she took towards other people, although it always made me feel mad with her.

'She's having an affair with the gardener," she hissed, her face a mask of disapproval. 'His wife doesn't know it, but we all do. She's quite brazen about it. There'll be trouble there, you mark my words."

'Goodness me, that's awful."

'Yes, you don't know the half of it. She's pregnant now. She'll have to get rid of it, there's no way we can look after it for her. I don't like her, and I don't want to get involved. Brazen, she is." She shook her head for emphasis, lips thin.

I sneaked a surreptitious glance over my shoulder, but the only other person in the room was a little nonagenarian in a wheelchair, who beamed and waved.

'Now you've done it," Mum said.

But no-one came over to pester us, and after an hour or so of exchanging innocuous comments about the weather, the birdlife in the garden, and Mum's current ailments, she was summoned to supper. I pushed her to the dining room in her wheelchair and asked where she'd like to sit, there were at least a dozen tables with old people scattered at them.

'Oh, by that old Mrs Jones over there. She's a bit of laugh, not like some of these others, always moaning on about this and that. Not like a Welshie at all."

I winced. Opened my mouth... But she was nodding vigorously in the direction of the table where sat none other than the little nonagenarian. I forced myself to take a slow breath, to take no notice of the racist slur, manoeuvred her into place and they both waved brightly as I disappeared back to the car, heads together chatting earnestly to each other before I'd even got to the door. I guess I'll never know what tales emerged out of that confabulation.

*

Mum's jumbled memories and tangled wires never ceased to disturb and amuse me equally while she was still capable of communicating, her life reduced to some synaptic muddle that had all the elements of a Breton novel or a Schoenberg composition It was as though she handed me the shards of her own broken mirror. But a mirror that would never reflect an ordered universe ever again. I wept for my mother then. And for us, all those lost years. For that brief space of time at the end of her life, we were released. I hugged her thin shoulders, wheeled her down to the beach to watch the cockle-diggers and the swooping gulls, and wedged open my heart finally to the human being within us both.

*

With Harry's going, I realized I no longer needed the wedge, it would stay open all by itself.

**

Water from a stone

1962

One sudden evening Evan's decades-long diet takes its revenge on his heart – or perhaps it is his own shame that he cannot out-work – and fells him by the gate as he throws a bale into the tractor for the cattle. Annie, cold and indifferent to the last, finds him in the morning, stiff and shining with frost, the cattle treading the ground into mud around him as they snatch mouthfuls of the sweet clover scented hay.

At the funeral Annie is dry eyed and string-like. It is all her neighbours can bring themselves to do, to come up and proffer their condolences in the face of her, and their, grim dislike of each other. Dilwyn nods to her, and watches as she walks down the path after the service is over. She refused his offer to come with her, hold her arm, protect her from what she surely knows she has invited. But it is Dilwyn she ran to, braving his wife's coldness, to come and move Evan into the house. To arrange the doctor, the undertaker, order the coffin, choose the prayers, the hymns, do all that is necessary at the end of a life.

By the time the winter's snow melts she has made up her mind. She opens the kitchen door, looks across to the blue painted gate at the top of the garden. It is not so far. She has not dared go in for years except through the lower gate, to the *tŷ bach*. She takes a deep breath and walks over, lifts the latch and takes a step inside. The old apple and the plum tree, as she knows they will, draw her eyes to the small unquiet grave under the arching branches. And as she also knows she will, she backs out, step by careful step, too scared to even turn around and run.

She tries the next day, and waves of nausea rise up until she has to turn and run. Each day she penetrates further, until she stands before the guardians, as she thinks of them. The profusion of snowdrops, spread out at their feet as though from an artist's careless brush, blinds her with their whiteness. So copious, so unexpected, are the tears, that she is reminded of the story her mam used to read aloud, the one where the tailor pretends to squeeze water out of a stone when really he is squeezing the whey from a cheese.

She knows she must propitiate. There is housekeeping to do. She cuts the grass, puts a bench between them, and takes to sitting there in the evening sun, listening to the bees working in the blossom. Thoughts, too, she can now let buzz in and out – memories of Jan, how old her little boy would be now and how he would look, guessing what might have been.

Her instinctive feel for colour and line re-asserts itself and as she works and heals a love for the garden and all growing things steals into the vacuum of her spirit. The peace and beauty that elsewhere continue to sit uncomfortably in her soul she materialises now in the lilacs, azaleas and rhododendrons, the lavenders and pinks, scabious and thrift she plunders on her solitary walks. She plants the wild things – bluebells, primroses and violets – she digs out of the woods or banks. Red campion rambles along the banks and meadowsweet thrusts its germolene-perfumed umbels out along the hedge bottoms. She allows them to grow wild amongst the rhubarb and artichokes, the runner beans and lettuces, along with the cranesbills, delphiniums and daisies. Giant horsetail and the myriad ferns that flourish in the damp, shady areas of the garden she leaves, judiciously, because she likes the ancient feeling they impart. In summer the garden is a riot of colour and painted ladies and small yellow fritillaries flitting, a picture within which she wanders for hours. Among them all wave the roses, Nain's roses, scattering their fragrance on the breeze.

*

1997

She is grown brown and leathery, her skin deep-wrinkled, and her hair thin. Her hips and knees have succumbed to the ravages of years of damp and cold, and it is hard to pick up and hold an axe or coal hammer. She is drawn more and more often to the seat by the snowdrops, from which she watches Dilwyn, long widowed now, and his friend George as they stump energetically along the footpath up from the beach, wiry and strong, staving off the immobility of old age. They wave. Dilwyn occasionally brings her whinberries from the hill, succulent and tart. She doesn't tell him she throws them out once he's gone, their acidity making her face twist and grimace. It is difficult to bend down.

From time to time in warmer weather she manages to walk as far as the cliffs and rocky shore at the eastern end of the bay. The small walled garden outside the kitchen door is a treasure trove of all the shells, fossils and driftwood she collects; old cages of ivy, the tree-trunk they strangled long rotted; buoys of all colours; bits of fishing net, a roman coin she secretes inside a lump of fossilised coral on the windowsill. The dunes are rich with shell fragments and pyramidal orchids. Grey plover, dunlin and shelduck, panicked at her passage, burst out in all directions. She learns to stop and wait, leaning on the blackthorn stick Dilwyn carved for her, if she would observe them at close hand, for, walking, she brings with her this bubble of human threat, they zing off its circumference.

A man from the council erects a stile and a kissing-gate, and a post with a yellow arrow pointing along and up the hill; another man comes round with a scythe and clears the paths once a year. Every so often she hears the clump of marching boots and hides in the shed or the kitchen, wherever she happens to be, and peers out at the walkers with their shorts and rucksacks. Although they peer back they see nothing of the dark interior behind the dusty panes, and she hears them wondering if anyone still lives here, what a quaint little cottage, wouldn't it be nice to retire to, it would be a lot of work to set it right though. Look at that view.

One night she is gripped with an excruciating pain in her bowels and heaves herself up from the hard pine settle where she sleeps sitting up, out into the icy night. To the *tŷ bach*. Before she can reach it, she turns and catches the white glimmer of the snowdrops by the light of the moon high overhead. They call her. It is time.

*

Dilwyn never quite told the whole truth about Annie's death. He didn't obviously distort it, just left out a couple of little things, personal things, things you wouldn't think had much significance. The significance lay in his head alone, he admitted that, when the floodgates finally opened. We were sitting in his garden, Bwster drowsing in a patch of sunshine by the door. Somewhere inside, I could hear Tylluan whistling as she made the tea. It reminded me of my father. I missed the whistlers, they hadn't come well down the generations, and it was a rare sound, one that ate up the years, like the hoot of a steam train passing under a bridge, the clacking of cylinder lawn mowers. More and more Tylluan was to be found at Maesgwyn. Neither of them gave a damn for what anyone else thought. I was happy for them.

"George and me, we weren't the first people to find Annie. You know, the night she died? I felt I'd neglected her, even though she wasn't exactly very welcoming. I did all I could for her, but I knew I'd let her down. I'd had a share in what she'd become. Even if she didn't know it."

Guilt, yes, and shame also because, although he determinedly insisted, in the way of old men not to be gainsaid, that he and George always took the path through the farm and down the bank at nine o'clock sharp, every day, looking in to say 'Bore da' to Annie on their way and see if she wanted for anything, they more and more often went by the less steep route down the road, and sometimes missed calling in for days, and, in bad weather, even weeks at a time. Nobody else bothered to visit or pass the time of day, they hadn't for years. Annie had made sure of that.

"The morning they found her, George was knocking on my front door at about half past ten for a *panad* and a biscuit. We saw the ambulance race past. There wasn't no people, traffic or other obstacles at that hour – that's the way of modern villages isn't it? No longer any heart or reason for being in any particular place? So it didn't have its siren going, just that blue light whirling silently, and throwing ghostly veils over the kiddies' swings and roundabout. We could see it wink its way along the windows. We turned to each other and both said 'Annie!' in unison."

"I pulled on my old overcoat and picked up the old stick, and we went as fast as we could to the turning down to the beach. When we got to the track to Bron Felen we could see the ambulance about half way along, prevented from driving closer by that old narrow sunken lane. Nothing could get through in winter. We could see the blue flash through the trees."

I knew well what he meant. Until we'd built a tiny stone bridge, the swollen stream gushed over the track and fell a waterfall into the deep gulley bordering the field, rushing its way down to the wetlands below.

"I'm sorry. You can't go any further, there's been an accident," said a person who identified himself as a member of the emergency team.

"But she's my cousin," Dilwyn bent the truth. "We always look in on her in the mornings. I'm her sole surviving relative" he added pathetically, remembering a phrase from a television serial that always seemed to open doors and relax official disapproval.

The man's manner became sympathetic. "I'm so sorry, of course you can go on up; but I think you'd better be prepared for the worst."

Dilwyn didn't pause to ask further. Leaning into his stick he stumbled up the track, George puffing a few yards behind. He cursed the ill maintained lane, with its ruined stile and badly hung gate, flinging it open to crash and reverberate like a cracked bell against the bank. George could see him, a wild cardboard cut-out of a cartoon figure, backlit in the shady lane by a weak sun, hair awry and scarf flapping.

"When I got to where this group of people was standing around a bundle on the ground, I could see a figure strapped on a stretcher, its face all covered up. I knew it was Annie from the hair escaping from under the covering, though it was faded by then. But you could still see it'd been that sort of red, like a conker. I thought my own heart would stop, so wild was it revving, and it was some minutes before I recovered enough to speak.

Mr Goddard, the Cornishman who's got the old coastguard's place down on the beach was there. It was him who found Annie. I wish it'd been me...

He told me his German Shepherd had whined and pulled away as they crossed the field below the house. He followed and found Annie stretched out on the ground.

"I couldn't think what on earth she was doing out in this weather. I ask you! She had coal, and milk, everything was to hand she was likely to need. She had no business she couldn't see to inside.

"They said she probably thought of something. Old folks, they forget things, and think they're back in another time when they were perfectly capable of getting about never mind the weather. As if I didn't know! Perhaps she was on her way to the outhouse... But it can't have been that, that's the other gate.

I asked how long she'd been d... – lying there like that, and I nearly dropped down on the spot when the paramedic bloke said he reckoned a couple of days. A couple of days! I can't hardly tell you how that made me feel. What sort of friend had I been when it counted? It looked like she must've fallen and not been able to get back up... almost certain she died of hypothermia. Often the way with old folk, he said. They say it's a kind death, too, though I don't know about that.

"He was quite a caring sort of man. Said to me, 'Come on, old feller, you can't stand out here in this bitter cold. It's been a shock.' Too right, it was. They tried to get Goddard to take me on home and get me a hot cup of tea. A cup of tea!? I had to laugh. A strong tot would've been more like it.

"Anyway I wasn't going to be put off and said blunt like, 'I'll be coming with you when you take her'. But they wouldn't let me in the ambulance. I'll say this for Goddard, he went straight down and brought his car back up, didn't need no telling, and him, me and George followed the ambulance to the hospital. That's the hospital where you work, isn't it? I wonder you didn't see us."

"But I didn't know you then, Dil. Even if I had seen you."

"Oh, aye. Well I can tell you this, when I saw them heft her into the back of the ambulance and drive off, it was like my ship went out to sea without me. I asked old Goddard exactly where he'd found her – and you'll be able to guess... Aye, under the plum tree. Face down on the grass, she was. He said it looked like she was clutching handfuls of snowdrops. He thought it was odd, like she'd gone out there specially to pick them."

On the drive to the hospital Dilwyn was curt with George's fussing. Forced to sit and wait in the morgue's waiting room, he kept his silence, and only broke it to be uncharacteristically abrupt and hostile when the vicar knocked and enquired if he could sit and pray with them. George apologised for his friend, outside the door in case he had it in him to raise a fuss.

"He don't hold with all that religious stuff, Vicar. It got knocked right out of him during the war." The Vicar smiled understandingly and promised to look in again before they went.

"It won't do you no good. It'll be a waste of your time."

"But we will need to discuss what funeral arrangements to make. I understand your friend is a distant relative of the deceased, er... Mrs Annie Williams?"

"Miss Annie Williams," George corrected him. "She never married. Yes, Dil's her only family, leastways what we know of."

The pathologist, a kindly man, came out to see the two old men – the one wracked with guilt or shame – he hardly knew the difference; the other concerned for his friend.

"I can tell you that Ms Williams died some days ago, but further than that it's not possible for me to say with any certainty. From what the paramedic tells me she was covered in snow which would indicate she had been lying there for a couple of days. Nor can I tell at this stage whether or not hypothermia was the cause of death. If I may suggest, there's nothing useful you can do here today. If I were you I'd go home now and someone will get in touch with you as her next of kin about funeral arrangements. I'm sorry." He put out his hand to Dilwyn in a gesture of sympathy. Dilwyn flinched, still looking at the floor. Said nothing.

"Thank you, Doctor," George said, "we'll do that. C'mon, Dil."

When the pathologist had left, George shook his head, "What was she up to?"

'Leave it be, George. I hope she's found some peace at last. It's been a long time coming."

George looked at him then, embarrassed. He, too, put out his hand and touched his friend's, wet from the tears that were coursing down his rough old cheeks. Dilwyn straightened and stabbed his stick at the floor.

'I'll be fine. Better get going though. Goddard'll be waiting for us. We'd best shift ourselves and go and find him in the WRVS. I don't fancy catching the bus today!"

**

Epilogue

'It is easier to perceive error than to find truth, for the former lies on the surface and is easily seen, while the latter lies in the depth, where few are willing to search for it.'

- Johann Wolfgang Von Goethe

Cnidarians

The text message said simply, *'Can you get a couple of weeks off? Do you fancy a jaunt round the Irish west coast? I thought Donegal and Connemara... Hxx.'*

The train from Chester to Holyhead meanders along the North Wales coast and across Ynys Mon, sometimes hugging the shore and sometimes veering inland among the flat fields and salt marshes and streams, with otters hiding among the roots and under the banks, and crowding waterfowl. As the sun sinks, the long shadows of the fastigiate black poplars, popular as breaks for the cutting coastal winds, reach their fingers towards the fleeing locomotive, the edges of the clouds gathering in the west turn pink then red, filling the ponds and streams with blood. The inhabitants of the moonlight begin to flutter and stretch, ready to pounce on their prey, those creatures inhabiting the sunlight, now preening and comfortably settling themselves, unconscious of impending death, flying fur and feathers, bleeding wounds, the screaming to come.

She likes to pass this journey as dusk deepens looking in the window at the reflections of the other passengers in the carriage. In this way she can observe without being observed. The darkling glass imprisons this outside world and the one inside, together, within its hard silicate atoms. By defocusing her gaze she is able to commingle them in bizarre juxtapositions. She looks on this living screen as silent reeds flutter through a young girl's locks of curling hair, disturbing not a strand; and at the fat man in the seat opposite, oblivious to the dull red bricks that decorate his stiff leather jacket; leaves bunch themselves into hats and scarves flirting with style and coquettish angles, or festoon the luggage racks; a lamp-post sprouts for the merest instant from a small child's head, a weird luminescent fungus, grotesque and scary; darkened doorways and blacked out windows replace faces, begging what, if anything, is within.

At first the outside is more powerful, more substantial, and the people sitting inside, locked in their own thoughts and day-dreams, are faint wraiths. But as dusk deepens the balance changes, the outside retreats, and molecule by molecule the passengers assert their dominance. Their boundaries lose their fuzzy edges. They pulse their cnidarian way from the depths to the surface of the world like monstrous jellies. There they bob, confident in their corporeality, and as minute flows into minute so they brighten and sharpen until they are solid once more. Then, shocking in its suddenness, from one moment to the next, they are alert to her stare, other eyes meet hers, and frown, or smile, or pretend indifference, as, disconcerted, she again knows them to be inhabitants of the same universe. She is one of them.

She turns away, and as she does she sees, as always, as she knows she will, out of the corner of her eyes for the briefest nano-second of time, there between the two worlds, molecules still dancing, whirling on and on in the panes that shiver with the spinning of the wheels. A shred of skin, a single hair, a pale hint of pearly teeth, a red splash that smears the window in the process of disintegration. Or perhaps in becoming. She finds it hard to distinguish.

Her heart lurches with the sway of the carriage, swings left, right, up and down, plummets to her knees, fills her throat, then finds its old familiar place, settles into its strong cage of bone, resilient sponge and tubes, and dozes. She seeks and holds her own reflection in her gaze. She smoothes her hair, adjusts her hat, steadies her breath and smiles. When she is ready, she opens her book and finds her page.

**

From Death to Decomposition

'Old Annie has scowled enough' said the soft fingered moon
As he grazed the coalhouse roof
Erased the ruts and troughs between her eyes, unseeing soon.
'I shall strip away the years and show the tears instead'

'Yes, where did he go? What deed was done?
We'd like to know'
Sang out the apple trees who stretched their
lichened boughs shady
Over the young man and his lady
Many fruit and blossom, leaf fallings ago.

The lilac and the buddleia dreamt on, remembering.
Secret whisperings were heard
As each tiny bird fluffed its feathers in the cold
The old hare crouched still listening in the grass
As the white owl passed overhead –
There'll be more will meet their maker before
this night is dead.

Between the slip and the stumble and the stilling
of her breath
Annie gathered all the pruning, the digging and
the weeding
The ivy climbing, plantain seeding
Wove a bridal gown that stretched to every corner of her land
Slipped resolutely on her calloused hand
A bright and golden wedding band
Forged and hammered, tempered with her longing
Etched with ne'er abandoned grief.

Reached out arms like strings but tender
Wrapped them round her skinny breast
Rocked the cold womb's emptiness.
Wept and watered bulbs still hiding

Melted snow and thawed the ice
Where shy white blooms raised green edged skirts
Peeped timid in the guttering light

The babe dead, the man never wed
A hard life lived on the land loved
Now bone cold to the fox's slink
The stink of betrayal curled her nose these fifty years
or more
Lipsink, teethgrind, fistclench, the bones of her face,
Those iron bars once home of strangled pride
Unlocked, swung wide, invited her outside
The space behind her eyes snow smooth
Clear as mountain water, falling water –
Annie cried.

The protozoa did their work
The fungi, beetles, worms and flies
Fluids ran, acids bit, and gases vaporised.

Formicidae, Muscidae, Silphidae, Histeridae
Sepsidae, Araneae, Sphaeroceridae
Piophilidae, Staphylinidae, Sarcophagidae and Phoridae
All did their bit.
Then along came Isopoda, Collembola, Dermaptera, Pauropoda.
And molecule by molecule she sank into the earth's caress
Where snowdrops curtsied, bluebells rang
To eternal Annie-ness

WITH A LOVE
FOR BOOKS

With a large range of imprints, from herbalism, self-sufficiency, physical and mental wellbeing, food, memoirs and many more, Herbary Books is shaped by the passion for writing and bringing innovative ideas close to our readers.

All our authors put their hearts into their books and as publishers we just lend a helping hand to bring their creation to life.

Thank you to our authors and to you, dear reader.

Discover and purchase all our books on
WWW.HERBARYBOOKS.COM

HERBARYBOOKS